FOOTPRINTS IN PARIS

Fly Away Home

The Intruder

Give Them All My Love

The Fields Beneath: The History of One London Village

The Born Exile: George Gissing

City of Gold: The Biography of Bombay

Countries of the Mind: The Meaning of Place to Writers

Célestine: Voices from a French Village

The Journey of Martin Nadaud

The Man Who Drew London: Wenceslaus Hollar
in Reality and Imagination

The House by the Thames

Footprints in Paris

A Few Streets, a Few Lives

Gillian Tindall

Chatto & Windus
LONDON

Published by Chatto & Windus 2009

2 4 6 8 10 9 7 5 3 1

First published in Great Britain in 2009 by
Chatto & Windus
Random House, 20 Vauxhall Bridge Road,
London SW1V 2SA

www.rbooks.co.uk

Addresses for companies within The Random House Group Limited can
be found at: www.randomhouse.co.uk/offices.htm

The Random House Group Limited Reg. No. 954009

A CIP catalogue record for this book
is available from the British Library

ISBN 9780701181024

The Random House Group Limited supports The Forest Stewardship
Council (FSC), the leading international forest certification organisation.
All our titles that are printed on Greenpeace-approved FSC certified
paper carry the FSC logo. Our paper procurement policy can be
found at www.rbooks.co.uk/environment

Mixed Sources
Product group from well-managed
forests and other controlled sources
www.fsc.org Cert no. TT-COC-2139
© 1996 Forest Stewardship Council

Typeset in Janson Text Light by Palimpsest Book Production Limited,
Grangemouth, Stirlingshire

Printed and bound in Great Britain by
CPI Mackays, Chatham ME5 8TD

Contents

List of Maps

List of Illustrations

Plate Section One

Arthur Jacob as a young doctor. From a now-lost portrait
Arthur Jacob's half-minute glass for taking the pulse
The Cour de Commerce St André at the beginning of the twentieth century
Demolition for the construction of the Boulevard St Germain, late 1860s
Sketch of the Rue Hautefeuille made at the end of the nineteenth century
Sketch of the refectory of the Cordeliers
Bertie Tindall as a little boy, early 1880s
The four Tindall children, Bertie, Howard, May and Maud, late 1880s
A studio model, drawing by George du Maurier for his novel *Trilby*
'Life on the Boulevard', from the *Illustrated London News*, *c.*1870
Watercolour painted by Bertie from his window in the Rue de l'Abbaye, 1895
The steam engine that crashed through the buffers at the Gare Montparnasse in 1895

Plate Section Two
Albert Alfred Tindall in old age
The Rue des Carmes, early twentieth century
The Rue de la Parcheminerie, c.1900
The Rue des Noyers, 1917
From the diary Bertie kept during his stay in Paris, 1895
Number 12, Rue Bonaparte, 2006
Maud Tindall as a young woman, c.1910
The Rue de l'Abbaye
The Hôtel des Carmes, with the Marché des Carmes
    below it, 1920
The water fountain that stood in the centre of the Marché
    des Carmes
Ursula with Tom's car, mid-1930s
'Tom' as a young soldier in 1939
'Julia' beside the Seine, c.1957
The Rue de l'Ecole de Médecine as it is today

The painting on the jacket by Emmanuel Lansyer is
looking south towards the Place Maubert, 1860s

The maps are by Martin Collins

The author and publishers have made every effort to
trace the holders of copyright in illustrations and text
quotations. Any inadvertent mistakes or omissions may
be corrected in future editions

'On garde la trace de son passage au Quartier Latin toute sa vie.'

Jules Vallès (1832–1885)

'. . . Our task is to revivify life that has passed away. We know that ghosts cannot speak until they have drunk blood; and the spirits which we evoke demand the blood of our hearts.'

Ulrich von Wilamowitz in 1908

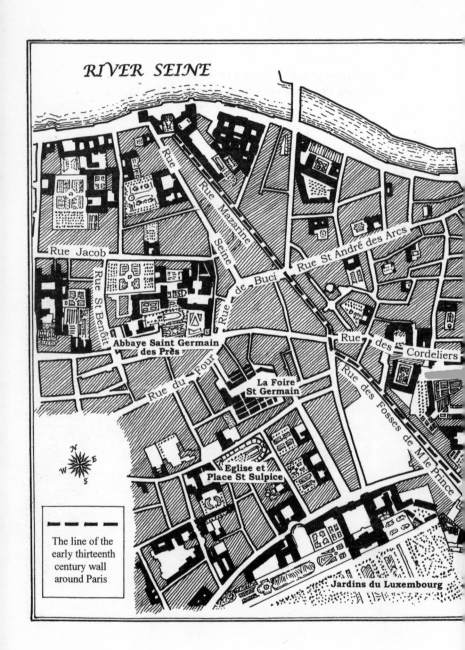

RIVER SEINE

Rue Jacob

Rue St Benôit

Rue

Rue Mazarine

Seine

Rue de Buci

Rue St André des Arcs

Abbaye Saint Germain
des Prés

Rue du Four

Rue des

Cordeliers

La Foire
St Germain

Rue des Fosses de Mʳᵉ Prince

N
E
W
S

Eglise et
Place St Sulpice

Jardins du Luxembourg

The line of the
early thirteenth
century wall
around Paris

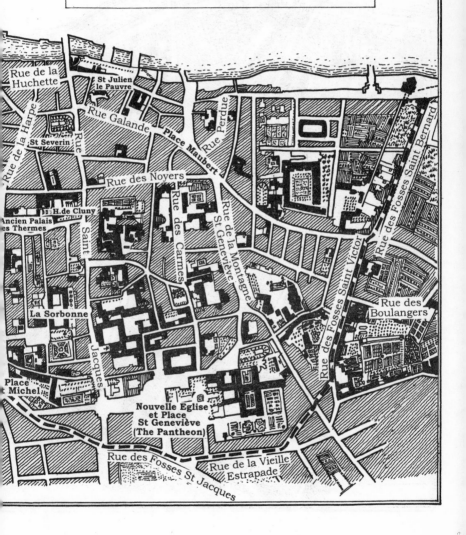

Adaptation of Jaillot's pre-French Revolution map, showing the medieval streets, alleys and squares of the Latin Quarter

Rue de la Huchette

St Julien le Pauvre

Rue de la Harpe

Rue Galande

Rue Perdue

Place Maubert

St Severin

Rue

Rue des Noyers

H.de Cluny

Ancien Palais des Thermes

Rue des Carmes

Rue de la Montagne St Geneviève

Saint

Rue des Fosses Saint Bernard

Rue des Fosses Saint Victor

Rue des Boulangers

La Sorbonne

Jacques

Place St Michel

Nouvelle Eglise et Place St Geneviève (The Pantheon)

Rue des Fosses St Jacques

Rue de la Vieille Estrapade

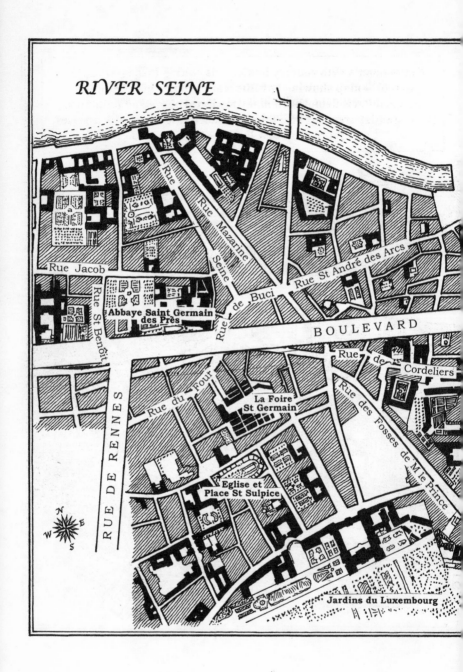

RIVER SEINE

Rue Jacob

Rue

Rue Mazarine

Seine

Rue St Benôit

Abbaye Saint Germain
des Près

Rue de Buci

Rue St André des Arcs

BOULEVARD

Rue de

Cordeliers

RUE DE RENNES

Rue du Four

La Foire
St Germain

Rue des Fosses de M le Prince

Eglise et
Place St Sulpice

Jardins du Luxembourg

N
E
W
S

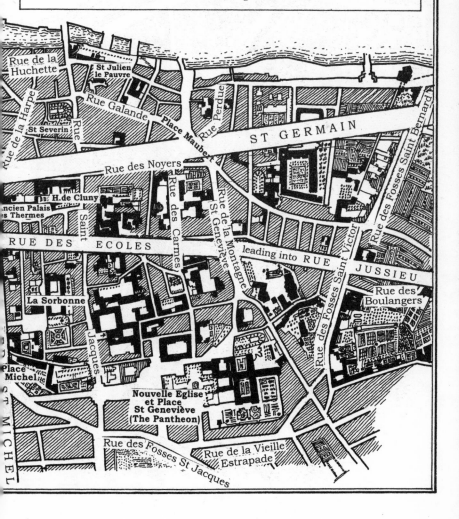

Haussmann's 19th century boulevards cutting through the old streets - map showing how the main arteries of the newly designed Paris demolished many medieval alleys and buildings. A substantial area was also rebuilt on each side of the new arteries, and there were new linking streets as well.

Rue de la Huchette

St Julien le Pauvre

Rue Galande

Place Maubert

Rue Perdue

ST GERMAIN

Rue de la Harpe

St Severin

Rue

Rue des Noyers

H. de Cluny

ncien Palais es Thermes

Saint

Rue des Carmes

Rue de la Montagne St Geneviève

Rue des Fosses Saint Victor

Rue des Fosses Saint Bernard

RUE DES ECOLES

leading into RUE JUSSIEU

Rue des Boulangers

La Sorbonne

Jacques

Place Michel

Nouvelle Eglise et Place St Geneviève (The Pantheon)

ERT

ST MICHEL

Rue des Fosses St Jacques

Rue de la Vieille Estrapade

Family Trees

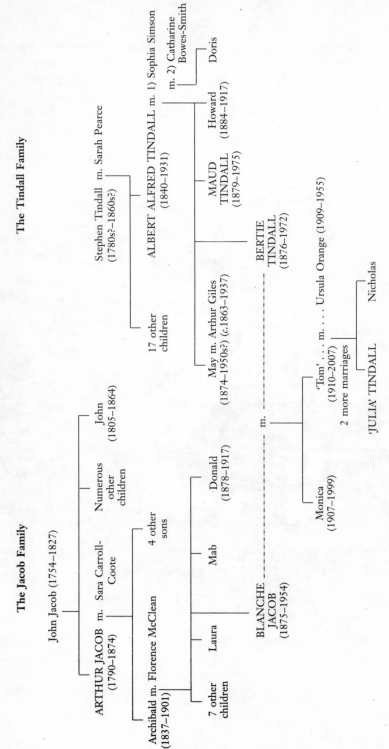

The Jacob Family

John Jacob (1754–1827)

ARTHUR JACOB (1790–1874) m. Sara Carroll-Coote

John (1805–1864)

Numerous other children

Archibald m. Florence McClean (1837–1901)

7 other children

Laura

Mab

4 other sons

Donald (1878–1917)

BLANCHE JACOB (1875–1954)

The Tindall Family

Stephen Tindall m. Sarah Pearce (1780s?–1860s?)

ALBERT ALFRED TINDALL m. 1) Sophia Simson (1840–1931)

m. 2) Catharine Bowes-Smith

Doris

17 other children

May m. Arthur Giles (1874–1950s?) (c.1863–1937)

MAUD TINDALL (1879–1975)

Howard (1884–1917)

BERTIE TINDALL (1876–1972)

m.

Monica (1907–1999)

'Tom' . . . m . . . . Ursula Orange (1910–2007) (1909–1955)

2 more marriages

'JULIA' TINDALL

Nicholas

Prologue

Long ago, one afternoon late in the Second World War, a woman and a small girl are walking along a potholed gravel road that skirts the edge of Ashdown Forest, in Sussex.

Once, Ashdown was a true forest, densely filled with oak, ash and birch. But little by little charcoal-burners, iron-smelters, gravel-diggers and herdsmen stripped most of it to a great heath, rising in tier upon tier of heather and gorse and bracken and copse to the blue hills of Colemans Hatch and Gill's Lap. To the child, who, till recently, has known nothing but the streets of a provincial town dingy with War, and walks beside someone else's pram, it seems like the world opening out before her.

That afternoon there is already a hint of expectation in the air, of something stirring in dank ditches or beneath the beaten brown fronds of last year's ferns. But it is only a hint as yet. This day that will arbitrarily lodge itself in the child's memory must be in winter still, or in the cold early spring, for both she and the woman are wearing winter coats. The woman's is brown, square-shouldered, with a belt, a little shabby in its fifth year. The child's is an odd, purplish tweed, made over by the village tailor from an adult garment: it grazes her bare knees above her gumboots. New clothes are hard to come by, near the end of the War. The woman and her child are walking to see old Mr Waters, in whose carpenter's shop down an appropriately watery side lane a kitchen table and a wardrobe are slowly being constructed. Furniture, too, is hard to come by. The furniture they used to have, which the woman remembers but the child does not, burnt brightly in a depository in the London Blitz of 1940: sizzling varnish, peeling inlay, dense upholstery smoke, the prints and photographs of stored memory reduced to a drift of black flakes.

The child is young, not yet at school. Because her legs are short, she and the woman walk slowly. The damp air condenses into a drizzle, and then into a fine, driving rain. The woman takes the child's hand and they trudge on, side-stepping the puddles now forming in the pot-holes. The child is conscious of being good, a Big Girl not making a fuss.

By and by the creaking and iron tread of a slow horse and cart approaches from behind, then draws level with them. The horse has huge, fur-hung hoofs that the child watches warily. The cart is empty but for a pile of sacks, and the carter has a sack over his head against the rain. He stops the horse with a throaty noise and a jangle of harness and looks down at the woman and her child.

'Should you like a ride, Missus? You and the little girl?'

– Or '*You and the little maid*'? Could he possibly have said that?

With awkward gratitude, the woman accepts. The child, shy but delighted, is lifted up. On the rough boards there is a pleasing smell of fresh sap and old manure: every-thing smells of something, and so do people. She knows the cart must be going to the broomyard at the top of Waters Lane.

For a very long time the willow and broom that grow in profusion on Ashdown Forest have been harvested each autumn and turned into household brooms.

The ageing men like this carter have worked in the yard all their lives – but not for much longer. All sorts of trades and habits, including horse-drawn carting, which were declining earlier in the century, have been prolonged by the privations and shortages of War and even given a fresh lease. But by the time the child is a grown woman a whole way of rural life, including the two-thousand-year European civilisation of the horse, will finally be extinguished. She will come to marvel at the memory of that afternoon lift in the rain, knowing it is a true one yet seeing it as something that must have happened to some other girl, in some other life, or in a novel by Thomas Hardy.

The grown-ups say the War will come to an end by and by, but this means little to the child who has known nothing else and so regards war as being in the natural order of things. She has also been told that 'after the War we shall be able to have as much butter and sugar and meat – and sweets! – as we like,' but this seems so improbable she thinks the grown-ups must be lying about it, as she has noticed they do about Father Christmas and fairies. Then there's that other story about how 'when the War is over Daddy will come home.' Daddy is a very young man in a leather photograph frame in Mummy's bedroom. His coming home sounds interesting, exciting even, but largely mythic. Like the prospect, confided to her when they were sharing the house of another family in Reading, that 'when we have a home of our own again we'll have it all decorated as we like.' Now they do have a home of their own, but the walls are mostly white and the curtains mostly blackout stuff. The beds come from Granny or from Auntie Someone in the village, and there is disappointingly little sign as yet of the hoarded tinsel, paperchains or holly that the word 'decorated' meant to the child when she heard it.

It's all just a story really, like the seaside and Paris, both places that Mummy is going to take her to when the War is over. The child has in fact been to Brighton, to go to the dentist and buy shoes, but does not associate the word 'seaside' with that. The shore at Brighton has mines and is covered in rolls of barbed wire, and the two piers are shut and derelict with a big, heaving hole of sea in the middle of each. This, to the child, is in the natural order of things, just as it is natural that the red iron chocolate machines on stations are always empty. She does not connect Brighton's forbidden and forbidding beach with the seaside pictures in children's books: boys and girls jumping about on yellow sand, with a beautifully made castle and a red bucket, and perhaps a small white dog jumping too.

So the after-the-War seaside and the after-the-War Paris, of which her mother speaks so longingly, have got themselves into the same story in the child's mind. Paris is a white city with towers and gold bits on them, like the magic castles in the big fairy-story book in Granny's house. There are knights in armour and unicorns and a forest behind. Paris also has a seashore, with very blue sea and ships with white sails. And magic swans, who sing. She can't quite square this with her mother's wistful remarks about having 'so many friends in Paris', but then Mummy talks a lot about other times – what has been or what will be.

The mother does not seem to notice the folds of Ashdown Forest, to which the child's eyes are continually drawn from her new vantage point up in the jolting cart, but this is probably because the mother is severely short-sighted and has never accepted her need to wear glasses. This physical myopia will, in the passage of years, evolve into a mental myopia also, a self-inflicted prison.

She retreats into literature, poetry mainly. She does her earnest best to share this with the child, talking and reading to her as if she were a small adult. So, by the time school will intervene, and each child in the class is asked to choose a poem to learn by heart, the child rejects the suggested ditties about primroses and fairies and brings to the school the Lyke Wake Dirge, banged out by her mother on an upright Remington with a worn ribbon. The headmistress is not pleased, which puzzles the child rather. It can't be Mummy's fault, so it must be her that Miss Spencer is cross with. Perhaps it is because she hasn't actually learnt to read the letters yet? But this does not matter (she thinks dismissively) as the words are in her head already. She does not understand quite all of them, but the graphic picture is there: a scary journey across the heather and bracken of Ashdown Forest in the winter, almost in the dark, probably in the rain, and only a flicker of candlelight to find the way.

> *On Whinny Moor when thou hast passed,*
> *This aye night and all,*
> *To Bridge o' Dread thou com'st at last*
> *And Christ receive thy soul –*

The traveller has no shoes on, she thinks, and maybe nothing else either, not even a nightdress. There is some abyss there that she senses with dread, though knowing it is beyond her comprehension.

> *If hosen and shoon thou ne'er gavest nane,*
> *This aye night and all,*
> *The winnies shall prick thee to the bare bane*
> *And Christ receive thy soul –*
> *. . . To Purgatory fire thou com'st at last –*

With a shudder of fear that, in the daylight and in company, is half-pleasurable, the child looks over the end of the cart to the great rain-blown expanses that lie ahead for her to cross when she is grown up. And it's all right, because some lovely house – in Paris, or Purgatory or somewhere, with gold and silver decorations on it – will be waiting at the end of the road.

Prologue

'Awfully bumpy, wasn't it?' says the woman brightly when the cart, going out of its way, has deposited them right beside Waters' place and disappeared back up the deep churned mud of the lower lane. She takes out a small packet of Players Weights and lights one, firmly regaining the modernity by which she sets store. She is, for a moment again, a clever young woman with a degree from Oxford and friends in Paris, who are just waiting for the War to end to invite her there again. Only, by some unfair quirk of fate, it would seem, has she found herself here in the depths of Sussex, in the depths of a War she has not tried to understand and takes as a personal setback, under a sodden sky.

Part I

Arthur: 1814

Chapter I

Walking to Paris

The child grew up, and went away from Sussex for ever, but Ashdown Forest remained lodged in her mind. It was that landscape that rose before her in memory when she heard the Lyke Wake Dirge again, or encountered the 23rd Psalm with its still waters, green pastures and valley of death, or John Bunyan's lifetime pilgrimage.

'*As I walked through the wilderness of the world...*' Bunyan's archetypal book begins. For him, this was matter-of-course. Long ago, everyone who wanted to move from one place to another, except the rich or unusually fortunate, simply turned their legs on to walk. Carts were for transporting heavy loads over short distances; over longer ones, when packhorses were used, they went at foot-pace, their masters walking alongside, on immemorial paths of a width not for wheels but for feet. It was on foot that armies moved to War until the twentieth century, and on foot that Dick Whittington and all the other unnamed Whittingtons over time came to big cities to seek their fortunes, or simply their daily bread. For many centuries itinerant labourers, harvesters, hedgers and ditchers, sheep-shearers, tinkers, pedlars, drovers, ballad-singers and preachers measured out their lives in footprints up, down and around the high roads, the byways, the sunken lanes and the downland paths of Britain. Some even ventured abroad.

What the child (whom I will call Julia) was not told, and what I did not discover for many years, was that a great-great grandfather had once made an epic journey on foot all the way to Paris, for his own work's sake. Like Wordsworth, Coleridge, Hazlitt and Leigh Hunt, all young like him at the beginning of the nineteenth century, and with more talent than means, he automatically walked as the logical way of covering any substantial distance. His name was Arthur Jacob, and when he set out to cross the length of England and northern France in the summer of 1814, his lifetime's career was just opening out before him. Paris was to be a determining factor of that life. So it was also to be, for different reasons, for his great-great granddaughter some hundred and forty years later.

Arthur arrived in a Paris which had an enduring tradition of young men travelling to the great city on foot, to take it on as an apprenticeship or a challenge. In some trades, particularly stone-cutting, building and roofing, men from the mountain villages of central France would leave home and family each spring once the snows receded and take the long road to Paris, Lyons or Marseilles. There, they spent the summer months on building sites, living sparingly, saving the bulk of their wages to carry home, still on foot, as the autumn chill set in. These great forays, out of the unlettered fastnesses of the rural world and into the evolving world of the cities, were known to the men themselves as 'campaigns'.

Except for a mere handful of surviving known names, those of individuals unusual enough to move from the building site into social and political prominence, nearly all these labouring men who trudged across France and through the generations are now forgotten. They have, in the biblical phrase, no name in the street. But it was

they who built the streets and the impressive buildings of
Paris. In doing so, they were a key part of an evolution
that was eventually to transform the human relationship
with landscape. For hills, moors, hidden paths and streams
were substituted buildings, paving stones, avenues, alleys
and quays. When a city is small enough to be walked out
of in an hour or so, as Paris and London still were in the
early nineteenth century, then the surrounding fields
continue to provide a context: identification with the urban
structure is not complete. But once a great city has become
a world in itself, then the allegiance of earlier generations
to the land, the emotional importance with which they
have invested standing stones, crags or tall trees, is transferred to urban landmarks. An urban peasantry is born.

Even more than the London that Dickens immortalised,
later-nineteenth- and twentieth-century Paris became a
city to which its inhabitants developed a visceral
attachment, almost regardless of their own places of
origin. The sentimental song with the refrain '*J'ai deux
amours – mon pays et Paris*' belongs to the 1920–40 era,
but its huge success then was surely due to its putting
into words a feeling that had been current already for
two or three generations. This extraordinarily strong pull
that Paris exerts has something of a literal, physical explanation, for Paris is a highly concentrated city. Even today,
when there has been a large, belated suburban expansion,
the population density of Paris proper, the Paris of the
twenty *arrondissements*, is roughly twice that of London.
The French concept of townscape is of something distinc-
tively urban, consciously grand, developed and fostered
over the last two hundred years. In contrast, the vague
English preference for leafy suburban sprawl has created
a quite different habitat.

The geographical heart of Paris has remained in the
same place for the whole seven hundred years since
the building of Notre Dame cathedral on the original
city-island in the Seine. The scholars, students,

foreigners, wanderers and idlers, who come and go on that small section of the Left Bank that lies opposite the cathedral across a narrow strip of water, are walking in the same patterns, and often on the very same named paths that their predecessors walked before the cathedral towers were raised.

Abelard, the young monk famous in his time for his learning and his persuasive debating skills, but more celebrated in subsequent centuries for his love affair with Héloïse, crossed from the island to deliver lectures to students sitting among hay fields before the name 'Latin Quarter' was current. The Rue St Jacques runs on the Roman route from the Paris island to the south: it acquired its name when the shrine of St Jacques of Compostela was established in the ninth century. The Rue de la Montagne Sainte Geneviève follows the irregular trace of the rocky goat path that led to the top of the steep hill long before Robert de Sorbon founded his modest teaching hall there in 1257. The Clos Bruneau, an insignificant alley off the Rue des Carmes, is the last flicker of an extensive vineyard of that name, one of many that flourished on that slope. The Carmelites remembered in the Rue des Carmes arrived in the place in 1309, but they were relative newcomers in comparison with the Jews who, denied residence on the city-island itself, had a settlement on the Montagne before being expelled around 1200. Some of their bones still lie a little way off, deep under part of the Rue Hautefeuille, a very old street in its own right and one we shall visit again – but then this Left Bank territory is mined with bones, a hidden chequerboard of small cemeteries long since buried under stone, timber, piping, concrete and iron.

Waves of itinerant masons have passed through; buildings have risen, remained for centuries, been chopped about, extended or replaced. Ancient streets have been bisected by new, wide ones; narrow rights of way have been swallowed up in boulevards, one-time central gathering places have become odd-shaped, tree-hung corners. Crowded tenements have become empty air. Yet if the psychic imprint of all that human living, hundreds of years of daily movements along personal routes within a square kilometre of space, could have left some visible trace, we would find ourselves treading directly in innumerable packed footprints. We share the same territory, both physically and psychologically, with troops of vanished others, all in their time as real and as involved in their own intricate lives as we ourselves are.

Some fifty years after that rainswept afternoon on Ashdown Forest, I wrote a book about the French masons and their epic journeys across France in thrall to the seasons. It was only then that I discovered, almost by chance, my own ancestor's long walk to Paris and his involvement in the very streets that I had by then made my own.

In the early summer of 1814 Napoleon had been despatched to Elba and the Bourbons were restored to the French throne. For the first time in thirteen years the British could visit France freely, and so Arthur Jacob set out from Edinburgh. In his pocket, he had a brand new qualification as a physician from the Edinburgh School of Medicine, and not much else. He journeyed on foot from the Scottish capital to Dover but not by a direct route, for it was part of his purpose to visit all the hospitals and infirmaries he could on his trek southwards. The little memorial book that was published by his colleagues on his death at the age of eighty-three, in a world transformed by trains and telegrams, chloroform and disinfectants, says 'it was in subsequent years a source of pride with him to be able to state that during the six weeks so occupied he traversed 960 miles.' Given that many of the days of those six weeks must have been spent looking round wards and dispensaries and talking to other doctors, the figures suggest an average, on walking days, of well over thirty miles.

He paused for some intensive hospital visiting in London, then set out for Dover. There he crossed to Boulogne and, still on foot, continued to Paris. His journey ended in the Rue de l'Ecole de Médecine – a stone's throw from where his grandson-in-law would live and work near the end of the century and where his great-great granddaughter, another sixty years later, would have her being. It is almost as if habitats, and even affinities for particular corners and views, persist in family DNA down the generations, unbeknown to the carriers, like a taste for poetry, a tone of voice or a turn of the head.

Chapter II

OUT OF IRELAND

B ut the journey, in fact, did not start in Edinburgh.
Arthur Jacob hailed from Ireland, a place with a
different image. And he did not even come from
Dublin, the elegant, miniature eighteenth-century townscape built under British hegemony, but from a remote
rural place. It was the damp, soft greenness of County
Wexford and Queen's County that formed Arthur. But
tempting as it is to link him therefore with the Irish
scholar-monks who came to Paris to live in the Collège
des Irlandais just a little to the north of the Carmelites,
leaving their invisible footprints all over the streets that
Arthur would come to tread, this would be false. Arthur
Jacob was not authentically Irish; he was neither Celtic
nor did he belong to the Old Faith, the Ireland of the
beggar-child's song, of the 'holy londe of Irlande'. When
that child was singing, some time in the fourteenth
century, Arthur's ancestors were probably Lombards –
bankers and moneylenders in northern Italy. Though,
by a maze of paths, some of them could have reached
the same territory in Paris as the Irish, since the Collège
des Irlandais in the Rue des Carmes had belonged earlier
to the Lombards.

The History of the Jacob Families (compiled by Arthur's
son together with a professional researcher the year

Arthur died, privately printed, and now in a crumbling, disjointed state, as if beginning to fall into dust itself) admits to a probable Jewish connection but plays it down. It ignores the seventeenth-century physician Hildebrand Jacob, even though his first name was used and reused in the family. This Dr Jacob, who attended members of the Royal Family, and was known to the gossipy John Aubrey as 'a person of great worth', seems to have been identifiably Jewish. But the family *History* places emphasis, instead, on a William Jacob (1610–1688) who was a lieutenant in Cromwell's army and was given a grant of land in County Wexford as a reward. He was, claims the book, first cousin to Sir John Jacob, 1st Baronet of Gamlingay in Cambridgeshire. He was also related to a raft of ecclesiastical persons by the name of Jacob in both Kent and Dorset. The Jacob family (never with an 's' at the end) was therefore, by implication, safely Anglo-Saxon. Arthur and his forebears were members of the Protestant Ascendancy, the Anglo-Irish who – according to your perspective – either oppressed the starving native peasantry, whose land they had stolen, or made a contribution to Ireland out of all proportion to their numbers, in that it was they who created the social structures, the schools, the colleges, the hospitals, the elegant buildings and eventually most of the literature of that past-racked island.

A hundred-odd years after William Jacob acquired his land his great-great grandson, Michael, was settled in Queen's County – 'a clever medical man and a pleasant companion; his company was sought often by the best in the county.' He was to be the first in a line of Jacob surgeons which ran unbroken till 1914.

Maryborough, the tiny chief town of Queen's County, is today called Portlaoise and is celebrated only for the large maximum-security prison which is the main local employer. Once a pretty place built within the remains of a fortress, with a winding high street of old houses and a nineteenth-century courthouse-gaol right in the middle, it has today been rendered physically incoherent by the building of a new shopping centre just beyond the town. A similarly featureless luxury hotel (surely too grand to offer accommodation to those come to visit their relatives in the prison?) has invaded a large parcel of land near the ruined fortress tower. The old gaol has been turned into a theatre and arts centre: its complete evisceration has removed all trace of the complex history once enacted there. A plaque 'commemorates the memory of eleven people whose remains were discovered in 1997 during the construction of this Arts Centre . . . May they rest in Peace.' There might have been twelve of them, had it not been for the humane efforts of Arthur Jacob and his brothers John and Thomas. (See pages 105-7).

I knew, more or less, what I was looking for, but had no real expectation of finding it, now after so long and so much change. In the new Public Library, somewhere beyond the shopping centre, any memories of the reachable past seemed to have been demoted to make space for coloured cut-outs of dinosaurs. However, as I drove out through the twentieth-century sprawl along the old Dublin Road, I braked at an unexpected glimpse of a blue plaque. It was on a house right by the road: a large, plain house with a classic Dublin-style doorway and porch, and walls that were probably stuccoed before they were covered in the grey porridge of pebble-dash of which Ireland today is unaccountably fond. Before the traffic came, and before a shopping centre (another) and a large modern Roman Catholic church were built opposite, the house must have had fine green views. Ruins down the lane behind it, and a steep rocky hill nearby with gravestones here and there upon it, hinted at earlier incarnations for the site.

'This was for many years the home of the famous Jacob medical family. An early Dr Jacob founded the first infirmary in Maryborough (now Portlaoise) in 1756. His son, Dr John Jacob, founded the County Infirmary in 1808 and built this house c.1810. John's son, Dr Arthur Jacob, discovered the membrane of the eye, afterwards called "Membrane Jacobi" . . .' And the rest of the plaque's inscription was about how the building became the Parochial House after 1912 and was lived in by a series of much-loved parish priests – presumably associated with the church opposite and its huge plastic pietà. The house now appeared empty.

So I left Portlaoise with a warmer feeling for the town and its uneasy relationship with the past than I would otherwise have had. I discovered afterwards that the old stone vestiges down the lane were what remained of a very ancient building that had been reused by John Jacob, father of Arthur, as the first County Infirmary.

The traditional system at the end of the eighteenth century, throughout the United Kingdom, was for local medical men to tender individually each year to the Poor Law Overseers for contracts to look after the sick poor. Naturally the lowest tenders were apt to be accepted, often from useless or negligent practitioners; no one was satisfied with the situation and money was wasted. Go-ahead country surgeons, like Jacob, were coming to realise that if the sick could be brought to centralised places, thus saving time and effort, good local surgeons, physicians and apothecaries could be induced to come together to pool their experience and develop standard procedures: all would benefit. Just look, said the modern-minded men, at the success of such schemes in Edinburgh and Vienna, those famed centres of progress. They could have added Paris but did not, for the moment, since Britain had hardly yet recovered from horror tales of the French Revolution and anyway was at War with France.

So it was here, in the newly opened County Infirmary, and in the farms round about that Arthur, who was born in 1790, became a teenage apprentice to his father. He saw the handsome new house begin to go up nearby when he was sent to study medicine in Dublin. It was to this house that he eventually returned from his Paris adventure. He was in practice himself in Dublin, and already making his mark in research, by the time a brand new Infirmary was built further along the Dublin Road, with money badgered by Dr John Jacob out of the local great and good.

So, as it turned out, it was Arthur's much younger brother, another John, who took on the Infirmary and the extensive country practice at the father's death. This son 'was alike to rich and poor, to the peasant and the peer . . . honest, straightforward and outspoken almost to a fault'. (Obituary, 1864.) Family lore has it that he had an obsession, possibly well founded, with tuberculosis and the need to combat this with fresh air, and used to bang his stick through the windows of wretched little houses if the occupants were unwilling to open them. His local name was Old Danger, from the speed at which he drove the buggy that was kept ready to visit patients day and night, but the same energy and eagerness made him loved. His own children, sadly, were afraid of him.[1] He followed his father in keeping a diary on all the families he treated, of every class – a record which, passed down in the family and progressively augmented with succeeding generations of patients, became a medico-social account of nineteenth-century rural society.

The bust of John now in the Royal College of Surgeons in Ireland shows mutton-chop whiskers, a high stock and a determined look. The companion bust of brother Arthur – clean-shaven, neck bare above Roman drapery – creates a more spiritual impression, perhaps more fitting to a distinguished pioneer in diseases of the eye. He wears no glasses, though other likenesses throughout his life always show him with these. Perhaps it was in the need to wear spectacles from boyhood that the origins of his particular interest lay. Did the father understand in good time that his youngest son and namesake was the one more suited than Arthur to driving out to patients over the hills and bogs of Queen's County?

Or perhaps there were family arguments about this. There must have been good reason why the father's nickname went down the generations in family lore as Old Squaretoes. There were other sons, older than John, who might equally have been expected to step into their father's professional place but apparently did not. The eldest of all, Michael, mysteriously disappeared to Australia, which was not yet a place of respectable emigration. Was he discarded as a ne'er-do-well? Two others went to India and succumbed there to the infections that claimed many European lives.[2] John was in fact the youngest of the twelve children, almost all of whom survived into adulthood. Fifteen years younger than Arthur, he was still in baby petticoats when the Infirmary was founded. When Dr Jacob died in 1827, leaving the newer and purpose-built Infirmary behind as a memorial, John was a just-qualified practitioner not yet twenty-two. He took over, and flourished. But surely this was not what Dr Jacob had originally planned when he sent Arthur, who had by then stepped into Michael's place as eldest son, to study in Dublin with a celebrated surgeon, a chance that he himself had never had?

By custom, surgeons had till then existed on a lower plane than physicians and their training tended to be more modest and pragmatic. No previous Jacob had had a formal diploma in surgery from a medical college in Dublin nor had gone on to take a separate course as a physician in Edinburgh. But times were changing and there was a scent of progress in the air. 'Dr' Jacob, with his Infirmary on the model of others that were opening or shortly to open up and down the British Isles, prided himself on being part of the change. His son was to have the joint qualification and MD after his name.

There had long been a tradition of young doctors

completing their studies in Edinburgh, which was both cheaper and better organised for the purpose than Dublin. An MD from Edinburgh, where the likes of James Gregory, John Bell and James Hamilton the obstetrician were already making their mark, was much prized. There medicine itself, for so long sunk in an unprestigious trough of bleeding, leeching and cupping, was beginning to quicken to a few glimmering ideas to do with careful observation, precision and hygiene, and these would become more focused as the century went on. In any case there were many historic links between the Scots and the Anglo-Irish community to which almost all Dublin doctors belonged. Although the Penal Laws keeping Roman Catholics out of the professions had been largely revoked by Arthur Jacob's day, the medical establishment were still mainly 'of the Protestant persuasion'. Abraham Colles, the renowned surgeon and anatomist under whom Arthur worked in Dublin, had taken his degree in Edinburgh and no doubt recommended it to his pupil. So to Edinburgh in 1813, for a final year of study, Arthur went.

While he probably did not subsist, like the traditional hard-up Scottish student, on a barrel of oatmeal a term and another of salted herrings, a young man with ten brothers and sisters at home could not expect to live extravagantly. Quite as hard-working and determined as Colles, Arthur may have stayed with the same landlady, a Mrs Smellie in the old town, who used to interrupt her student lodger late at night 'to prevent him from reading himself into a coffin'. Food was not expensive; 'a piece of good cod' for tenpence would provide dinner for several days for two men sharing, and sixpence a head would buy a Sunday feast in an inn by the Firth of 'good kele broth, bacon and eggs, oaten bread and butter'. Butcher's meat, though, was a rare treat.

By March the following year the Russians, and other of Britain's intermittent allies in the Napoleonic Wars, were forming up to attack Paris. As Napoleon's minister, the arch-survivor Talleyrand, remarked with his habitual cynicism: 'This is the beginning of the end.' Napoleon's support was haemorrhaging from him. Paris, ill-prepared for any assault, fell on the last day of the month. Six days later Napoleon abdicated, theoretically in favour of his infant son who was already in safety elsewhere, and departed to 'rule' Elba. This insignificant realm the size of the Isle of Wight, between Italy and Corsica, was ostensibly a Ruritanian imperial seat in which he could salvage his pride, but in practice it was an island prison which he soon began scheming to leave. The restored Bourbon king, arbitrarily known as Louis XVIII since his unhappy nephew, the little Dauphin, had disappeared in the Revolution, was in Paris by early May. The Parisians, punch-drunk with successive regime changes over the preceding twenty-five years, obediently stuck white cockades in their hats. Continuing loyalty to Napoleon was muttered in the old streets, but in the wealthier quarters the royal lilies and bees were quickly sewn back onto curtains.

The hostile armies had all vacated the city by the end of that month, just about the time that Arthur Jacob in Edinburgh was being awarded his MD. For this he wrote a dissertation in Latin on one of the arteries from the heart. Diplomatically – or perhaps, who knows, with sincere gratitude? – he dedicated this opus to his parent – '*quo rudimenta non solum attigit, sed omnibus postes nummis adeptu professionis in cultu fructus est filius*'. ('From whom did he attain not only the rudiments but all subsequent provision for the professional art: the son is the fruit.')

Since Arthur did not return to Ireland before his momentous journey, any dispute with his father over the plan must have taken place by mail. One can imagine the nature of it in an era when letters were composed with a certain formality, even between close relatives.

'. . . *I have spent money on you, my son, money that I have laid out gladly but, as you are aware, Samuel is now studying for the Church in Dublin and so costing us money also for his fees and keep. I don't speak of the Michael business, but his debts are now paid. Four of your sisters are now off my hands, but each had to have her portion, there will still be Susan and Mary to marry not to mention William, Thomas and little John to launch into life. I shall be sixty this year and have pinned many hopes on you. I know you have been a devoted scholar, but it is now your duty to return to Ireland and take up your place here as a grown man.'*

'Sir, the chance of a lifetime is before me. Paris can now be visited again, and my professor here, John Bell, is willing to give me introductions to Dupuytren, who is soon to become chief surgeon of the Hôtel Dieu, and to Dubois who has been physician to the Empress. Professor Colles will help me too: with such recommendations I believe I can readily find some work in Paris as a dresser or even as an assistant. Do you not see, Father, that I cannot possibly ignore these offers?'

'. . . did not send you to Edinburgh for you to work as a dresser. You know of my plans for a building more fit for the Infirmary, and that Eyre Coote and Sir James Grattan have pledged their support. I have devoted my life to this. I shall need you, Arthur.'

'. . . I too am devoting my life to medicine but – forgive me, Father – medicine today is becoming much more than . . .'

'. . . these French ideas! Jacobins. Many of our best medical men distrust them, you know . . . Well, you must act as you think fit. No doubt in any case you will. But please under-stand that not a penny more . . .'

Old Squaretoes. But no, perhaps I have got it wrong. Perhaps, at that stage, Arthur did have the family busi-ness in his own sights, and initially the main purpose of the walk to Paris was the chance to survey comparable institutions, both in England and in France.

'. . . So, Father, making the journey on foot, I shall have the opportunity to vary my route to visit many hospitals and infirmaries on my way south and form an opinion of their

methods. This will be of the greatest use in the future, to you as well as to me . . .'

Maybe, indeed, it was not till Paris was attained, and further experience had there, that Arthur's ambition evolved definitively away from the life of a country surgeon towards a more specialised career.

Chapter III

Arthur's Journey

A better-off young man than Arthur Jacob would have climbed onto one of the coaches that then plied between Edinburgh and London. The journey, undertaken all at once, was arduous in itself, for the coaches kept going for six days and nights with breaks only for meals. Relays of horses were replaced at specially equipped inns all along the route. (The mail coaches did it in sixty hours, but with them the changeover of horses had developed into a coordinated exercise timed to the minute.) The great north road resounded to hoofbeats at that period, for it had a better gravelled surface than ever before. In a number of once-quiet provincial towns on or near its route new industries had changed life entirely. A new breed of commercial and business travellers rattled constantly through tracts of country that before had known only the great slow-motion gatherings for cattle fairs and the transactions of the immemorial wool trade.

Coaches were never a form of mass travel. They were not cheap. They hardly could be, with the high-quality performance of man and beast on which they depended, though it was no doubt also true that the coaching inns profited from having a captive market of relatively well-off travellers to rack up prices. William Smith, one of the first geologists and land surveyors, wrote in his memoirs, which cover the years of Arthur Jacob's youth: 'Everyone who travels knows that ready money must be provided for the road. There is no credit at coach offices. A man's hand is constantly draining his pocket, and so pressing for fees were all the lackey attendants . . . that I used to say a civil answer could scarcely be obtained on the road for less than sixpence. In taxes and tolls alone the man obliged to travel much pays heavily, however abstemious and economical he may be . . .'

Signs from his later life suggest that Arthur was abstemious or, at any rate, not fond of lavish living. Let us suppose, for a moment, that he *had* taken the coach. He would have travelled 'on the outside', that is, on the top, unprotected from wind or rain, as men routinely did. Only old or infirm gentlemen thought it their place to join the ladies in the stuffy interior, which normally accommodated only four to six people anyway. But, even outside, a journey of no more than sixty or seventy miles from central London to the south coast cost a pound, and Edinburgh to London by the shortest route was over five hundred miles. So locomotion alone would have cost Arthur seven or eight pounds, before any of the tolls, taxes and tips that William Smith mentions. And then there would be meals. Travellers' manuals of the period suggest that the standard coaching-inn meal, with service, would cost each time something like three to four shillings, a far cry from the sixpence (half a shilling) a head that had procured a Sunday feast in a simpler Scottish tavern. So, at twenty shillings to the pound, over six days at least another three pounds must be added, bringing the total cost of the journey to something like twelve pounds. Or far more, of course, if Arthur had used the coaches to pursue his more circuitous route from one town to another. Similarly if, on the direct six-day route, he had permitted himself the luxury of a night or two in an inn bed, to rest from the ceaseless shake and clatter and dust and night-time chill of the journey, the figure would rise much more steeply. At exactly the same period, a young French iron-master, visiting England to try to find out why English iron was of better quality, paid fifteen shillings and sixpence (just over three quarters of a pound) for a brief sojourn in an inn at Deal, where a storm at sea had landed the ship's passengers precipitantly, and then fourteen shillings for a night and dinner in a hotel in Dover. This, in an era when many ordinary working men did not earn fourteen shillings a week and a servant-keeping member of the modest white-collar class only about three times that.

So, Arthur set out to walk. The summer of 1814, which followed one of the coldest winters on record, was not a warm one, but perhaps, for the comfort of a walker, this was all to the good. For Arthur was not a labourer or yet an impoverished poet, who would sleep out under the stars or seek a night's shelter in a barn. He could not tramp the muddy or dusty roads of England quite unwashed, in shirtsleeves or a smock. He was a quali-fied physician; when he reached the town that was his next objective he had to appear presentable at the gates of the infirmary or private house where he hoped to be received.

I do not know exactly what medical centres he visited on his zigzag path. He seems to have started with Scottish ones, probably Glasgow and Dumfries. Nine hundred and sixty miles, almost twice as far as the direct route to England's south coast, took him, as he told people long after, as far as Wales on one side and East Anglia on the other. Britain had a fair number of hospitals and infirm-aries by then, most of them established in the preceding sixty or seventy years and many of them, like the one in Maryborough, much more recently than that. Arthur would surely have visited the ones at Newcastle-on-Tyne and at York. The growing industrial cities of Hull and Huddersfield had yet to acquire theirs, but Leeds had one. So did Manchester, Sheffield, Stafford, Worcester and Birmingham. Newcastle-under-Lyne, in the Potteries, only opened theirs the following year, but Nottingham, Leicester, Northampton and Bedford each had one, and another had recently opened in Derby. In towns such as these Arthur would have sighted for the first time the ponderous, noise-filled buildings and great smoking chimneys that the new industries had brought in the previous fifty years to England's ancient agricultural land-scape. In the west, he reputedly went to Chester, Shrewsbury, Hereford and Bristol. Did he get as far as Exeter, an old foundation like the one at Bristol, and also to the infirmaries in the other cathedral cities of Salisbury and Winchester? He would not have wanted to miss the one at Oxford, named for the seventeenth-century physician John Radcliffe but only founded in 1770. He certainly visited the older one at Cambridge, since he made the journey into the east as far as Norwich.

Progress was in the air, and Arthur Jacob's voyage of discovery was in itself part of this stirring. The old Poor Law system, based on individual parishes, had broken down as people moved from one place to another far more than they had in the past, drawn or driven towards jobs in the expanding towns. In the new mills and work-shops, with their unguarded machinery, terrible accidents occurred – limbs torn off, faces battered by grinding stones run too fast – adding to the more traditional ailments of the labouring poor as listed in medical hand-books of the period: scrofula, tuberculosis, ophthalmia, hernia, pleurisy, lumbago and abscesses, not to mention more opaque diagnoses such as 'swollen brain' or 'vita cutis'.

In an effort to cope with the new urban working class and their ills, old and often inefficient institutions, each run by a handful of surgeons and apothecaries, were being revamped, and new ones opened. There had been passionate arguments in Edinburgh Royal Infirmary itself about which doctors and students had the right to attend patients. The Bristol Royal Infirmary had been founded in 1742, but it was rebuilt in the 1790s and, for the first time, acquired a room specifically designated for operations with an operating table donated by 'one of the sawbones'. But a set of operating instruments was not bought there till 1811: till then each surgeon carried his own knives with him. Worcester Infirmary was in financial trouble all through the 1800s, and the not-yet-qualified man who was brought in to run it in 1812 was even younger than Arthur. But medicine was rising in status. That boy was to go on to a long career as a pioneer of cleanliness and suitable diet, and eventually a knighthood.[1] The year before Arthur's great walk, the Northampton institution 'for the Relief of Sick and Lame Poor' was also reforming itself, and drew up a detailed list of rules about diet, nurses' duties, visitors and regular inspections.[2] Full meals for those considered fit enough to eat them consisted of milk porridge for breakfast, meat on most days for dinner and bread and cheese for most suppers. No strong liquor (i.e. gin or port) was to be allowed in the wards, and 'no Patients to be, on any account, suffered to drink tea' anywhere in the Infirmary. Presumably this related more to tea's status as a luxury commodity than to any supposed harm it might do. Also 'that no Patients do presume to give to their friends who come to see them, or others, any of their allowance of bread, meat or beer'. It is not hard to guess, from this, and from the insistence that all washing and dressings were to be done early in the day, what the older, un-reformed hospitals were like.

So, pulling the iron bell-handles at the gates of these old and new institutions, Arthur came, dressed for the road probably in 'buff' or light brown Irish linen breeches rather than the cream ones then fashionable in summer, and good solid boots or shoes. (Wordsworth, for long tramps, favoured shoes.) Arthur would have worn a waistcoat, a cutaway coat like a riding coat, a neck-cloth folded to cover the top of his shirt, and some sort of traditional broad-brimmed hat rather than the newer town-style that was then in the process of evolving into the ubiquitous nineteenth-century 'stove-pipe'. William Blake, another fervent walker of the time, showed just such a hat on his little drawing of a traveller 'hastening in the evening'. Arthur Jacob must also have had a small shoulder bag of leather with a spare shirt, nightshirt and socks, some letters and papers – perhaps a pocket French dictionary to study – and one of the small-scale, approximate maps of the time. He no doubt had his doctor's pocket knife and lancet in a little case, but not much more than that: the stethoscope had not yet been invented. A shave could be had in any town or village through which he passed, and no one of any class then considered it necessary to bath often, or to change their outer garments.

Sometimes he would have been received with reserve or open condescension by an elderly surgeon-in-charge in the tie-wig and long, snuff-stained waistcoat of a previous era, but sometimes his newly acquired Edinburgh knowledge would have been welcome and solicited: here and there he would have encountered known faces. No doubt he was accommodated with dinner and a night's stay, either in the infirmary itself or in the home of one of the medical men, with a servant to clean his boots and brush his coat for the morning. But what about the nights in between towns?

'If you're passing by Berwick you should look up my people.' That is the sort of thing a fellow student in Edinburgh would have said. Or –

'I've an uncle who's a surgeon in Shropshire, Ludlow way. I'll write and tell him to expect you.' Or yet –

'I've some cousins in Lincolnshire. Mostly females. Haven't seem 'em for some time, but I'm sure they'll take you in. It's a quiet life there.'

For in that pre-railway world, out among the hills and pastures of a still very rural England, the number of those who could be classed as educated gentlefolk was relatively tiny and social life correspondingly restricted. Everyone in this small world knew each other or knew *of* each other. A new face, with fresh conversation, was readily welcomed, and then passed on as a desirable guest to an acquaintance or relative in the next county ('Ask for Mr Bailey at the courthouse. I'll give you a note for him . . .'). Arthur could have reciprocated hospitality here and there with useful advice on Bessie-Jane's poisoned finger or an up-to-date opinion on Mother's dizzy turns. Without means he might be, sustaining himself during his long marches on a few penn'orth of bread, cheese and milk bought from the farms he passed. I suspect he had a distinct Irish accent, perhaps ironed out a little by Edinburgh gentility, but he had his professional credentials and the manner and dress of a gentleman and, as such, many doors would have been opened for him.

If other resources failed, and another dusk began to overtake him, he could simply seek out the vicarage in the next village to which he came, knowing that the vicar would be unlikely to turn him away. Vicars were honorary members of the network of rural gentry, and as an Anglo-Irishman Arthur was a member of the Established Church of England. He could claim cousins who were churchmen themselves, in the West Country and in Kent, and a great uncle had been an Archdeacon in Armagh.

In point of fact, Arthur's later life reveals a man who had little truck with God. Darwin's theory of evolution was not to be published till Arthur was old; but already, in his youth, progressive opinion was advancing observations on human and animal physiology which were beginning to lay a long fuse of doubt and uncertainty regarding the conventional Christian view of mankind. Arthur's eldest son – who later took Holy Orders and ended up as the incumbent of a fashionable church in Bayswater, west London – was, as a teenager, worried by his father's lack of faith. He wrote him an anguished letter and left it on his plate at breakfast:

> 'I thought indeed of *speaking* to you on this subject, but found myself quite incapable of facing the great dislike you have always entertained to conversation on religion . . . I dare not, as a Christian, or as a *son*, hold back from this *painful* task . . . Perhaps the obstacle is *procrastination*, putting off religion to a *more convenient* season. Are we sure that this season will come? Is there no such thing as *sudden death*? . . .'

Addressed to a doctor, this appeal seems particularly inept. However, Arthur must have been to some extent touched by it, or by the emotion behind it, for he did not throw away the little, tightly folded missive but kept it for the rest of his life. It survives among his sparse papers today.

But in 1814 a long road still separated the eager, energetic, supremely fit young man with the scholar's eye-glasses and a mop of curly hair from the austere, formidable figure he was to become. Trying to concentrate on the young man, coming in and out of focus in the mind's eye, I have the same tantalising feeling that is produced when looking at tiny people in an engraved landscape: surely, if I gaze hard enough, I will eventually, as in an enlarged photograph, be able to discern every expression, every thread of cloth?

No good. He's off down the winding road, back view as ever, a flickering figure busy on his way to many other places. Somewhere along the road his twenty-fourth birthday has recently occurred. Paris calls.

But first he has the excitement of London, and the negotiation there of a few formalities. Judging from his subsequent career, Arthur would have done his research thoroughly. Perhaps he had acquired a copy of a small, fat, leather-bound book which is still to be found from antiquarian dealers – *A New Picture of Paris, or the Stranger's Guide to the French Metropolis*. The edition I possess is the sixth, published in 1817. It claims to have been 'much enlarged and entirely recomposed' in consequence of the Restoration, but it is in essence a description of the imperial Napoleonic city of the preceding decade, the city that Arthur was shortly to discover. Arthur's earlier edition would have told him all he needed to know about procuring a passport from the Foreign Office (still a requisite that year, though, with Napoleon on Elba, it was hoped that the Wars were over), and another paper from the French ambassador at his house off Portman Square. It would also have told him how to purchase French gold and silver coins, at a rate advantageous to the traveller, from Mr Solomons, New Street, Covent Garden, or from Mr Smart, 55 Prince's Street, Leicester Square (a district full of French émigrés since the Revolution), 'or from Mr Thomas, 102 Cornhill, on whom the tourist may confidently rely for punctuality and integrity'. Since passports and foreign exchange all cost money, it must be assumed that whatever savings Arthur had made by his long tramp were ready waiting for him at a London banking house.

I do not think he paused for long in London this time, though he may have taken the opportunity to introduce himself to Astley Cooper. Cooper pioneered research into blood vessels. He was soon to be appointed chief surgeon to a succession of royals, and later knighted. Abraham Colles had worked with him as a young man and must have recommended his promising pupil, Jacob, to him, for on his return from France the following year Arthur himself worked with Cooper for several months.

If he did seek Cooper out in Guy's Hospital, this would have fitted conveniently into his route. Guy's, founded a hundred years earlier, stood, as it does today, just off

Southwark High Street, and the road to Dover led from there. The street was lined then with galleried coaching inns and yards, of which the George today is the only survivor. Not that Arthur was about to succumb to a coach, especially after an invigorating day or two in London, but Southwark was the place anyway to start the journey. There were bakers' shops where, for a couple of pennies, could be bought kidney pies into which gravy was poured with a spout, and in Borough Market fresh raspberries from the market gardens of Camberwell were sold wrapped in cabbage leaves.

It puzzled me at first that Arthur set out for Dover, since, before the railways came, that was not the most obvious route to France. Many ships left from Brighton, which is not as far from London as Dover is, and arrived at Dieppe which is nearer to Paris than are Calais or Boulogne. However, the reason is not far to seek. There was a large, old infirmary to visit in Canterbury, directly on the way to Dover, but none near Brighton. In Dover, he would take one of the packets, still under sail then, which would, for a sum of about ten shillings (half a pound), deposit him in France. According to winds and tides 'the passage is frequently completed in three hours, but it is sometimes prolonged to five or six. It will therefore be advisable to take some slight provision on board.' (*The Stranger's Guide.*)

So, early in the morning, he leaves London again. It is high summer now. The streets soon fall away behind him, giving place to hay fields innocent of the houses that will come to cover them during the next thirty years. But the road is busy. It will take him over Blackheath and Shooters Hill, past Greenwich into the deeper country-side and on and on to Rochester thirty miles distant. In the afternoon, in some chalky rise of the North Downs where a white haze hangs in the sunlight, he sees yet another London-bound coach approaching him, and steps once again back against the hedgerow to avoid the worst of its travelling cloud of dust. The heavy vehicle, not an express coach but one that takes twelve hours from Dover to London, picking up and setting down passengers at many places on the way, lumbers noisily past him on iron-clad wheels, with its team of sweating horses and its roof crowded with hatted heads.

The coachman on the box is a young man called Stephen Tendall or Tindall, son of a small Sussex farmer, who has seen in coach-driving the chance of a life more entertaining and modern than the drudgery of the plough and the slowly turning seasons. In his own obscure way, he is as go-ahead as Arthur Jacob.

In the long future, when both these coming men are dead and gone, the grandson of one will marry the granddaughter of the other. But this improbable wedding will be a dynastic one, engineered by both families, for by then a link will have been formed between them which is traceable back to Arthur Jacob's stay in the Latin Quarter of Paris in the months before the Battle of Waterloo.

Chapter IV

The Walled City

A great many other people besides Arthur Jacob were visiting France that summer. Seat of the bloody Revolution of 1789–94 that had sent tremors of fear round Europe, then at War with Britain for much of the intervening time, France was a focus of fascinated curiosity, particularly for those who also regarded her as the main source of the Enlightenment. By 1814 travellers could again easily visit Paris, for the first time since the short-lived Peace of Amiens in 1802. Both British and Americans took advantage of this, and a few of them have left diaries to tell us what it was like. Morris Birkbeck, a leading exponent of new agricultural ideas and owner of much land, set out from Dieppe by the huge, swaying French *diligence*, so much slower than the stagecoach of England. He was already in middle age, although his energy and enthusiasm were yet to carry him on a few years later to found a Utopian settlement on the other side of the Atlantic, that obsession of visionary spirits. Although the French roads were much quieter than those in southern England, he found the countryside and the towns between the coast and Paris more cheerful and prosperous than he had expected:

'Since I entered the country I have been looking in all directions for the ruins of France; for the horrible effects of the revolution of which so much is said on our side of the water: but instead of ruined country, I see fields highly cultivated and towns full of inhabitants . . . Everyone assures me that agriculture has been improving rapidly for the last twenty-five years . . . and that vast improvement has taken place in the condition and character of the common people . . . I ask for the wretched peasantry of whom I have heard and read so much; but I am always referred to the revolution: it seems they vanished then.'

Later on his long journey round France, he commented on 'the general politeness of all classes and the lack of heavy drinking in spite of the relative cheapness of wine'. He did, however, also remark that 'our English eyes look in vain for respectable homes [i.e. the comfortable though unpretentious country house which had by then become such a feature of the British landscape, like the Jacob house outside Maryborough] . . . Remote from large towns and manufactures, there seem to be no habitations but those of small farmers and cottagers.'

It depended, of course, on what your expectation was. *The Stranger's Guide* that Arthur Jacob may have had in his pocket describes Calais as having 'a mean and dirty appearance' surrounded by 'a dreary expanse of country . . . infinitely inferior to that which [the traveller] has so lately admired at Dover'. Boulogne, which is where Arthur landed, finds rather greater favour as being more 'picturesque': Boulogne had a long tradition of trade with England, both licit and illicit (*'Brandy for the parson, 'baccy for the clerk, laces for a lady, letters for a spy . . .'*) and was now poised to develop a more genteel British community. However, Montreuil, on a hilltop, the next place of any size on the hundred-and-sixty-mile road to Paris, is stigmatised in the *Guide* as forming 'a miserable contrast with the beauty of the situation. The streets are narrow and dirty, and an appearance of poverty pervades the place.' The writer also remarks, as did all travellers at this period, on the inconvenient fact that French towns were still walled with gates that were shut at night, a practice long abandoned in England. And he has a further complaint:

'The poor laws are unknown in France. No public provision is made for age, sickness or misfortune; it is not, therefore, surprising that the number of mendicants should be great. The natural frivolity of the French character contributes to increase this evil. The common people live merely for the passing day; they lay up no provision for the future; and when age or misfortune overtakes them, they have no resource but the charity of individuals.'

There speaks the archetypal English voice, certain of his own superiority, a voice that was to boom louder as the century went on and Britain's wealth and world influence increased, while France seemed to progress only by means of repeated uprisings and regime changes. But if the landscape and towns of Picardy and upper Normandy did not make the same unfavourable impression on the well-informed Birkbeck, they are still less likely to have disconcerted Arthur Jacob. Growing up in rural Ireland, visiting his father's poorer patients in tiny turf-roofed cabins, he would have encountered a way of life considerably more primitive than that of post-revolutionary northern French peasantry. Nor would he have been a stranger to beggars: the beggars of old Dublin were notorious. He would also have been unsurprised by various other inconveniences listed on the debit side by the scrupulously fair Birkbeck, including 'the habit of spitting'; 'the Cabinets d'aisance, and, in some places, the utter want of them'; unpaved streets, smelly towns, dirty water thrown from windows, 'increasing numbers of priests', over-loquacious ceremonial greetings, and (in contrast) the casual way servants would enter a room at any and every moment.

It was true what the *Guide* said about the French beggars. Dickens, at a slightly later time, remarked that 'every cripple at the post-houses, not blind, who shoved his little battered box in at the carriage windows [asked for] "charity in the name of Heaven".' Many of these would have been ex-soldiers from Napoleon's Grande Armée, or their dependants. The numbers of deaths and injuries among young conscripted Frenchmen during the Wars were comparable, in proportion to the population, with those suffered just over one hundred years later in the First World War. But the Napoleonic Wars were, like the Revolution that had preceded them, consigned quickly to the receding past: no one, from 1814 onwards, wanted to think about the disastrous retreat from Moscow two years earlier. The damaged survivors of this and other battles had little attention paid to them, outside Paris's military hospitals of Les Invalides and the Val de Grâce.

However, the *Guide* was wrong about France having no provision for the sick and old poor. On the contrary, almost every town of any size had an ancient religious foundation that served this purpose, and though the Revolution had battered many of them, it had not – unlike the Reformation in England two hundred and fifty years before – destroyed them. There was one in Montreuil, one in Abbeville, both on Arthur's direct route, and the large town of Amiens had two. There was an Hôtel Dieu, the 'Lodging of God', the traditional name for the last refuge of the poor: this one had been founded in 1100. There was also the large Hôpital St Charles, which was partly funded by a lottery. It had two hundred beds for the old, two hundred for needy children, and accommodation for some fifty to sixty newborn babies, most of them foundlings. This establishment must certainly have been in Arthur's list to visit, en route to the very large number of such institutions – many more than in London – that were to be found in Paris.

In Amiens, and in many places in Paris, the sick were cared for by the Sisters of St Vincent de Paul, a nursing order founded in the seventeenth century. It had clearly been much too useful to be disbanded at the Revolution as the older, grander convents and monasteries had been. Another young British doctor, following in Arthur's footsteps several years later, remarked apropos of the Hospital for Incurable Women on Paris's Left Bank that the inmates 'are waited on with great tenderness by the Sisters, instead of being obliged to drag out a miserable existence in filthy lodgings or an ill-managed workhouse'.

It was to be another forty years before Florence Nightingale, in the Crimea, commented that the wounded French had devoted Sisters to care for them and that something of the kind should be done for 'our own poor fellows'. Such was the paradox of France at the end of Napoleon's rule: though, by many measures, it was far less prosperous than Britain, old-fashioned in many ways and politically highly unstable, the forces that had made it the intellectual centre of Europe in the previous century were still at work. People who could now visit Paris again did so partly because it was a source of exotic fashions and ways of living and was a great deal cheaper than England for daily expenses. It was already, as it was to become far more emphatically in the future, an escape route, a place of dreams, a personal Other Place. But people also went, as Arthur did, in search of practical new ideas, and customs old and new that they could admire and emulate; and they were not, overall, disappointed.

The Paris in which Arthur finally arrived in the late summer of 1814 had a population approaching three-quarters of a million. London, at a million-plus, had overtaken it and would, in the following decades, become bigger and bigger, leaving Paris and every other world capital behind. But Paris, in its own way, was growing too.

The essential physical difference between London and Paris, which is as clear today as it was two hundred years ago and more, derives from the different histories of England and France – the one, an island realm which has never been successfully invaded since 1066, the other a Continental kingdom constantly vulnerable to the incursions of other powers. In the early Middle Ages both London and Paris were compact walled cities designed to keep enemies at bay. Paris consisted of the original settlement on the Ile de la Cité, which had gradually become the heart of a semi-circular swathe of development on the right bank of the Seine reaching about a kilometre from the river at its furthest, and another of roughly the same extent on the left bank. Centred now on the newly constructed Notre Dame, Paris went on accreting round her cathedral like a coral reef round a great rock. A fortified wall was built right round this city about the year 1200, under the reign of Philippe Auguste. In the next century and a half Right Bank Paris expanded a little more, and so new sections of the wall were built further out under Louis XIII and Charles V. However, the wall round the Left Bank remained where it was, a fixed urban contour. Even today, when it has disappeared, streets follow its lines, and buried fragments of the massive structure are still to be found – in the Rue Clovis behind the Panthéon, and in an underground car park near the Rue de l'Ecole de Médecine.

It is this small, contained city, north and south of the river, with its great old gates – Porte Montmartre, Porte St Denis, Porte St Martin, Porte St Antoine, Porte St Jacques, Porte St Germain, the Porte de Buci and the others – that formed old Paris, an intricate mass of streets and buildings, which did not change its essential lineaments for hundreds of years. In England, the gates of the City of London fell into disrepair, the walls were pillaged for building materials, the town began to expand north over Moorgate Fields and Finsbury and to stretch out robust tentacles along the Strand and Holborn towards that other city at Westminster. By the late seventeenth century London and Westminster were merging into one large built-up area, with a new western quarter burgeoning round St James's, and the medieval walled City was a distant memory; but then time ran differently in England . . . Paris still clung to her walls, and her centre was still the island in the river as in the days of Abelard.

Outside the walls Paris had, by the eighteenth century, begun to spread, but only in a tentative, suburban way interspersed with gardens, vineyards, tanneries on the south side along the Bièvre river, and other small works. The smell of the tanneries mingled with that of hawthorn and lilac and washing laid out to dry. Montparnasse was still countryside, and so was Montmartre in the north, with its windmills. However, by the reign of the ill-fated Louis XVI this spread had become important enough financially for a new wall to be built encircling Paris much further out. This so-called wall of the Fermiers Généraux measured twenty-four kilometres round. It was a relatively light fortification intended as a tax barrier, with customs posts at intervals for goods entering Paris. It was not popular – 'le mur murant Paris rend Paris murmurant' – and by and by the murmurs swelled and joined the cacophony of the Revolution.

But meanwhile the first tentatively grand road plans, based on circular meeting points of the sort we associate with Paris to this day, began to be laid out, between old Paris and the new wall, on the high ground above the Latin Quarter. On the Right Bank the remains of the old walls of Louis XIII and Charles V were converted into grassed walks for bowling games – the origin of the word 'boulevard' – then, later, gravelled and planted with elms. (The ghosts of these pleasant walks are today drowned in relentless modern traffic and high commercial buildings: Boulevard Haussmann, Boulevard Poissonnière, Boulevard Bonne-Nouvelle . . .) Other more central improvements were suggested, some of them prefiguring the huge road-piercing campaign that actually got going under Préfet Haussmann some seventy years later. These did not get built at the time, since the Revolution over-took such rational plans along with many of its own initial ideals.

However, when Napoleon came to power, he continued the grand avenue schemes, mainly to the west, where the Champs Elysées and the Arc de Triomphe would eventually appear, ousting fields of cows. He set about a massive rebuilding of the old fortress of the Louvre, and made a beginning on the arcaded Rue de Rivoli to run along its northern side from the Tuileries palace and provide an eventual cross route for the capital. He had four new bridges constructed, an aqueduct, and a canal to bring water to the city. He built three kilo-metres of new quays, a big wholesale wine depot on the river east of the Latin Quarter, and several covered markets. He had the slaughterhouses and the cemeteries moved to the edges of Paris. He built the Bourse – the Stock Exchange – and continued the building, which had already been planned before the Revolution, of fine new medical schools on the western edge of the Latin Quarter – the Ecoles de Médecine. Paris overall was beginning to assume some of the shape and logic that are still part of its structure today.

But not old Paris. Old Paris, within the ancient limits, remained the same tight-packed maze that it had always been. Even its main thoroughfares were narrow, and often there was no obvious route across town from one small district to another. And this was especially true of the Latin Quarter, known by that name ever since the time when Latin was the universal language of European learning.

This Quarter, when Arthur Jacob took up his abode there, was still, physically, a district of monasteries, convents, learned institutions and *collèges*. (These last were halls of residence, sometimes religious and sometimes secular, for those who came to study or just to imbibe the atmosphere of Parisian discourse.) By 1814 many of these institutions had been emptied of their former occupants, but their structures remained, sometimes ruinous, more often put to other uses. All these walled enclaves, many with their own gardens, created a chequerboard through which lanes twisted and turned, often at right angles. The traditional Latin Quarter, then as in all the centuries before, extended from the Place Maubert at the foot of the Montagne Sainte Geneviève on the east for about a kilometre as far as the site of the wall of Philippe Auguste on the west, roughly where the Odéon Metro station is today on the Boulevard St Germain. It had one main north–south route, the Rue St Jacques, and a subsidiary one more or less parallel, the Rue de la Harpe. It had one slanting east–west route near the river, consisting of the Rue de la Bûcherie, the Rue de la Huchette (both very narrow) and the Rue St André des Arts, which ended at the westward limit of the old wall near the ancient crossroads of the Rue de Seine and the Rue de Buci. No other clear transversal routes, no direct access to the Sorbonne either from east or west. The newly named Rue de l'Ecole de Médecine (previously Rue des Cordeliers, from the monastery there of that name) snaked up from the Odéon area as it does today, but stopped at the Rue de la Harpe, which was more or less on the line of the present-day Boulevard St Michel.

The Rue des Ecoles was not extended eastwards into the heart of the old Quarter till the mid-nineteenth century, sweeping convents and churches and graveyards away in its path. The two great Haussmann boulevards that bisect the Quarter east–west and north–south were not constructed till the 1860s and '70s. These were to change the entire geography of the Quarter, altering the relationship between one old street and another, losing old vistas, gaining new ones and destroying many ancient landmarks. The unseen footprints of innumerable successive generations were still there, but the old routes were dislocated.

To someone from Arthur Jacob's generation, returning to Paris as an old man, it would seem as if the Quarter, so familiar and dear from his youth, had been broken up as in a kaleidoscope. Some street corners would have been instantly recognisable – the slant of old walls, the shape of shopfronts low under the huge beams on which the rest of the building was supported, the line of the open gutter running down the centre of the street – but effects of light and shade would be puzzlingly altered: suddenly, rounding the known corner of a lane, the walker would be out in an unrecognisable cityscape of standard blocks, shaped to fit along a space where no space should have been. Many were those who, living from one era into the other, mourned the loss of this personally internalised geography. Charles Baudelaire, born in Paris (in the Rue Hautefeuille by the medical schools a few years after Arthur Jacob's time there), died while only in his forties, but nevertheless lived long enough to write:

Le vieux Paris n'est plus; la forme d'une ville
Change plus vite, hélas, que le cœur d'un mortel

(Old Paris is no more; a town alas,
Changes more swiftly than does the human heart.)

I don't know how deeply Arthur took Paris to his heart, but there is evidence that at least one acquaintance he made there, in the Rue Hautefeuille itself, stayed with him for life. I also know that he was a man very interested in places and responsive to them, and that he took the trouble to acquire foreign languages in addition to the Latin that, as a doctor, he had to be able to write. His French must have been serviceable already in 1814 for him to plan his great expedition.

When he died, he left his books to the Royal College of Surgeons in Ireland, of which he had twice been President, and they are there to this day: battered, leather-bound, well read, tied up with tape now and awaiting laborious further conservation. There are numerous works on medicine, as you would expect, some from the eighteenth and even the seventeenth century, a few vellum-bound, some handed down from the earlier Jacob surgeons. Many of the ones published in his own life-time are in French, a few in German. There are also a good many on related subjects, such as chemistry and zoology; many on birds, fish, insects, fossils, and on gardening and fruit-growing. During his long professional career he lived in Ely Place, Dublin, where there were still a few walled orchards till late in the century. Maybe he owned one of them. Some books are very fine, and minutely illustrated: there is a reprinted edition of Robert Hooke's discoveries made under the first micro-scope, and some works by the Swedish naturalist Linnaeus. There is John Evelyn's discourse on trees and Gilbert White's *The Natural History of Selborne*. There is Erasmus Darwin's *Laws of Organic Life* – but nothing by his grandson, Charles: the seminal *Origin of Species* did not appear till Arthur was almost seventy. There are forty-odd volumes of a French encyclopaedia of 'prac-tical matters', complete with illustrations, published in a steady series from the late eighteenth century onwards.

But what is striking is the very large number of books on foreign places, some old but many published during Arthur's lifetime, ranging from travellers' tales, through memoirs of the 'Twenty Years in North Africa' variety, to historical and philosophical studies of other cultures. Among the countries covered are Sweden, Finland, Lapland, Iceland, Greenland – Arthur seems to have had a particular taste for these northern fastnesses – Labrador, Newfoundland and North America in general. The American continent was opening up progressively throughout his life, and evidence of this appears in journeys of exploration into 'the West', the Rockies and 'New Spain'. South America interested him also – Brazil, Peru, Paraguay and Chile figure. Sub-Saharan Africa is also there but to a lesser extent (Dahomey, Sierra Leone, the Cape . . .). The interior of Africa was hardly explored for much of the nineteenth century. But Australia figures, and the islands of the Pacific, including Tonga, also China, Tibet, India, 'Bootan', Ceylon, Mauritius, Persia, Turkey, Syria, Algeria, Morocco, Cyprus, Greece and Italy. Nothing, however, on 'the Holy Land', that staple of Victorian popular geography. The main bulk of Europe does not seem to have appealed to his imagination either, perhaps because, once he had worked in France, it was accessible and known. He was stirred, rather, by the amount of new information now becoming available on exotic and far-flung parts of the earth, including the polar seas.

I do not think he ever voyaged to these parts himself. To do so would have been immensely expensive and time-consuming, and his busy professional life overtook him. But he voyaged extensively in his mind. Other books, such as the Letters of Madame de Sévigné, translations from the Portuguese of the poems of Camões, and various philosophical treatises, suggest further realms of mental voyaging.

Chapter V

LIFE IN THE QUARTER

When Arthur arrived in Paris the enduring ecclesiastical character of the Latin Quarter was already a thing of the past, but there was no hint of the changes to its contours that the century would later bring. Old Paris was as it had long been, and all foreign travellers described it in much the same way: high, ancient, fortress-like houses rising six or seven floors above narrow, shadowed and dirty streets. These were almost all without pavements and were chaotically crowded with both pedestrians and wheeled traffic, which regularly broke axles lurching over old pavings as huge as stone pillars. Gas lighting would not begin to arrive for another ten years or so. At night oil lamps were lit, suspended on rope from the houses on each side. These illuminated the centre of the street for those with carriages rather than the hazardous edges for those without, and were not lit at all in the short nights of summer. Mounds of refuse and stable sweepings stood at street corners each morning, even beside grand private mansions. Much of this was never fully carted away, and was ground down by feet and wheels into a stinking black mud. In the daytime tradesmen used the street as a workplace; tinsmiths mended pots and pans with soldering irons dangerously close to passers-by, mattress-cleaners spread out flock to dry. It took an unusually perceptive foreign visitor to remark that Paris, in spite of all this, was 'a magnificent place . . . *character* is indicated by almost every surface . . . In the English capital, your ideas and feelings are less frequently and forcibly excited than in the French.'[1]

It was also noted with some surprise by British and American visitors that Paris houses were most often socially layered, with commerce and workshops or stabling at street level, often extending round an inner courtyard. On the spacious first floor there would be a tenant of some social standing – 'He perhaps pays 300l. [£300] per annum for the rent of his share of the edifice. Above him are tenants possessed of different gradations of fashion or opulence, to the sixth or seventh floor, which are inhabited by the milkman, the cobbler or the scavenger, and who only pay a rent of ten pounds.' Thus states the author of *Picture of Paris, the Stranger's Guide* – who also notes disapprovingly that it seemed to be no one's job to clean the shared staircase and that the richer tenants did not appear to care about this. Evidently, the time when the gabled and timbered houses of old London were socially mixed in the same way had passed from British memory, as the town had spread into new quarters, purpose-built for the gentry, leaving the older areas to exclusively working-class occupation. In fact, in many parts of Paris the pattern of social mix survived till recent times, for the mid-nineteenth-century building prospectors who made fortunes under Haussmann continued the tradition of building blocks to house different kinds of tenant on different floors. Only in the last decades of the twentieth century has the rise of property values deprived the working class of their old eyries on top of bourgeois blocks in central Paris and driven them off to distant outskirts on the Anglo-Saxon model.

Where did Arthur stay in Paris? Somewhere within five or ten minutes' walk of the Ecoles de Médecine, one may

be sure. Another young British doctor, also newly qualified from Edinburgh, arriving in Paris four years later,
easily found lodgings for himself and an American friend
with a Madame Rousseau: three rooms between them for
sixty francs a month plus five for the concierge. (The franc
was then reckoned at twenty-four to the pound.) This
house was in the Rue de la Vieille Estrapade, which was
to the north-east of the medical schools, on the high
ground just above the Sorbonne and the Panthéon, almost
on the line of the old walls near the Porte St Jacques. It
seems to have been a respectable establishment, and indeed
the streets round there were particularly favoured by the
six hundred-odd students attending the Ecoles de
Médecine at that period, because they were thought to be
slightly healthier than the district near the river. But I
have a sense that Arthur, no longer a student and independent by nature, may have sought somewhere cheaper
than Madame Rousseau's rooms, knowing that in any case
he would be spending little time at home. To him, after
Dublin and Edinburgh, living in the midst of working-
class Parisians would not have been a novelty, as it classically was for a boy from provincial France; but in any
case he seems to have been robust enough in temperament and dedicated enough to his profession not to mind
much where he lodged. The notoriously corrupting nature
of Paris, which was generally recognised long before Balzac
made it one of his principal themes, was hardly likely to
affect a man who had voluntarily walked over a thousand
miles to get there.

The Balzac family moved from the Touraine to live
in Paris that same autumn; Honoré de Balzac was then
in his teens. In a later literary work he placed his young
provincial character in a little room near the Hôtel de
Cluny – the fifteenth-century abbot's palace between the
Rue St Jacques and the Rue de la Harpe that concealed
then-unexcavated Roman baths. The young man pays
fifteen francs a month for a room on the fourth floor:

he complains in a letter to his sister that it is 'one of the poorest and darkest little streets of Paris, squeezed between three churches and the old Sorbonne buildings'.[2] But then this particular young man soon gets tempted from his studies by ill-fated money-making schemes. Not, you note, by the seductions of the *vie de bohème*. Although Balzac did use that phrase just once, in 1830, in his great Parisian novel cycle, it was not till 1845 that Henry Murger applied it to his world of the passionately feckless young and, in doing so, transformed the concept into a romantic idyll that would be copied and played out again and again in the Latin Quarter down the generations to come.

I am inclined, though, to see Arthur Jacob, too, for practical reasons, in the very heart of the Quartier Latin. Perhaps he found a room in one of the cross-streets between Harpe and St Jacques – Rue de la Parcheminerie, for instance. Laid out about 1270 beside the cemetery of St Séverin, it was known then as the Writers' Street because it was largely populated by public letter-writers and copiers. It later became the main centre of the parchment sellers. Houses were rebuilt several times on the same foundations and at some periods they were quite grand. Photos taken in the early 1900s, just before some substantial municipal demolitions in the name of hygiene, show fine doorways and windows ornamented with stone carvings in the style of the early eighteenth century. By Arthur's time the houses were all hotels where people lodged long term, thus preserving the old meaning of the word 'hotel' as a fixed residence, and they were more respectable than they would later become: Hôtel des Pères Tranquilles, Hôtel St Séverin, Hôtel de la Paix, Hôtel Garantie, Hôtel du Centre 'founded in 1806' . . . Writing materials were still sold in the Rue de la Parcheminerie; there were many book-dealers round the church of St Séverin, and others already established, as today, on the riverside quay. In 1812 an antiquarian book-dealer set up shop in the capacious, derelict grandeur of the Hôtel de Cluny, which had been emptied of its ecclesiastical inhabitants at the Revolution. Just the area for a book-loving young man.

Immediately to the east, the other side of the Rue St Jacques, lay the section that had been the medical quarter for centuries, before the building of the new medical schools shifted this focus a few hundred yards to the west. The first medical schools had existed across the water, on the island by Notre Dame, in the early fourteenth century, next to where Paris's Hôtel Dieu stood right on the river. The Hôtel Dieu remained there till the mid-nineteenth century, when it was rebuilt on the other side of Notre Dame where it stands to this day, but the medical schools shifted over time. For a while they were in a church near the Hôtel de Cluny ceded to them by the Mathurins, an order of monks who specialised in buying back Christians who had been imprisoned during the crusades. At the beginning of the sixteenth century the aspirant doctors moved again, to the Rue de la Bûcherie, running parallel to the Seine and very near it, where much of the firewood that Paris consumed was landed and chopped up. Here, at the corner of the Rue de la Bûcherie and the Rue des Rats (later more elegantly renamed Rue de l'Hôtel Colbert), a fine domed amphitheatre was built in 1744. It served as a lecture hall, a theatre for such operations as were performed, and then as a dissecting room till at least 1810. It may still have been in use for dissection when Arthur arrived in the Latin Quarter, for dead bodies were a passion with French doctors at that time. No doubt the presence very near to hand of the church of St Julien le Pauvre had long been convenient for the amphitheatre, for this ancient little place of worship was the mortuary chapel for the Hôtel Dieu, just across the water by a covered wooden bridge. Many of those who died penniless and friendless in that last refuge must have been swiftly transferred from the chapel to the domed building on the next corner.

By the mid-nineteenth century the amphitheatre was recorded as being used variously as a *lavoir* for local washer-women, the warehouse of a wine merchant, and as a discreet brothel. Against all the odds, it stands to this day, a monument to the past of that particular knot of streets, which is the oldest kernel of the Latin Quarter.

In fact, you could say that the tradition of science here antedates even the arrival of the medical school. It was here, some hundred years after Abelard taught philosophy among the cornfields and the vineyards, that Maître Albert, a great Dominican philosopher, chemist, naturalist and polymath, gave public lectures that drew a large audience, including the young Thomas Aquinas. Albert the Great was perhaps the first person to define the principles of observation, experiment and logical conclusion that form the basis of medical science. His presence is often invoked in the area, but the crooked thirteenth-century street now called after him was, till the nineteenth century, called the Rue Perdue, the Lost Street. I suspect that this poignant name was a deformation of some quite other word, just as the Rue des Rats was originally the more benign Rue d'Arras – Tapestry Street. In Maître Albert's day lectures were still given in the open air, with the speaker standing on a bench or table and listeners sitting round respectfully on the ground or on bales of straw. A wisp of remembered straw survives in the name Rue du Fouarre, 'fouarre' being an old word for animal forage.

There is no mistaking the origin of another street of much the same date: the Rue des Anglais signifies that a *collège* of English students was established here, but there were plenty of students from other countries also. At the time that these lanes were beginning to fill the fields on the bank opposite Notre Dame, Dante Alighieri studied here. The street to which his name is now attached is a relatively modern one: he actually attended the institute of higher learning by then established in the Rue du Fouarre, and lodged in the Rue de Bièvre. This followed the course of the then-open river, the Bièvre, on its way down into the Seine. (The street follows it to this day, but the once-bright river is, like London's Fleet, in a dark pipe many feet below the paving.) Another century and a half and another poet frequented these streets: bastard son of a high-ranking priest, student-in-name, member of a secret criminal fraternity:

> *Cy gist et dort en ce sollier,*
> *Qu'amours occist de son raillon,*
> *Un povre petit escollier*
> *Qui fut nommé Françoys Villon . . .*

(Here lies in this attic one cast low by love's jest – a poor and little-regarded scholar called François Villon.)

This knot of streets became known as the Maubert Quarter, from the name given to the triangular open space into which several of the streets ran, and from which, in the other direction, up the steep slope, ran the Montagne Sainte Geneviève and the Rue des Carmes. (Since the late nineteenth century the shape of the space has been largely extinguished by the Boulevard St Germain cutting across it.) The name Place Maubert has been generally said to be a corruption of 'Maître Albert', and so another echo of the Dominican preacher, but this strikes me as unlikely. The word Maubert, or Mauberge, crops up in various places in northern France: it comes from a Germanic word Malberg, meaning a place of formal assembly, law-giving and judgement. This would seem to fit, since, in its early days, the district round Place Maubert was favoured by wealthy citizens, particularly lawyers. Later, there was an execution block here, a pillory, and at one time a wheel on which miscreants were broken. In the mid-sixteenth century Protestants were burnt here, including the humanist and printer Etienne Dolet, who was accused of disseminating heretical ideas by the new, powerful medium of the printing press. A place of judgement, indeed. By that time Place Maubert had become associated with popular assemblies and with general trouble, a reputation that then clung to it for centuries and has only faded in recent years.

Even when the neighbouring streets still harboured respectable establishments of learning, and when the fine medical amphitheatre was built, and when Voltaire worked nearby as a clerk, a faint aura of the disreputable or sinister hung about the Place Maub'. At the time when Arthur Jacob was in Paris, the negro servant of Madame du Barry, the mistress of Louis XV, who had lost her head to the guillotine twenty-one years before, was living at 13, Rue Perdue. He was trying to keep a low profile in this appropriately named street, not easy for someone conspicuously black in the Paris of that era. His neighbours all knew who he was and cold-shouldered him. When he died, not one went to his funeral. Having been a spoilt favourite under the Ancien Régime, he had transformed himself into a municipal officer under the Terror and had (said the neighbours) betrayed to the authorities his lady employer, who had been so kind to him.

On the other side of the Place, where the equally narrow and ancient streets ran up towards the not yet rebuilt Sorbonne and to the Panthéon, a greater gentility was apparent. Bordering on the Place was a lateral lane, Rue des Noyers – Street of the Nut Trees – named after a line of trees that had once run there along the bottom of the Clos Bruneau vineyard. Here, in 1814, in an apartment in a substantial stone house of the previous century, with an inner courtyard, lived the de Musset family, with their four-year-old son Alfred. The father of the future

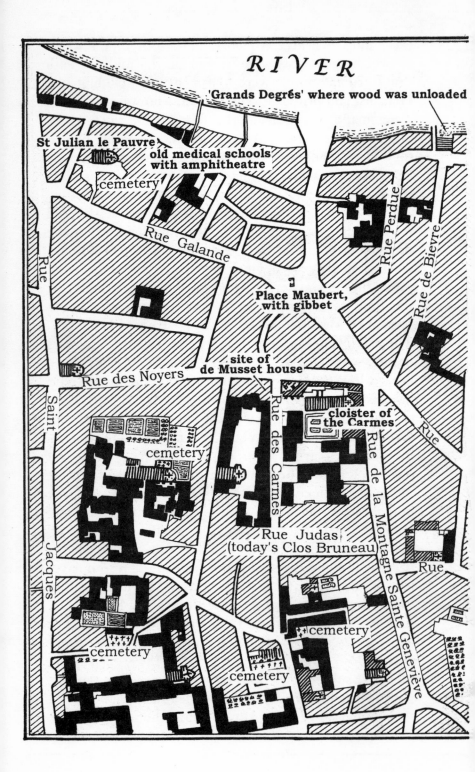

RIVER

'Grands Degrés' where wood was unloaded

St Julian le Pauvre

old medical schools
with amphitheatre

cemetery

Rue Galande

Rue

Rue Perdue

Rue de Bièvre

Place Maubert,
with gibbet

Rue des Noyers

site of
de Musset house

Saint

cemetery

Rue des Carmes

cloister of
the Carmes

Rue

Rue de la Montagne Sainte Geneviève

Jacques

Rue Judas
(today's Clos Bruneau)

Rue

cemetery

cemetery

cemetery

cemetery

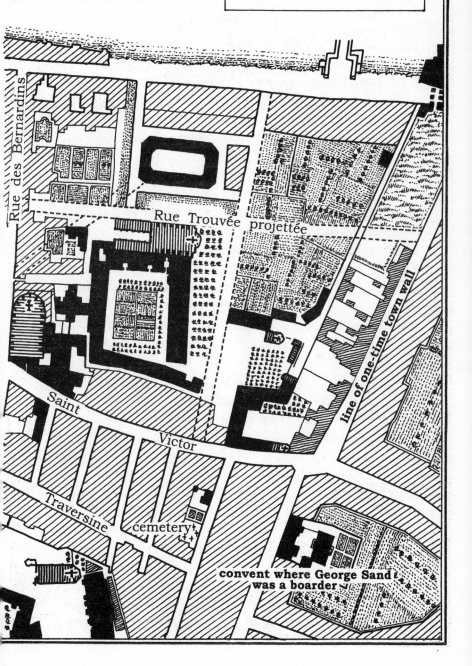

SEINE

The Maubert District

Rue des Bernardins

Rue Trouvée projettée

line of one-time town wall

Saint

Victor

Traversine

cemetery

convent where George Sand was a boarder

romantic writer was listed in the register of births at the
local Mairie as a *propriétaire*, someone whose income
came chiefly from other properties he owned and rented
out; one of the family friends who signed the register as
a witness was a legal consultant. The premises on the
ground floor were occupied by someone in the less exalted
profession of wig-maker, but the lane was secluded and
respectable in an almost rural way. The small church of
St Yves, in ruins since the Revolution, stood at one end
of it, a nesting place for pigeons and crows. Behind it,
the great trees in the gardens of other one-time religious
buildings – the Carmelite monastery, the Collège de
Lisieux, St Jean de Latran – ran in a vista of greenery
all the way to the Hôtel de Cluny.[3]

Further up the hill, and to the east of the Rue de la
Montagne Sainte Geneviève, immediately outside the
line of the old city wall, there existed in 1814 a still-
thriving religious enclave with an entirely rural and
provincial air, swathed in gardens.[4] This conventual
property was not seized at the Revolution, since it could
not be considered a *bien national*. Its owners, *les Dames
Anglaises*, were English Catholic Sisters who had owned
the site since they had fled from Oliver Cromwell. A
similarly protected Irish seminary and a Scottish college
were near to hand, although canvas was nailed over the
gate-grilles of the English convent so that the Sisters
and their charges could not see these male neighbours.
Three years after Arthur Jacob's stay on the Left Bank,
a young French girl called Aurore Dupin was sent to
board here by her grandmother, herself an ex-pupil.
Aurore grew up to become the lover of Alfred de Musset,
among many others, and to take on a literary identity
as George Sand. She described the convent as having
been like a prison, but one with a big garden full of
chestnut trees and huge old cellars to explore. The
Mother Superior was a well-upholstered, worldly, loqua-
cious lady known as Madame Canning. All the Sisters

had English, Irish or Scottish accents, as did two-thirds of the boarders: 'Once inside the gates it was as if one had crossed the Channel.' English jokes and reprimands abounded ('Oh fie, Miss!') and Mary Queen of Scots was venerated as an unofficial saint.

No diary or letters survive from Arthur's stay in Paris. Any domicile I give him can only be an informed guess. But I think I see him most clearly on the rising ground just above the Maubert huddle of streets, near the Rue de la Parcheminerie, St Séverin and the Hôtel de Cluny but a little more secluded among the neglected greenery east of the Rue St Jacques. Perhaps in the Rue des Carmes, which ran, and runs today, up the steep hill towards the Panthéon? Although it has been tidied and widened since those days, there are still a few old houses in it which, under accreted crusts of cement and plaster, hide seventeenth-, sixteenth- or even fifteenth-century stones, great beams, and the glassed-in remains of paved courtyards, the whole structure supported on cellars of a still older date. Here Arthur could have rented a moderately priced but airy room with a view. Leaning out of the window one way, he would see the neo-classical church of Sainte Geneviève (as the Panthéon was now, briefly, once again) and the other way the perpendicular-Gothic towers of Notre Dame.

The street was originally a path running through the Clos Bruneau vineyard. The first few Carmelites who were to give it its name arrived in Paris in the thirteenth century, drawn there, like many other groups, by the sainted King Louis IX. They settled first in the Marais, on the Right Bank, and then migrated in the following century to the developing Quartier Latin. They acquired much of the Clos Bruneau, and also the site of what had been a Jewish settlement before the first expulsion of the Jews at the end of the twelfth century, and which still appeared on plans as '*vicus Jude*'. They built themselves living quarters, a cloister, a chapel and then, as their numbers increased, a grander one, swallowing up a *collège* or two in the process. On the finely carved façade of their wall on what was now the Rue des Carmes they erected a pulpit, from which both Albert the Great and St Thomas Aquinas preached at different times. They flourished, and ornamented their cloister with paintings. It was regarded as the most beautiful one in all Paris, and became a favourite burial place for important citizens of the Quarter, including a prominent sixteenth-century printer and chronicler of the Paris streets.

Such a well-established and wealthy institution stood no chance when the Revolution came. In 1790 (the year of Arthur Jacob's birth) the place was shut down.

In the years that followed, the building was used as an armaments manufactory, which seems to have been a common fate for ex-religious structures. Then, under the Empire, it became a military school. But Napoleon had another scheme in mind for the site: in 1811 demolition began, and by 1813 the cloister on the Rue des Noyers was being rebuilt as one of the new covered markets – the Marché des Carmes. The square shape of the cloister was still clearly apparent in this new guise, and remained discernible for the next century and a half.

So here, perhaps, a little uphill of the market, near ground that had once belonged to the Lombards and then to the Irish, and where a Rue Judas still recalled yet older times, Arthur Jacob had a high room to himself. It would not have seemed very strange to him to be here in a hidden corner near the flower pots and bird cages of his Parisian neighbours, for the high houses of old Edinburgh where he had been living for the past year were of the same kind. It would have had one of those red-tiled floors that were and are quintessentially French, and that the fussier English visitors considered 'naked' and 'poor' – 'Why no carpet?' It would have been furnished with a canopied bed, a cupboard, a washstand with basin and slop-pail, a table, a bookshelf, a chair or two. It probably had no fireplace, but small charcoal stoves, with a chimney stuck into an adjacent flue or simply through the roof tiles, were in standard use. Paris, unlike London, still burnt only wood at that time, huge boatloads of which arrived in the Quarter at the boat-steps by the Rue de la Bûcherie. This attachment to wood, and the virtual lack of industry by British standards, made the air of Paris far cleaner than that of coal-burning London, in spite of the time-honoured Parisian smell of open street-gulleys and drains.

There was no water on tap anywhere in the house, nor yet in the courtyard. Nearly all the drinking and washing water used in Paris, in dwellings of all classes, then and for another half-century, was still carried into houses and up many flights of stairs in wooden buckets, as it had been in the Middle Ages. The water might come from the Seine, or from the new Canal d'Ourcq, or from one of the seventy-odd public fountains within Paris. An elegant example of one of these[5] stood in the middle of the new Marché des Carmes, probably on the site of a well used by the convent. But the water still had to be carried about on yokes, a bucket of twenty litres on each side at a time, by a small army of strong men. These were traditionally Auvergnats, come to Paris from the mountainous heart of France. There were well over a thousand of them at work all day long in the city at the Restoration of 1814, and the usual price of a full bucket to a customer was ten centimes – fifteen for two buckets bought at the same time. Ten centimes was worth roughly one old penny, a small sum of money even by the standards of the poor. A water-carrier did not earn his family's income easily, but at least it was a steady job once he had built up a clientele.

Water closets, called *cabinets à l'anglaise* since they were by then beginning to proliferate on the other side of the Channel, were still virtually unknown in France.

There had been one each for Louis XVI and Marie Antoinette at Versailles before the Revolution, but courtiers there had continued to relieve themselves in palace corridors. Parisians behaved similarly on the streets, 'just as if they had been in the open country-side' complained the English, and sometimes apparently used the communal staircases of their own living quarters. Within their homes, the better-off used chamber pots and close stools. Even when a lodging house was well kept, it only had one latrine, usually on the top floor with a shaft descending the whole height of the house to a cess-pit at cellar level, which was pumped out at long intervals. The latrine (*lieu d'aisance*) cannot have been a pleasant place to visit; indeed ordinary workmen, arriving in Paris from France's deeply back-ward rural regions, found the very idea of an indoor convenience disgusting, and said so. However, our ancestors, even those inclined to clean linen and new concepts of medical hygiene, necessarily took a more relaxed view of such things than we do today. The tall houses of Edinburgh had the same system as the Parisian ones. There would have been few flush toilets in the Dublin Arthur Jacob knew as a young man, and certainly none in rural Ireland.

The Parisians were not particularly dirty in themselves, though the British liked to imagine them so. Although some French medical men were of the opinion that frequent bathing caused infertility, there were many public bath houses and also floating baths on the edge of the Seine, like shallow swimming pools. These were carefully designated according to sex and price – *Bain pour Dames, Bain pour Femmes, Bain pour Hommes*, etc. Legions of washer-women also scrubbed clothes on the edge of the river, sometimes on the flat stones of the quays, some-times in specially constructed *bateaux lavoir*.

These activities would have been impossible, by that date, on the Thames in the centre of London, where the quays were lined with industries and wharfs and there were boats everywhere going to and from the great port below London Bridge. But Paris was not a port city. Her river, too far from the sea to accommodate large ships, is not tidal. The only activity to disturb the calm waters round the Ile de la Cité came from slow barges unloading the heavier and less perishable merchandise that Paris needed for itself: wood, charcoal, wheat, wine, building stone . . .

'The peculiar cleanness of the air of Paris – (at least, peculiar as it seems to an Englishman) – gives a glancing brilliancy, an almost startling distinctness to every object. Distances are lessened by the pellucidness of the medium . . . through which they are seen . . . The general effect here, on a fine day, is that of a Venetian painting . . . Angular peninsulas of lofty buildings jut out from the opposite side of the Pont Neuf: a gigantic facing of stone houses, stained, irregular, and uncertain in their indications, looks from its height on the green crystal of the river, and is depicted far downwards in its depth.'

This unusual view of the Latin Quarter, seen at an angle from across the river, is from the pen of John Scott, editor of *The London Magazine* and friend of Hazlitt, who came to Paris at the same time as Arthur and with the same eagerness. Half a dozen years later Scott's strong emotions were to carry him into a duel with a rival editor, in which he was killed. Large numbers of his fellow countrymen had by then met a similar violent end on the field of Waterloo, which he also visited, and described in passionate detail.

But in the autumn of 1814 the Battle of Waterloo was unimaginable. Napoleon was apparently consigned to Elba. English people came in increasing numbers, rattling to Paris in the swaying French *diligences* or in hired post-chaises, sending enthusiastic or critical bulletins home. They found a city enjoying, with a rather febrile gaiety after all that had gone before, the novel idea of being ruled by a king once again.

Chapter VI

Richelieu's Head, and Other Revolutionary Mementoes

Few people familiar with Paris today, if asked to delineate the Latin Quarter, would place its core as far east as the Place Maubert. But while it was the construction of the Boulevard St Michel in the 1860s, bisecting the district north to south five hundred metres west of Maubert, that created a new central axis for the Quarter, some degree of westward shift had taken place before that. At the end of the eighteenth century the building of the Ecoles de Médecine, so near the wall-line of old Paris, and a new theatre just beyond it (later to be known as the Odéon) introduced a sense of expansion into a Latin Quarter that for six centuries had been a fixed territory, self-contained within the corset of streets that followed the one-time fortifications.

On this western side, the phantom wall was the raised Rue des Fossés St Germain (today's Rue Monsieur le Prince), which met the Rue de l'Ecole de Médecine at the point where the present Boulevard St Germain cuts across, and then continued to the river along the line of the short Rue de l'Ancienne Comédie and then the Rue Mazarine. The narrow lane with an arcaded entry off the boulevard, called the Cour de Commerce

St André, runs closely parallel to the Rue de l'Ancienne Comédie as far as the Rue St André des Arts: it is on the line of the ditch that once ran below the wall. Till the boulevard cut through it, the Cour was longer, extending all the way from the Rue des Ecoles. In the seventeenth century it was laid out as a bowling alley: it acquired a Turkish baths (sure sign, as in London's Covent Garden, of a place of slightly disreputable enjoyment) and it was in this bath house that an enterprising Sicilian opened Paris's first coffee shop, the Café Procope. With one entry from the bowling ground and another convenient for the actors at the Ancienne Comédie, who were the King's players, Procope's was frequented throughout the eighteenth century by such men as Voltaire, Jean-Jacques Rousseau, Diderot, Beaumarchais, and (with a darker nuance) Robespierre, Danton and Marat. By the end of the century the alley was lined with houses on both sides and had become an arcade of small workshops, the forerunner of a number of glassed-in passages that were to be constructed in Paris over the next generation. Shopping became an elegant Paris pastime, and shoppers were happy to avoid the medieval dirt of the open streets, both the stinking black mud underfoot and the danger of having filthy water poured down your back from an overhead window.

Beyond the exit from the Cour onto the Rue St André des Arts the immediate district was already an animated one, spilling beyond the old city gate at the west end of the street into the lively market on the Buci crossroads. This is still a market today. From there, St Germain des Prés, a name whose celebrity today eclipses that of older Latin Quarter landmarks, is a very short walk away.

Until the Revolution, the great Abbaye de St Germain was the largest and richest of all the Left Bank religious communities, and also the oldest. It had been founded in the mid-sixth century under the Merovingian dynasty and became the burial place for their kings. It was rebuilt about the year 1000. The church we see today, floodlit after dark above the noisy Boulevard St Germain, is essentially this thousand-year-old construction, though its accompanying grounds and buildings have all gone under streets. Over the next two and a half centuries a brilliantly decorated Chapel of the Virgin was built and also monastery buildings: cloister, refectory, dormitories, parlour, chapterhouse, library, scriptorium, infirmary, kitchens, vegetable and physic gardens, and a palace for the Abbot with its own garden. Later came a stable yard, and the Abbey's own prison was added on the south side as the secular power of the institution increased, for the Abbey owned all the land running westwards along the Left Bank of the river for many miles.

It was called St Germain des Prés – 'in the fields' – to distinguish it from another St Germain church on the Ile de la Cité, but the name was apt, for on the medieval map of Paris the packed streets stop short at the walls and at the Porte de Buci. The Abbey, barely two hundred metres distant, is indeed out in the green fields, surrounded like a storybook castle by its own fortified walls and by a moat fed from the Seine. (Today the narrow Rue de l'Echaudé runs down the line of the one-time Abbey moat on its eastern side, while on the west the citadel extended as far as the present Rue St Benoît, to the north as far as the present Rue Jacob and to the south almost to the Place St Sulpice: the Rue du Four there remembers the Abbey's *four* – its bakehouse.)

By the seventeenth century the moat had gone. A hospital for the poor, La Charité, founded by Marie de Médicis, was constructed alongside. Queen Marguerite de Valois had built herself a palace and gardens between the Abbey and the river, and a new suburb, mainly of rather grand private houses, had spread beyond La Charité to the west. The Abbey itself, under Benedictine rule, had become something of an intellectual centre, and the Faubourg St Germain adjacent to it was the chosen quarter of cosmopolitan aristocratic families. The English Resident (King's representative) had a house there in the Rue Taranne,[1] and during the Civil War and the Commonwealth, when Royalist sympathisers took refuge in Paris, an English colony was established in the Faubourg.

The young John Evelyn discreetly left England for some time and lived in the Rue de Seine, just on the frontier of the Latin Quarter and the Faubourg: he ended up marrying the Resident's daughter. Shortly after Charles II made a triumphal return to England to claim his throne, Evelyn's friend and Royal Society colleague John Aubrey also visited the Left Bank. Aubrey's finances went through periodic crises, so it is perhaps indicative of one of these that he did not stay in the select Faubourg but in the heart of the old Latin Quarter, lodging in the time-honoured way of visiting scholars '*dans le cloistre de St Julien le Pauvre*'. A letter addressed to him there is in the neat hand of Thomas Hobbes, the philosopher, who was another long-term Parisian Englishman.

Throughout the eighteenth century the Faubourg St Germain, keeping aloof from the Latin Quarter on its doorstep, continued to flourish socially and architecturally. Streets of handsome houses *entre cour et jardin* were built, and a roll of the distinguished family names associated with the Faubourg reads like a history of both the Ancien Régime and the Enlightenment. This state of affairs was too good to last, and it did not. By one of the many violent reverses of fortune that the French Revolution threw up, the Place Maubert, so long associated with popular uprisings and judicial brutality, did not feature much, whereas the hitherto tranquil area

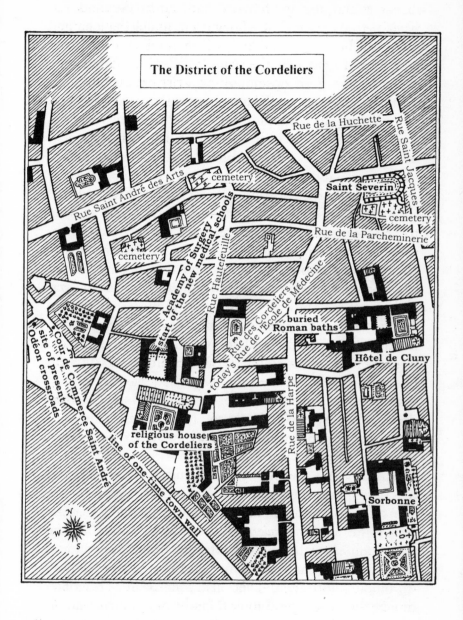

The District of the Cordeliers

Rue de la Huchette

Rue Saint Jacques

Rue Saint André des Arts

cemetery

Saint Severin

cemetery

cemetery

Rue de la Parcheminerie

start of the new medical schools

Academy of Surgery

Rue Hautefeuille

Rue des Cordeliers

Rue de l'École de Médecine

today's Rue de l'École de Médecine

buried
Roman baths

Hôtel de Cluny

Cour de Commerce
site of present-day
Odéon crossroads

religious house
of the Cordeliers

Rue de la Harpe

Rue de Commerce Saint André

line of one-time town wall

Sorbonne

N
W   E
S

between the new medical schools and St Germain des Prés became steeped in Revolutionary associations and in actual blood.

The old name for the Rue de l'Ecole de Médecine was the Rue des Cordeliers, from the large monastery of the Cordeliers on its western side, one of the many institutions that settled in the Quarter under Louis IX. Humble barber-surgeons had long had a presence in the street, and towards the end of the seventeenth century a handsome amphitheatre was built there for what was by then the socially grander Royal College of Surgeons. Then, in the late eighteenth century, the fine new medical schools were planned on the opposite side of the street on the site of an ancient *collège*. By the Revolution, they had been partially built. When the monks were dispossessed in 1790, their chapel was requisitioned by the more extreme wing of the Revolutionary movement headed by Georges-Jacques Danton, Jean-Paul Marat and Camille Desmoulins. All lived nearby, and thus the lethally influential Club des Cordeliers was born.

Marat was a medical doctor and had had some success in this capacity in Britain, but by 1790 he had abandoned the study of gonorrhoea (for which he had been awarded an MD from the University of St Andrews) in favour of journalism. He had his own printing press in the Cour de Commerce St André, with which he published a Revolutionary journal, and it was at his lodging in what was to become the Rue de l'Ecole de Médecine that he was famously stabbed by Charlotte Corday while he was taking a medicinal bath.[2] Not that the street was unused to blood before then. There had long been a slaughterhouse there, serving the old Marché St Germain, and it is characteristic of the visceral invective that drove the Revolution forward that a local butcher, Legendre, was a prominent member of the Club des Cordeliers and made much of his slaughtering trade. The cobbler Simon, in whose brutal custody the ten-year-old son of the King and Queen was later to vanish, was also a local man and Club member.

Just up the road, the small Abbey prison became a Revolutionary one, into which were packed more than three hundred prisoners whose crime consisted of showing a lack of Revolutionary enthusiasm. These included some aristocrats from the Faubourg and eighteen priests, but also a number of quite ordinary citizens of the Quarter and some unfortunate actors from the theatre. When the September massacres of 1792 launched the Terror the Abbey prison became the site of one of the most violent: the long association of the Abbey with the burial of kings gave an extra edge of profanation to these mass killings. The victims were cut to bits one by one with sabres as they tried to escape back into the building, collapsing on a huge pile of clothes in the centre of the prison courtyard which soon became saturated with blood. Although the massacre had been begun by a street mob, it turned into an organised ritual of execution. Benches were placed for spectators – men and women separated, as if to respect prim convention even in this scene of carnage. After some initial nervousness, the audience settled down to talk and hoot, commenting on how 'well' some victims died and booing the 'cowardly' ones – a neat illustration of the fact that there is always a section of society that will accept any regime, however grotesque, provided it appears to have official sanction. The bodies were left there for days as a festering spectacle.

It may have been the September massacres, or it may have been the execution of the King the following January, that decided Charlotte Corday to act. A girl from an impoverished family of minor aristocrats, with intellectual tastes and the moderate Revolutionary sympathies of the pre-Terror period, Corday left her native Normandy in July 1793 and travelled to Paris by *diligence*. She took a room off the Rue St André des Arts, made a trip to the Right Bank to buy a knife in the shopping galleries of the Palais Royal, and managed on her second try to gain entry to Marat's lodging. Having stabbed him, she made no attempt to flee, and was quickly arrested by a police sergeant who came upon the excited crowd gathered in the street. This was in what was officially Year Two of the new republican universe, when even time was supposed to run differently. It is rather disconcerting to find the regular forces of law and order still taking charge of a murder inquiry and 'confronting the accused with the body' in the traditional French way, when so much blood had already flowed on other pretexts. She was taken to the Abbey prison. 'I have killed one man to save a hundred thousand!' she told the judges at her summary trial. She was sent to the guillotine four days later. Her high-principled act did not save anyone nor halt the relentless progression of the Terror. It was Marat who became a popular hero: little effigies of him were sold to replace the discarded crucifixes. By the autumn of the same year Queen Marie Antoinette had followed the King to the guillotine.

The following spring it was the turn of Danton and Desmoulins themselves to be arrested at dawn by Section-leaders beating rifle butts on the doors of their houses. Danton's home was near where his statue stands today, at the Odéon crossroads, by what was then the entry to the Cour de Commerce. Three months later, with even the semblance of a trial abandoned, the intellectual leader Robespierre and his disciple Saint-Just met the same inevitable fate. With their beheading, the Terror had essentially consumed itself and was extinguished. In any case, France was already at War with Austria and her allies, and Napoleon Bonaparte was in the ascendant.

At the start of the Revolution, when the monks had been dispossessed of the Abbey, a huge quantity of saltpetre for making gunpowder had been stored in the refectory. In August 1794, just as the cycle was reaching its end, an explosion took place. This, and the fire that followed, destroyed many of the buildings on the north side, including the library and the Chapel of the Virgin. After this, time, neglect, the long-term effects of saltpetre and the spread of urban Paris did for much of the rest. The Rue de l'Abbaye was laid out over the northern ruins as early as 1800. A few battered pieces of masonry and statues are preserved in a little railed garden which is all that remains of the monks' cloister. Other, more substantial stones underpin, like folk memories, the foundations of several of the houses in the street.

The whole Revolutionary experience had been so traumatic, so far-reaching in its effects both geographically and in time to come, and yet so brief, that within a few years it came to seem almost incredible even to those who had lived through it. In Paris, there had been no oppressed, landless peasantry for the Revolution to emancipate. The great upheaval was seen by most Parisians as a disaster, which directly brought about the death of nearly three thousand mainly harmless fellow Parisians.[3] The monetary inflation and the economic and social disorganisation that followed in its wake temporarily ruined great swathes of the bourgeoisie, including all those shopkeepers whose trade depended on prosperous upper classes, and brought no material gain at all to the mass of the Parisian poor. It also, as part of the ideological assault on closed societies and cartels, dismantled the collegiate and teaching structures of the Latin Quarter. Doctors of Letters at the Sorbonne were butchered, faculties and academies were swept away, as were exams and professional qualifications. In the medical field it was declared that, in the name of equality, anyone could be a doctor or surgeon who claimed to be one. Antoine-Laurent Lavoisier, who for thirty years had been advancing the study of chemistry and laying the foundations of much that we regard as essential to the subject today, was guillotined because of his upper-class association with the former government. He had discovered oxygen, invented the first periodic table and indeed the metric system that the Revolution itself adopted. He asked for a few weeks' stay of execution to give him time to complete his memoirs, but this was denied him by Robespierre with the notorious remark that 'the Revolution has no need of learned men'.

This state of wilful chaos could not last. With the coming of the Directoire, a little order began to be restored. Under Napoleon, the whole structure of formal medical education was reinvented, this time on a national scale, helped on by the need for competent surgeons to attend to battlefield injuries. Napoleon himself took a closely focused interest in these matters: it was during his campaigns that the first field hospitals were set up, and several Parisian hospitals were improved. There was now much greater emphasis on clinical training and hands-on practice, and here the more positive, longer-term effects of social upheaval begin to become apparent. The intellectual vision that had fuelled the Revolution had been overtaken by fanaticism, yet enough of it had survived to release a rush of energy and creativity. Old methods and hierarchies were questioned; a new spirit of enquiry and imaginative conceptualisation was abroad.

Some of the leading medical figures that Arthur Jacob was to encounter twenty years later passed their teens in the maelstrom of the Terror and the abolition of the institutions where they were supposed to be studying, yet that decade saw the emergence of an outstanding group of young men who became known as 'the School of Paris' and were to change medical and surgical practice for good. Among them were Guillaume Dupuytren, who was to preside over the Hôtel Dieu for twenty years from the Restoration, and René Laennec who invented the stethoscope. New disciplines in anatomy, pathology, physiology and statistical evaluation, all based on close observation, had begun to develop. Surgeons, who had by long tradition been classed as inferior to physicians, were now their equals and worked along-side them. In any case, the status of both had never been higher. No wonder, by 1814, Paris had become *the* place to study, for foreigners just as much as for the French themselves.

So, when Arthur Jacob arrived in the Latin Quarter, although it was the downfall of Napoleon that made his visit possible, the Napoleonic organisational struc-tures were securely in place and throughout subsequent dynastic upheavals were not essentially to change. The Rue des Cordeliers, after being briefly named Rue Marat and then Rue de la Santé, had become the Rue des Ecoles de Médecine; the building of the Ecoles had been resumed and extended.[4] There was now a fine amphitheatre there for anatomical demonstration, top-lit, holding twelve hundred, though within a gener-ation the number of aspirant medics wanting to attend lectures there would make its space inadequate. The inscription, stating that the Emperor in his kindness had encouraged the students in their zeal and progress, had just been modified to read not 'Emperor' but 'Sovereign'. The surgeons were now established in part of the one-time monastery of the Cordeliers, though they were not to take over the entire premises till 1825. For the moment, a manufacturer of decorative tiles had his workshop there in the monks' refectory. The slaughterhouse had been got rid of, as had the old and dirty Marché St Germain. A new market building had been built, arcaded like the one of the Carmes on the other side of the Quarter. Except for the smell from the live poultry being sold there, the Ecoles de Médecine area was now regarded as a salubrious district: the blood, animal and human, had been washed away.

In other ways, too, the Quarter had retained its old equilibrium. Most of the monastic institutions were gone and some of the churches were in ruins, but the others had reopened their doors again for business years ago as if the massacres of priests and parishioners had never been. The Panthéon, which had been built on top of the Montagne Sainte Geneviève just before the Revolution as an elegant replacement for the ancient church there, then re-named at the Revolution as a secular mausoleum for national heroes, now, for twenty years, became the church of Sainte Geneviève once again.

It was as if a collective amnesia had overtaken Parisians, along with the sense of accelerated time induced by the meteoric rise of Napoleon, his Empire and now his spectacular fall. It was the epic battles of Napoleon's wars that were lodged in the forefront of memory now, not that other blood shed less than a generation before which now seemed remote as if many more years had passed. If some still mourned their fractured families and lost inheritance, they did so in private. New titles, bestowed by the Emperor, were everywhere now, though the bearers of older ones too were, like the Bourbon king, regaining their old place in society. The grievances now were the grievances of hundreds of army officers, suddenly finding themselves on half-pay and without occupation, and of rank-and-file ex-conscripts who were reduced to begging for bread on the streets. Popular resilience was already strained by the abrupt collapse of all that Imperial might and the need now to wave enthusiastic flags at the returning Bourbons. If the Revolution was still present at all in memory it was for the time being unmentionable, inexplicable, thrust away out of sight like some embarrassing and toxic object. Like Richelieu's head –

Cardinal Richelieu, the towering political figure of the early seventeenth century, had been responsible for rebuilding the Sorbonne. He died in 1642 and was entombed in the new chapel attached to the university. At the height of the Revolution in 1793, the chapel was sacked, the marble tomb broken open and the body dragged out and trampled underfoot. In a grotesque mummery of what was being done throughout France to living representatives of former power, Richelieu's head – in a remarkable state of preservation and apparently recognisable from his portrait – was hacked off. Then it disappeared.

Twenty-two years later, when the supposed remains of Louis XVI and his Queen were given a ceremonial reburial, there were many in Paris who felt that this gesture disinterred a shameful past that would have been better left hidden. So no one was eager to bring to notice any of the Revolution's other detritus. When Arthur Jacob arrived in Paris to study the new, sophisticated medicine, Richelieu's head was actually sitting in the centre of the Latin Quarter, in a cupboard in a grocer's shop in the Rue de la Harpe. Its presence there was unknown to anyone but the grocer and his wife. He had picked the head up and made off with it on the day of the tomb-breaking. She objected to having 'that nasty thing' in the house, but her husband would not agree to dispose of it. Eventually, after his death, she confided in a neighbour and, with his help, sold the object. It then vanished again from the record and from men's minds for forty years and another two revolutions. Such was the history of nineteenth-century Paris.

Ordinary bodies were, however, a commonplace feature of the Latin Quarter. Some of them, unlike Richelieu's remnant, became embarrassingly public. The young medics of the time, spurred on by the new view that anatomical observation and understanding were fundamental to all branches of medicine, seem to have had a passion for bodies. In that era before refrigeration, dissection officially only took place in the winter months. But it was complained that, between April and October, students would secretly take bits from patients who had died in hospital and carry them home in their pockets to dissect at leisure in their lodgings. In 1818 human bones were found in the latrine of a baker who had been letting rooms to medical students for years, and later some more were discovered in a drain near the Ecoles de Médecine. Nor were the young medics above playing jokes by leaving body parts around the streets. The year before the discovery in the latrine, a dissected head turned up one morning, placed on top of a marker stone in the Rue Serpente, which wound its way between the Rue de la Harpe and the Rue Hautefeuille.

But how did Paris medics find bodies so easy to get? This was during the period when, notoriously, in London, Edinburgh and Dublin, bodies for dissection and teaching purposes were mainly obtained by raiding graveyards for newly buried corpses. Dublin, in particular, had several conveniently central burial grounds for the poor, which were free and therefore almost unmaintained and unguarded. The raids seem to have been carried out with the more or less open connivance of those in charge of medical education, who apparently took a view that might be classed as enlightened self-interest: on balance, it could be argued, the eventual social benefit of this grave-robbing outweighed the evil. During Arthur Jacob's period of study in Dublin, before he went on to Edinburgh, it was actually one of the officially recognised duties of those demonstrating anatomy to 'undertake the direction of the resurrection parties'.[5] These were headed by the dissecting room porters, who were paid a standard extra fee for the supply of 'subjects'. In fact so blatant and busy were the Dublin grave-robbers that by the mid-1820s envious anatomists began to arrive from London in quest of material. A shipment of Irish corpses was discovered being unloaded at Liverpool docks in a crate marked 'Irish Cheddar'. Arthur himself, by then a Fellow of the Royal College of Surgeons in Ireland and a rising figure in the Dublin medical world, proposed a committee to look into the matter, though it is not clear whether he was more disturbed by the resurrectionist activities in themselves or by the further illicit trade in bodies this engendered and the thought of London gaining from Dublin's loss. His proposal was defeated. Two years later one of the College porters was killed by an angry mob, led by aggrieved relatives of the freshly dead.

Not till Burke and Hare were found to be actually murdering people in Edinburgh to provide the schools there with 'subjects' was the whole traffic properly exposed. The resulting Anatomy Act of 1832 brought the resurrection trade to an end, by officially permitting unclaimed bodies from workhouse infirmaries, free hospitals and the like to be taken by medical schools. In this way Great Britain finally created the same framework for legal dissection that had long been accepted in France.

It becomes apparent that, until then, the liberal French law was a key reason, among others, that ambitious young practitioners such as Arthur Jacob were eager to make their way to Paris to further their clinical studies. In fact there were complaints from French medical students at that period that foreign students were competing for 'their' subjects. A Frenchman who qualified in Paris has left us a graphic description of the practical arrangements. A little younger than Arthur and the son of a family who were having to make sacrifices for his education, he had evidently agreed with fellow students to perform a paid service for them:

'In winter, I used to get up at five in the morning, to go from the Rue du Bac [on the edge of the Faubourg St Germain where the family lived] to the Hôpital de la Pitié [beyond the Latin Quarter to the east, where he was employed as a houseman]. It was imperative for me to get there before the arrival of the covered cart that picked up un-reclaimed bodies from all the hospitals in Paris. That way, I could choose for myself *my subjects*. Then, my scalpel in my hand, I could prepare, for my associates, the teaching material for that day. Our anatomical studies went on all the morning . . .'[6]

The sheer number of charity hospitals, hospices, orphanages and asylums in Paris drew to the capital the dispossessed and desperate from much of provincial France. After thirty years of social upheaval and War, this meant that very many people breathed their last in a Paris to which they were essentially strangers, with no family on hand to see them decently laid in earth. In any case, in the capital, grave-space had long been so heavily used and so rapidly reused, that all laying to rest was more token than permanent even for respectable members of society. After the hospital cadavers of the poor and unclaimed had been chopped about, all the bits of bodies were supposed to be decently buried, with prayers, in a common grave, but in practice they often arrived there in a state of advanced decomposition. Arthur Jacob's matter-of-fact view of dead bodies, and what seems to have settled, later in his life, into a private aversion to religious concepts, could only have been strengthened by his Parisian experiences.

Chapter VII

A WINTER OF HOSPITALS

The Hôpital de la Pitié housed about six hundred patients, many with chronic ailments, all poor, some of them prostitutes or girls who had 'fallen'. It was behind the large Left Bank botanical garden that stretched down to the river and was traditionally called the Jardin du Roi, the King's Garden. At the Revolution the name had been changed to the prosaic Jardin des Plantes, and when the place officially went back to being the King's Garden at the Restoration in practice both names went on being used interchangeably. By that time it had acquired, as well as the plants, a large menagerie of exotic animals and birds, an important natural history collection, an anatomy section used for animal dissection and lectures, and also a collection of human mummies, skeletons and waxworks. No public zoos as yet existed in other capitals, and so this one was an obvious port of call not only for any doctor or scientist visiting Paris but for anyone of an enquiring turn of mind. Nearly all the foreigners who arrived in Paris went there, for this was an era when most Europeans had never before seen a lion or a camel in the flesh, let alone an elephant or a penguin. (The giraffe which was to be a main attraction for many years did not arrive till 1827.) John Scott, the editor of *The London Magazine*, recorded the day he spent there with his usual vivid attention to detail. There is circumstantial evidence that similar close attention was paid by Arthur Jacob, probably on repeated visits.

Medical men doing the rounds of Paris naturally combined their visit to the Jardin with one to the Pitié, and also to the Salpêtrière nearby.[1] The Salpêtrière derived its name from having been installed, in the seventeenth century, in a disused saltpetre works, and by the 1800s it had become the largest refuge for the sick poor in Paris. In the women's building alone there were six thousand patients many of whom were more or less permanent inmates. John Sims, the young doctor from Manchester who, like Arthur Jacob, finished his training in Edinburgh and then came on to spend a season in Europe, visited the Salpêtrière but was less favourably impressed by it than by most of the Parisian hospitals he saw. He remarked that there were no day-rooms and 'no amusements of any kind . . . The accommodation for the lunatics . . . are of a very inferior description and it would require an entire reformation to render them as comfortable as their unhappy condition is capable of being made.' He noted that the Superintendant knew this, and had said that Napoleon himself had had plans to improve the place but that these had been aborted by national events.

Like Arthur Jacob, Sims was a dedicated and indefatigable student of his chosen discipline. He must have been richer than Arthur, since he travelled to France, and then across that country and to Switzerland and Italy, by *diligence*, but he was from a Quaker family with the habit of hard work and plain, decent living. During his time in Paris he set himself just as rigorous a timetable, with just as much walking about from one part of town to another, as Arthur undoubtedly did. (There were no buses in Paris till 1828, only *fiacres* for private hire.) Like Arthur, who preceded him, Sims had recommendations from tutors in Edinburgh and also from Astley Cooper in London. Unlike Arthur, he kept a detailed diary which has survived,[2] and so one can discern in his busy, documented itinerary, the shadow-figure of Arthur, who had already walked in the same paths all over Paris.

For both young men, the outstanding figure of the time was Guillaume Dupuytren who, when Arthur arrived in 1814, had just risen to the position of surgeon-in-chief at the Hotel Dieu. Dupuytren, too, was descended from several generations of country surgeons. He had grown up in the Limousin, part of the mountainous fastness of central France where (as Balzac said) most people couldn't read or speak the national language properly and believed in witches: a place not unlike rural Ireland. Studying in Paris, Dupuytren was taken under the wing of another from the Limousin, Alexis Boyer, who became official surgeon to Napoleon, but Dupuytren's own abilities carried him up and up. By the end of the Empire he had been decorated by Napoleon, and was to be made a baron under Louis XVIII. He figures in several of Balzac's novels as The Surgeon, Dr Desplein, and his distinctive name is still affixed to certain conditions today. He is credited with having reorganised the Hôtel Dieu, till then a byword for dirt and overcrowding. He turned it effectively into a teaching hospital, introducing a rigorous methodology and system of note-taking. His time in charge of the place, 1814–35, is generally considered the first era of something approaching modern surgery, though, even with his scrupulous care, the mortality rate following surgery in those days, before antiseptics or asepsis, never fell below twelve per cent.

Stories of rudeness and domestic brutality hover round Dupuytren's name, but all the evidence from those who saw him in the hospital is that he was kind and calm, with 'a soft, smooth voice' assuring patients he would cure them, and particularly good with children. Possibly he was more at ease with patients, students and hospital colleagues than he was with his professional equals and rivals. There was an especial animosity between him and Antoine Dubois who, as physician to Napoleon's second Empress, was made a baron before Dupuytren. Today the names of the two life-long enemies have been given to two short streets that run next to one another out of the Rue de l'Ecole de Médecine up to the old wall-line.

John Sims made numerous visits to the Hôtel Dieu to watch the great man operating. Sometimes his travelling companion, an American Quaker called John Griscom, came along too, for though he was not a doctor himself he was interested in everything and the two young men had been sharing digs and expenses since they had first met in Geneva. Dupuytren operating on a man with cancer of the penis made a particular impression, and Sims describes it twice, once in his journal and once in what appears to be a letter:

'He cut off the part with a single stroke of the knife, then began to tie the numerous arteries . . . He performed this operation with such dexterity as to give the man as little pain as possible. I observed the furnace with red hot irons was ready in case the bleeding should be unmanageable.' Either the furnace or the very nature of the operation was too much for Griscom. He began breathing hard, and 'his countenance indicated that if he did not speedily leave the theatre he would soon be upon the floor.' So they went out. Griscom, on Sims's advice, stretched out flat on a bench outside Notre Dame. Sims went back into the theatre and watched the 'very interesting case' of a woman who had just died on the operating table. Then came a ruptured uterus, where Dupuytren succeeded in dismembering the dead baby – 'If it had been living, he would have tried a Caesarian.' Presumably he used a simple trumpet-shaped device to help him to decide that the baby's heart had stopped, for Laennec's stethoscope was then only just in the process of invention. At the end of this early-morning session

Sims rejoined his friend, finding him much restored by the fresh winter air, and the pair went to eat a hearty breakfast at one of the cafés that were beginning to be a feature of Paris.

This, to modern sensibility, appears to come from the Chamber of Horrors of old-style, pre-anaesthesia surgery. However, Dupuytren and several of his colleagues were extremely skilled and, for their time, knowledgeable, pioneering intricate procedures that had hardly been attempted before. All were to some extent general surgeons, for specialisation itself was in its infancy. Even Dubois, who reigned over 'La Bourbe' – the big, well-appointed lying-in hospital in the suburbs south of the Latin Quarter – and gave lectures to the student-midwives (something that did not exist in London), turned his hand to many other medical procedures. This is why newly qualified medics such as John Sims and Arthur Jacob attended a whole range of operations, demonstrations and lectures, and saw over hospitals and asylums of every kind. They were trying to orientate themselves in a world of knowledge that now seemed almost overwhelmingly full of possibilities.

So they went to La Charité by St Germain des Prés; and to the Foundling Hospital in the Rue d'Enfer with 'pretty, curtained cribs', where some five and a half thousand babies were left each year, no questions asked. They went to the Hospital for Incurable Women on the Left Bank and to the huge Hôpital St Louis on the far side of Paris, originally a plague hospital, where those with skin diseases were treated by such modern methods as steam baths and statistical evaluation. They saw round the Sick Children's Hospital (another idea as yet untried across the Channel) and the new dissecting rooms in the old convent garden of the Hospice du Perfectionnement – Sims found these well lighted, with a black marble table in each, but 'dirty', though he acknowledged that the young anatomist giving lectures was excellent. They saw other dissections in the military hospital at the Val de Grâce (another ex-convent); they visited orphanages and asylums for the insane of all kinds, and for 'girls of incorrect life'. They saw a place in eastern Paris where deaf and dumb boys were being educated in language by being taught to read, and another where blind ones were being taught with very large letters embossed onto the wall for them to feel. They went to the Hôpital des Quinze Vents where incapacitated men lived, often with their whole families – the place had been founded six centuries before by St Louis for crusaders returning blinded from the wars. Paris was indeed well provided with 'receptacles' for life's casualties.

In time to come, Arthur was to focus particular interest on the diseases of the skin and on the eye. He founded Dublin's first opthalmic hospital, was the first person to identify a light-sensitive inner coating to the eye (*membrane Jacobi*) and became known as one of Dublin's first eye specialists: by the later part of his career he was concentrating entirely on eyes.

The only other eye specialist in Dublin was the father of Oscar Wilde, Sir William Wilde. The two ophthalmologists collaborated in visiting workhouse infirmaries when a contagious eye disease struck Ireland in the late 1840s, in the wake of the potato famine. I had nurtured the idea that the Jacob and the Wilde families, as near neighbours in Dublin, both in the same professional field and both with cultured tastes, might also have enjoyed socialising together. However, it turns out that, as the years went by, the Jacob interest came to disapprove of Wilde, professionally and personally. He was 'showy'. He had manoeuvred to get his knighthood. His wife, who wrote newspaper articles and rather bad poetry under the name Speranza, was worse. And when the scandal broke about Dr Wilde having had an improper relationship with a young female patient, and claims and counter-claims of libel followed, the Jacob family said that they had suspected him all along: look at those illegitimate children of his that he passed off as 'wards'. And why did he dishonestly avoid giving evidence in court himself when Speranza was accused of libel? Arthur wrote in *The Dublin Medical Press*, a paper he had founded with another doctor, that Wilde 'owed it to his profession, which must now endure the onus of the disgrace – he owed it to the public, who have confided and are still expected to confide themselves to his honour – and he owed it to Her Majesty's representative who had conferred an unusual mark of distinction on him, to purge himself of the suspicion which at this moment lies heavily on his name'.

Such was life among the elegant Georgian terraces in the heart of Dublin's Protestant Ascendancy, where Arthur forged a reputation for scrupulous expertise and for forthright speaking.

Brief, official accounts of Arthur's career suggest that a formative influence on his choice of speciality was William Lawrence, at whose Dispensary for Curing Diseases of the Eye and Ear he worked for a while when he came back from Paris to London. Lawrence, who was only seven years older than Arthur, had himself been much influenced by the French school of medicine, which viewed human physiology as part of the spectrum of natural history that covered all animals, rather than as a separate study. A public lecture he gave had even been denounced by the Lord Chamberlain as 'anti-scripture'. All this would seem to have accorded with Arthur's own evolving view.

But something in France must have set him on the path towards ophthalmology. In the early nineteenth century, eyes were being looked at medically almost for the first time. There had long been a French tradition of dislodging cataracts by prodding them downwards, but it had only recently been recognised that a cataract is distinct from the lens itself and is therefore removable. Dupuytren took an interest in cataracts and on occasions removed them successfully, but he was wary of doing so in any season or circumstances when infection might strike. It was recognised that inflammation in one eye could all too easily pass to the other, and then the luckless patient, from being poorly sighted before the operation, could end up blind.

Two years after Arthur returned to England, a series of lectures on eye surgery was given for the first time in London by George James Guthrie. For case histories of cataracts Guthrie relied a good deal on F.J. Gondret, who had worked in Paris and published a treatise on the subject. Did Arthur Jacob encounter Gondret? Did Gondret perhaps work at an eye clinic that was established at no. 6 Rue de l'Observance (today Rue Dubois) which led out of the Rue de l'Ecole de Médecine? Certainly the technique Gondret described to tease a cataract from behind the pupil of the eye, using a fine sewing needle that he bent just-so towards the point, was the same method that Arthur Jacob famously used in Dublin many years afterwards.

It was not as desperate a remedy as it sounds. Dr Guthrie wrote in his published lectures that people were mistaken in imagining the eye to be very sensitive and delicate and better not touched. The sensitivity is only in the lid, which can be rolled back – 'Who could bear quietly the sensation which must arise from pushing a needle into the eye if it were analagous to that arising from a fly or a dry solid substance between the eye and the lid? ... Few persons can duly estimate the liberties that may be taken with the eye until they have seen several operations performed.' Guthrie put the insensibility of the eyeball itself down to 'the benignity of the Creator'. I suspect that Arthur Jacob would have differed on this matter, but otherwise their approach was the same. In middle life, Arthur described his method – no form of anaesthesia was available for any surgery till chloroform and ether appeared, when he was already nearing sixty:

> 'I seat the patient in a chair and make him sit straight up or inclining, according to his height. If very tall, I raise myself by standing on a large book or two, or on anything which answers the purpose to be found at hand. [The Jacobs were not tall.] In my own place of business, I find old medical folios answer the purpose well; operating chairs, though very imposing and calculated to produce effect, I have not adopted, not finding myself at ease with such things. When he is seated, I lay the patient's head against my chest . . .'

One must suppose that being firmly held to the doctor's chest had a calming or at any rate subduing effect on some patients. If one winced away, Arthur supplied 'a word of encouragement or remonstrance'. His procedure must have been generally successful, or he would not have had a steady supply of candidates.

The young French medic who scrounged bodies for his fellow students from La Pitié was allowed twenty francs, something under a pound per month, by his family, but this was just spending money as he lived at home. (He did spend it each month, very rapidly according to him, on gambling.) Balzac's hard-up young student from the provinces had to pay fifteen francs a month for his small room in 'one of the poorest and darkest little streets'. Griscom and Sims spent twice that each on their relatively more comfortable rooms, with a sitting room between them, but neither of them was short of money: neither sought work during their lengthy stay in Paris. Arthur, I am sure, did work, in hospital, demonstration theatre or clinic, possibly coaching students himself. With his qualifications and contacts he would have found a niche without too much difficulty.

How long he originally intended to stay I do not know, probably a whole year. But in early March 1815 Napoleon escaped from Elba back to France and began to advance towards Paris, collecting troops as he went, fulfilling the prophecy of one of his less than loyal friends (Fouché) that 'Spring will bring Bonaparte back to us, with the swallows and the violets.' When Napoleon reached the capital, he was greeted neither with resistance nor with much jubilation: no one, except the unemployed army officers hanging about in cafés, wanted yet more War, and after the last twelve months, not to mention the last twenty-five years, the Parisians had become cynical about new dawns. Since all was quiet, the foreigners in Paris tended to wait and see – till Napoleon and his reassembled army marched north in June to confront Wellington and *his* army near Brussels, and it was clear a further great battle would take place. This was to be Waterloo, with Napoleon's definitive exile to follow, but, fearing it might be a defeat for England, the English hastily made for the Channel, Arthur among them. This time he travelled by *diligence*, so clearly his sojourn in Paris had left him modestly in funds.

In any case, for an Englishman Paris was not expensive, and this continued to be true for another hundred and twenty years, as generations of expatriates could testify. In 1815 England's Industrial Revolution and accompanying commercial gains had been advancing for half a century, while France, in today's terms, was still an underdeveloped country. Sims, passing by a steam engine used for pumping water near the recently laid-out Champs Elysées, remarked that it would 'disgrace the meanest manufactury in England'. It is true that Sims hailed from Manchester, a world centre of steam power. It was undeniable that, to British eyes, life within old

Paris seemed quaint, old-fashioned, almost medieval still; yet at the same time there were sophisticated developments which made it, in some ways, more like a modern city than the London of the time, and certainly more than Edinburgh or Dublin.

A few coffee houses such as the Procope had flourished throughout the eighteenth century, but after the Revolution had run its course many new cafés were opened. These were not yet the pavement cafés that would become so characteristic of Paris a generation or so later; they were all indoors and, while open to everyone, became assembly places for specific groups or professions. There was the Café Voltaire on the Place de l'Odéon, just south of the Rue de l'Ecole de Médecine, where Griscom and Sims liked to go.[3] There was another on the corner by the Ecoles and the Rue Hautefeuille, in an ex-chapel opposite the ancient dwelling with a tower that stands there still: this café was very popular with foreign doctors.

Many restaurants, too, had opened under the Directoire and the Empire, mainly founded by cooks from the great households that had existed before the Revolution and were no more. The whole concept of a restaurant – a 'restoring place' – was new then and specifically French. In England, and most other countries, there were only inns to serve travellers or parties gathered there for a special occasion. Otherwise, places to sit down to a meal, outside private houses or guest houses, hardly existed. For Griscom, who was from America but had been touring in Switzerland and Italy, this new French amenity called a restaurant was strange enough for him to describe it:

'On entering one of the houses and seating oneself at a small table covered with a neat white cloth, a printed paper is presented containing a list of all the varieties which the house affords . . . The price of so much as an individual ordinarily requires is attached to each article. Hence a person may call for just what he pleases, and pay for no more than he calls for.'

Freedom and sophistication indeed.

Restaurants in Paris existed at a lower economic level also. Some, called *gargotes*, were shacks catering for labourers working on sites at a distance from their home or lodgings. These were exclusively working class, but the same formula of plain dishes at rock-bottom prices was applied by the famous *restaurateur* who fed generations of Latin Quarter students, one Flicoteaux. By the end of Napoleon's empire he and his relations had five or six restaurants in the Quarter, and these are mentioned in novels and memoirs of the era. There was one in the Rue de la Parcheminerie – 'A big, dim room, tables and benches, no table cloths or napkins; main dishes at 3 to 5 *sous* [15 to 25 centimes], soup at one *sou*, not much wine and bring-your-own-bread.'

It was said that a student needed about fifty francs (just over two pounds) a month for food and coffee which, at Flicoteaux prices, sounds adequate. Obviously such establishments could not have run without a pool of extremely cheap labour, and the fact that Parisian labour was so cheap – to cook, to wash dishes, to clear and serve, to cart water in and slops out – explains why even the poorest students never cooked for themselves. It was socially unthinkable for an educated young man to do so, and anyway impracticable.

(This tradition lasted in Paris right through the nineteenth century and into the first half of the twentieth, prolonged through the 1920s and '30s by economic depression. Into the 1950s there were still elderly people of both sexes – teachers of a kind, librarians, commercial translators, would-be writers – living permanently in Left Bank hotels where they did not even have to make their own beds, much less housekeep. They ate all their meals in the remaining obscure *prix fixe* restaurants, where napkins were kept for them in rings with their names on. Traditionally, these individuals would claim to be too poor ever to have set up a home, unaware that, as the world changed around them, their antique way of life would be seen by most people as leisured and trouble-free to the point of luxury.)

Other expenses mentioned in Latin Quarter budgets of Arthur Jacob's time were fifteen francs a month to cover clothes and laundry, five for paper, postage and tobacco, and five for membership of one of the many reading rooms which provided a comfortable place with a fire for a young man to read or write away from his minimal lodgings. This would have been welcome to Arthur, for the winter of 1814–15 was cold enough to freeze the goldfish at the Jardin des Plantes in their pool. I am sure, too, that Arthur, judging from the wide-ranging library he later amassed, would have spent some money on books. There were the book and print dealers round the old church of St Séverin by the Rue de la Huchette, and the antiquarian who had set up his huge store in the Gothic cavernousness of the Hôtel de Cluny. The bookstalls along the river, that were to become such a feature of the Left Bank, were already beginning to appear opposite Notre Dame. There were also a number of well-known bookshops in the Rue Hautefeuille, round the corner from the medical schools, and others in the Rue de l'Ecole de Médecine itself that specialised in medical works. It was in one of these that Arthur seems to have formed a relationship that was to have long reverberations for his family.

Two years before Arthur's coming to Paris, a skinny boy of not yet fifteen arrived from northern France to begin work as an assistant in a bookshop in the Rue de l'Ecole de Médecine. He came from a family of skilled cloth-workers in Beauvais, who had been impoverished by the general dislocation of society that had followed the Revolution and by the trade blockade of the Wars. His name was Jean-Baptiste Baillière, and he was to prove extremely intelligent and able. He went on to open his own shop in the Rue Hautefeuille – at the spot where, a thousand years before, a Jewish cemetery had been. He became an expert bibliophile and then a publisher of medical and scientific works in his own right. He commissioned finely detailed and coloured engravings to illustrate the physical minutiae of the human body that was then being explored and revealed. He got celebrated surgeons to contribute to compendia that became standard works for the rest of the century. He developed contacts round the world: his work was carried on by Baillière brothers, sons, nephews and grandsons, and branches were opened in London, New York, Madrid and distant Melbourne.

By the time the young doctor and the teenage shop assistant were both old men, an intricate and fruitful link had developed between the Baillière firm and the Jacob family. But by the twentieth century the family story had been recast, assigning the entrepreneurial role in this business arrangement to a dynamic figure (one Tindall) who married into the Jacob family a generation later – a role which, on a closer look at dates and lives, appears implausible. The lost fact that the book-loving Arthur and the founder of Baillière et Cie were both ambitious young men on the same Paris street in the same year seems far more significant.

Given his interests, Arthur could not have failed to visit Jean-Baptiste Baillière's place of work and make purchases. Getting into conversation with the assistant, he no doubt noticed, as a number of other people had already, how bright the boy was and what a prodigious memory he had for books and authors and scientific details. There is evidence of ongoing contact between the two. Thirty years later Arthur brought out, under the imprint of his own recently formed Dublin Medical Press, a small bound volume of his previous papers and lectures: *Dr Jacob's Essays – Anatomical, Zoological, Surgical and Miscellaneous.* This was also published in London, by Hippolyte Baillière, Jean-Baptiste's younger brother, and in Paris by Jean-Baptiste himself.

From our vantage point in time we see past lives laid out in linear retrospect, everything equally present because it is all done. It is tempting to believe that the later, intricate tie between the two families was already in some sense there while the earliest contact was being made. As the young men stood chatting in the bookshop in the Rue des Ecoles, did the long future reach out momentarily to touch them?

Early in 2008, just as this book was nearing completion and almost two hundred years after Jean-Baptiste Baillière first arrived in Paris, a plaque commemorating him and his great enterprise was unveiled in the Rue Hautefeuille. It seems appropriate that Arthur Jacob's great-great granddaughter was among the crowd who gathered to honour him.

From Paris Arthur brought home, as well as books, something he was to carry on his person for the rest of his life. This was a tiny hour glass – actually, a half-minute glass – used to take a patient's pulse in that era when ordinary pocket-watches had no second hand. 'Pulse watches' that could count the seconds had existed for some time, but these were rare objects, expensively ornamented, favoured for display by fashionable London doctors but hardly by serious young ones starting out on their careers. Thirty-odd years later, it was a Dublin doctor, a near-contemporary of Arthur's, who established the importance of pulse-taking for a range of diagnoses, so one must suppose that Arthur put his glass to good use.

Fitted snugly into an ivory case of French workmanship, the whole thing takes up no more room in a pocket than a fat piece of chalk. When every other personal possession, excepting books, has gone, the pulse glass has survived through time and chance, a heartbeat lying quiet in its case.

I want to believe that Arthur, however focused on work, had fun in Paris too.

The great places for popular relaxation at the time were the gravelled, elm-lined boulevards encircling the Right Bank, where cafés had opened and chairs could be rented. Here, John Griscom watched

> 'ballad singers, dancers, both children and dogs; conjurors, puppet shows; merry Andrews and fortune tellers; men with castles inhabited by white mice . . . fortresses guarded by a regiment of Canary birds, which perform their evolutions with great precision; caricaturists or *grimaciers*, who change their faces into a rapid succession of odd and singularly grotesque forms . . . thankful for the voluntary *sous* that may be thrown at them . . . Fruit women, flower girls, musicians, hydrostatic experiments . . .'

John Scott, at the same scene, noted particularly the pervasive smell of roasting chestnuts, and of the fruit and nosegays thrust forward for sale. He watched jugglers, a dog turning a barrel organ, and a man with a painted castle on his back from which glasses of lemonade were tapped. He had seen the same man on the Left Bank quays, for on Sundays the caravanserai moved to the quays and the bridges to perform for a public that worked too long hours during the other six days to stroll on the boulevards. There would have been a cacophony of sounds from competing hucksters, adding to the cries of those who hawked their wares in the streets every day – the sellers of charcoal, fish, pans, glass, milk and hot rolls, the lavender girl with her plaintive song, the water-carrier with his stentorian cry '*A l'eau, à l'eau*'. There were the bird-trappers and -sellers too, the *oise-liers*. George Sand, who was from a slightly disreputable aristocratic family on her father's side, liked to say that her mother's father had been a *Maître-Oiselier* – 'My mother was a child of the streets of old Paris.'

All this was gayer and more engaging for Arthur than the hawkers and beggars of either Dublin or Edinburgh, whose abject urban poverty was the end result of rural poverty under despotic and often absent landlords. But I continue to think, for reasons that appear in his later life, that his favourite walking place was probably the zoo in the Jardin des Plantes.

Chapter VIII

ARTHUR IN ESSENCE

Arthur, we know, went on to become a well-known figure in Irish nineteenth-century medicine: his name is to be found in specialised histories, or on a gilded board in the Royal College of Surgeons in Ireland. But such people too, like all the rest, usually pass from the common stock of memory and reference. *The Medical Press and Circular*, which he founded, is no more. The teaching hospital he set up has long since been absorbed by other institutions. The part of the eye he discovered when he was not yet thirty is no longer known as the *membrane Jacobi*, nor is a particular kind of rodent face ulcer any more called 'Jacob's ulcer'. Cataracts are not now removed with 'Jacob's needle'. The big old house in Ely Place in Dublin, just off Merrion Square, where two generations of Jacob doctors practised their skills, now contains the smart modern offices of a PR firm.

I wanted to see if I could summon Arthur himself back from the great oblivion. I have handled the books with which he furnished his life and read some of the articles and letters he wrote. I have traced his epic journey: I have marked his footprints in Paris and seen the kind of life he led there and the people he knew. I have held his pulse glass in my hand to time my own heart's beat. But what was Arthur like as a person?

The limitation of obituaries is that they are usually written about old men, not about men as they were in their vigorous prime. The author of the memorial pamphlet published in Dublin in 1874 seems to have been overawed by the task, regarding himself as 'treading upon sacred ground'.

'Arthur Jacob is dead!' he begins, and goes on to describe 'an earnest, honest and pre-eminently intellectual man . . . punctual and energetic, attracting large classes of students, whose boast in subsequent years was that they had been his pupils'. He lists Arthur's numerous appointments, publications and professional interests, then continues:

'For many years of his life it was his unvarying habit, after the completion of a laborious day's work, and having dined, to retire to bed for a couple of hours rest, when he slept profoundly; he then got up, had tea, and devoted the greater part of the night to reading, writing, and preparing notes for his anatomical lectures . . . which were to him labours of love . . . To those who had but a superficial knowledge of Dr Jacob, his manner may have appeared brusque, but to those who were intimately acquainted with him the generous, disinterested, honest and thoroughly independent nature of his character was well known . . .

'Of Arthur Jacob, the worst which can be said is that those objects which were nearest to his heart he loved "not wisely but too well". [These seem to have been mainly the Royal College, and the reputation and circumstances of Irish doctors and medical services, for which he fought London rivals and governments ferociously for much of his life.] On more than one occasion the strength of his feeling and the vigour with which he went forward to his object gave him the appearance of intolerance in opinion and excessive zeal in action, and his unhesitating candour made for him antagonists whom a more cautious and disingenuous diplomatist would have conciliated.'

It looks as if Arthur, like his long-ago mentor Dupuytren, was better at relationships with patients and students (in whom, we hear, he took a great interest) than with some of his peers. The picture is a somewhat daunting one, particularly when we are also told that he had a great wariness of appearing self-interested or of courting that 'public and pecuniary advancement to which his labours and his talents justly entitled him'. No wonder he did not like the flamboyant Dr Wilde and his knighthood. When Arthur was seventy and some of his colleagues clubbed together to have a bronze medal struck for him, he rejected it with the remark: 'I cannot accept this or any other testimonial, but if at my death you still think that I deserve it, you may nail it on my coffin!'

I like to think that this was said with a wintry humour – there must have been a sense of fun in a man who chose to address his (female) housekeeper as 'Moses' – but it was surely rather galling for those who had planned and commissioned the medal.

Another obituarist wrote: 'He rarely indulged in even the mildest of festivities.' (Knowing what 'festivities' in Ireland can be like, and that he and his brothers had much trouble with a drunken cousin who was also a doctor, one is not entirely surprised.) 'He had an intense dislike to humbug of every kind.' The worldly dinner parties of Dublin High Society, which was headed by doctors and lawyers, may also not have been to his taste. The world, in a wider sense, was where he mentally belonged: in his library, he travelled to its furthest corners.

But what we are being shown here is a man at the end of his life, and a widower. His wife, a shadowy figure from a good Anglo-Irish family of County Sligo, who gave him five sons that grew up and a girl that did not survive infancy, had died fifteen years earlier. You do not father six children by going to sleep immediately after dinner and then staying up reading most of the night, so one may assume that in younger days Arthur had a less eccentric timetable. Witnesses from that period remembered a different man and a sociable one, forming a dining club with colleagues. And while his wife lived and the boys were growing up, there were cheerful visits between Dublin and Maryborough. Small sons in need of country air were despatched on the Maryborough coach in the charge of the coachman. Presents of plants and game went back and forth by the same means. On at least one occasion a whole family of little cousins was invited to stay in Dublin for Christmas. Arthur was evidently proud of his own family, for he had the four eldest painted while they were still very young. The future vicar of St Thomas's, Bayswater, two doctor-surgeons and an engineer stand round with faces scrubbed, hair curling over clean collars, surrounded by some of those folio medical volumes their father used to stand on to treat his cataract patients. Later in life – possibly after their only little girl, the youngest, had died – he took his wife on one or more visits to Paris. A well-thumbed *Guide to Paris* among his surviving books, with advice on shopping, seems to have been mainly for her.

When Arthur was a lecturer in the 1820s, first at the Park Street School he had helped to establish along with several colleagues, and then at the Royal College of Surgeons in Ireland when he was appointed Professor of Anatomy there at only thirty-seven, following on from Abraham Colles, the medical students of Dublin were an elegant lot, according to an Irish correspondent of *The Lancet*.[1] They were given to 'spear-pointed shirt necks', artificially frizzed curls, and heeled boots in the manner of the Duke of Wellington. They affected umbrellas, gold rings, and 'quizzing glasses' hung on decorative chains round their necks – but Arthur seems to have equalled, if not excelled them, in dandified airs of his own. Slight in build, he gave the impression of disdaining elaborate dress, favouring a dark blue coat and black stock, but actually gauged his appearance nicely. His spectacles fitted his face and eyes as if they had grown there – 'an expanse of the cornea spread out upon a delicate frame of silver wire. Over the springs of this beautiful piece of mechanism . . . hung two luxuriant ringlets of auburn hair, like the tendrils of a vine, and writhing into beautiful contortions.' He came up to the lecture table 'with a buoyant swing' and a grin that seemed at once pleased with the effect he made and self-mocking. No medical gravitas there.

An oil painting dating from this time shows him in just such a mode, though the curls are beginning to recede a little up his high forehead. His mouth is gentle and slightly sensuous, his expression mild. We seem far, here, from the austere old party who rarely indulged in festivities. We are near, however, to the young man walking in the Jardin des Plantes, observing animals and birds there that he could then have seen nowhere else, for it was agreed that when he lectured on anatomy he was a wonderful imitator:

'With the albatross he seemed about to take wing and leave us all behind him; the penguin soon brought him down again to the very depths of the ocean; with the snail his fingers crept along the wall, and now with the parrot he worked his way, *unguibus et dentibus*, through the dense heart of the forest; but we confess, when he came to illustrate the fantastic tricks of the monkey tribe, he looked the character to such perfection that we could not help considering it, of all the characters he assumed, as his forte.'

There is an edge of malice in this, but it is nothing compared with the invective that sometimes passed between doctors in those outspoken times. Arthur, and his main ally Dr Henry Maunsell, did not hesitate to use publicly terms such as 'rabble' and 'scandalous' about people of whom they disapproved, frequently the Fellows of the Royal College of Surgeons in London, and accusations of 'plots' pepper their letters.

The animal theme continued throughout Arthur's life. He collected books on zoology; he wrote a learned paper on his dissection of a whale that was washed up on the Irish coast. He also had a taste for exotic pets. In widowerhood, he used to let a parrot sit on his shoulder at dinner, for which ceremony he wore an especially shabby old coat. Parrots were not uncommon in Victorian homes, but at one time a small bear was kept in the drawing room at Ely Place, chained to the mantelpiece and released when Arthur 'wanted to converse with him'.[2] A medical student, come to collect some certificates, got bored waiting and undid the bear's chain. The doctor was summoned from the other end of the house by screams: amused, but rather annoyed, he managed to disentangle the young man from the bear's paws. When Archibald, Arthur's fourth son and the one destined to follow him into the practice, got married and moved in with his bride, the bear was housed in the President's room at the Royal College where Arthur sometimes stayed. All went well till the bear escaped one night, investigated other rooms, and tucked itself into the bed of the College Secretary, who discovered his bedfellow when getting in wearing only a nightshirt. After that the bear was given to the Dublin Zoo, but a monkey was installed at Ely Place instead.

Archibald was twenty-three when he married: he had graduated from Trinity College but had not yet completed his MD. His bride was younger. His mother was dead by then, and Arthur, who had not married till he was thirty-four and well launched on his career, seems to have disapproved of his son's early marriage. Possibly he disapproved of the bride too. Florence, the daughter of a fashionable Dublin dentist, was socially quite suitable, but Arthur may have thought she was silly, and such scraps of evidence about her as were passed down to future generations suggest that he may have been right. He showed a wounding lack of confidence in her by having the front windows of the house covered in whitewash. This was to deter the young gentlemen of the Queen's Service Academy opposite from making indelicate gestures to her or to the servants. It was a practical solution and possibly, given Arthur's mordant sense of the ridiculous, even a joky one, but it was one that Florence, naturally, much resented. Tears and scenes followed and the whitewash was removed, but then the monkey took against her as his master had. A crisis was reached in their relationship when poor Florence was about to go to a garden party at the Viceregal Lodge, the miniature Court of the Lord Lieutenant to which prominent residents of Dublin and their families were regularly invited. She was wearing a hat adorned with a bunch of artificial grapes. She passed too close to the monkey's perch and he made a rapid and devastating grab. A minute later, Florence was being pelted with crushed grapes.

After that the monkey followed the bear to the Zoo. Archibald and Florence moved, for the time being, into a place of their own, a house in the long, light Georgian vista of Harcourt Street, on the other side of St Stephen's Green. There, they took in medical students as lodgers, till their rapidly growing family made this unfeasible. It was said that, in any case, Florence sometimes found the students 'difficult to keep in order', as she later did her children. They did not take over Ely Place as living quarters till Arthur retired, when, to the surprise of his colleagues, he removed himself entirely from Dublin and from Ireland. His last years were spent in the home of another son, who was Chief Engineer to the booming industrial municipality of Barrow-in-Furness, across the Irish Sea. The three other sons were in London, India and Australia. Already the mould of Anglo-Irish life was beginning to break up.

Many years before this, John Jacob, Arthur's younger brother who had taken on the Infirmary and the practice in Maryborough, had written to Arthur apropos of some now-impenetrable row with a local dignitary: 'I suppose one of the marked features of the Jacob character is and has been a disregard and non-practice of the usual civilities of life.'

This trait, along with a basic decency and honesty to a fault, did indeed seem to run through that generation and was handed down. Archibald, too, had little concern for niceties of dress or behaviour, though he is said to have been much more charming and conventionally fun-loving than his father. His career, though respectable, was less distinguished. He and Florence had twelve children, of whom ten survived. They lived comfortably and hospitably, but never had quite enough money or much idea where it went. One of Florence's daughters always remembered her mother in tears over the simple lack of cash to buy groceries. 'You see this house and everyone in it?' Archibald is said to have told the tax inspector when pressed to state his income. 'Well, there's my wife, ten children, four servants and a governess and *I keep the lot of them*. Now go home, my dear Sir, and *you* calculate how much I earn.'

As for the Jacob clan in and around Maryborough, the small amount of Arthur's personal correspondence that has, by some quirk, survived, contains letters to and from the brothers, all dating from a brief period at the beginning of the 1840s. At one point both John and another brother, Thomas (a country solicitor), were writing

passionate letters to Arthur to get him to intervene in
the case of 'an unfortunate wretch' who had, in their
view, been unfairly condemned to death for the murder
of his mother. They wanted Arthur to raise influential
Dublin medical feeling against a Queen's County doctor
who, they thought, was the person really responsible for
the old woman's death. Her son was said to have caused
her to break her arm while he was drunk:

> 'Dr Edge was examined . . . He found the deceased,
> a woman between sixty and seventy, lying on *wet*
> straw, that the rain ran down thru the roof of the
> Cabbin [*sic*] upon her . . .' (Thomas).
>
> 'This is a bad case and the convict must not be
> permitted to be executed . . . Edge visited, ordered
> a warm plaster, castor oil and "the usual remedies"
> – *did not set her arm*. She lived in that state two
> months and half – in all probability would have
> recovered if sent to the Infirmary' (John).
>
> '. . . Edge has a dispensary in the Colliery and
> spends more time hunting hares than seeing patients
> and gets his grant in consequence of his family being
> useful in election offers to the party in the County
> who have the management of the Public money'
> (Thomas).
>
> '. . . The prisoner was *inefficiently* defended by a
> lawyer as provided by the Crown . . . Bushe [Chief
> Justice] has arrived at the lachrymose period of second
> childhood the wreck of a whole fabric not wishing
> to join issue with the profession and the Press of
> which I believe the judiciary here has become some-
> what fearful – charged strongly against the prisoner
> descanted on the atrocity of the parricide –' (John).

Neither brother seems to have had much regard for
the 'usual civilities' of punctuation.

John wanted Arthur, as well as marshalling the doctors,

to call on Bushe when he returned from the Quarter Sessions circuit to Dublin and 'talk it over with him privately'. Arthur agreed to respond to the various appeals, and evidently did so effectively: a few days before the due date for hanging, the sentence was set aside. There is no further written information on the young man's fate. He may have been transported to Australia, he may simply have gone free. He may have taken himself off to America, like so many of his fellow Irish, and prospered there, or not – but at least he was not laid in a felon's grave within the precincts of Maryborough Gaol.

Everything about this case – the drunken and penitent son, convicted on the evidence of a child; the victim saying he was 'a good and kind son to her unless when he was drunk'; the rain-sodden cabin, the family's poverty, the sister's children 'all but begging' and 'eating heartily of a meal of dry potatoes which were given by a neighbour' – all is redolent of the stereotype of the wretched Irish peasantry, who would die in their thousands in the potato famine three or four years later. But the other part of that stereotype is an image of the Anglo-Irish ruling class, which is now popularly held to have been responsible for that misery. It is cheering, therefore, to record the Jacob brothers banding together to remedy an injustice ('This will be judicial murder') and bringing their combined power to help what must have counted as one of the less deserving poor of Queen's County. However abrasive their manners, their hearts were evidently in the right place.[3] The next letter preserved from that summer finds John approving of a paper Arthur had written on the need to make smallpox vaccination free for all, and urging him to pursue the matter in the next edition of *The Medical Press*, since 'I find I cannot explain these matters without making enemies.'

* * *

When John Jacob could not get his way in the Infirmary, he formed the habit of co-opting his near relatives as life governors and extracting a 'subscription' from each. After he died, reputedly from overwork and not yet sixty, a question was asked in the House of Commons as to whether it was proper that one family should effectively own the Queen's County Infirmary. The Jacob clan were also, needless to say, Justices of the Peace, Poor Law Guardians and local Councillors. However, no one was able to point to any particular evil resulting from this hegemony, and the matter was dropped.

John was succeeded as County Surgeon by his son David, and he in turn by his son William, who was finally edged from power in the Infirmary in 1900, but continued in practice and was surgeon to the local regiment. William died while returning from visiting a sick patient in December 1914, and thus the one hundred and fifty years' medical link between Queen's County and the Jacob family ended. But a great many more things were going to end then, in the hurricane blown up by the Great War. In 1916 came the Easter Rising, followed by the Troubles and Irish Independence in 1922. By then, the greater part of the extensive Jacob family were no longer in Ireland. Arthur's grandsons and most of their cousins were scattered to 'the dominions'; his grand-daughters had married Scots or Englishmen, or were eking out lives of genteel penury in west London. The world of Anglo-Ireland was now vanishing as fast as that of Anglo-India was going to a generation later.

The Jacob Diaries, the record of the health and sickness of every local family from top to bottom of the social scale since the late eighteenth century, were bequeathed by William to the Infirmary. They were kept in a bookcase in the Surgeons' Dining Room, where they could be consulted. In 1939, on the eve of the Second World War, the hospital was being cleared for Army occupation. Though Ireland was to remain neutral, it was foreseen that, as in previous English wars, Irishmen would enlist and so might come home wounded, though it was no longer absolutely clear on whose side they would be. The Diaries were thrown out, and burnt. Apparently this was on the orders of the Fianna Fáil-appointed Manager of the County that was now called Laois, who said that they were 'useless old rubbish'.[4] In this way, a precious social record of the lives of countless ordinary Irish families was destroyed for ever.

Arthur Jacob as a young doctor

Arthur Jacob's half-minute glass for taking the pulse

The Cour de Commerce St André at the beginning of the twentieth century

Demolition for the construction of the Boulevard St Germain in the late 1860s

Sketch of the Rue Hautefeuille made at the end of the nineteenth century. The substantial house on the far side of the arched doorway was the headquarters of the Baillière company

Sketch of the one-time refectory of the Cordeliers, just off the present Rue de l'Ecole de Médecine

Bertie Tindall as a little boy, early 1880s

The four Tindall children, Bertie, Howard, May and Maud, late 1880s

A studio model, from George du Maurier's novel about would-be artists in Paris. *Trilby* was published in 1894 but the story is set back to the 1850s

'Life on the Boulevard', from the *Illustrated London News*, *c.*1870

Snowscape painted by Bertie from his window high up in the Rue de l'Abbaye, 1895

The steam engine that crashed through the buffers
at the Gare Montparnasse in 1895

Part II

FROM ARTHUR TO BERTIE: 1815–1895

Chapter IX

LES COMPTES FANTASTIQUES DE HAUSSMANN

etween the departure of Arthur Jacob from the Latin Quarter in 1815, and the arrival there of his grandson-in-law eighty years later, the Quarter was to experience greater change than it had in more than five centuries.

Here and there, of course, and most specifically in the creation of the new medical schools, change had already come before the nineteenth century had even begun. There had been plans, and dreams, and Napoleon himself had envisaged far grander schemes for the whole of Paris than, in the event, he had time to build. After he had been consigned to his final exile on the South Atlantic remoteness of St Helena, he wrote: 'If only Heaven had allowed me a twenty-year reign and some time to spare, then Old Paris would have been nowhere to be found; no vestige of it would have remained.'

For this reason, among others, one may feel thankful for the outcome of the Battle of Waterloo. But Napoleon was not, of course, alone in his conviction that old Paris, medieval within-the-walls Paris, would not do for a modern capital. Time tends to telescope change in the collective memory, simplifying events, creating spurious Befores and Afters. The popular myth now is that old

Paris remained intact in all its gabled, unhygienic picturesqueness till Baron Haussmann burst on the scene in 1853 like a satanic jack-in-the-box and, in his capacity as Préfet of Police under the Second Empire, imposed a new order. It is only partially true. The Restoration of 1814 may have cut short Napoleon's grand plans, but the task of modernisation did continue piecemeal, and was possibly all the better for being conducted with more pragmatism.

Between the re-establishment of the Bourbons and the revolution of 1830, which sent them finally packing and placed on the throne the Orleanist and last king, Louis-Philippe, more than a hundred and thirty new streets were opened in Paris. These were mainly to accommodate the great increase in wheeled traffic, but for the first time pavements for pedestrians became a normal part of street construction. Then, in the eighteen years of Louis-Philippe's reign, till he in turn was ousted by another clamorous revolution, one hundred and twelve more streets were opened. They were not particularly wide. The Comte de Rambuteau, Louis-Philippe's Préfet in charge of the capital, who had been born and bred in the heart of Paris, was respectful of the old geography, but the new streets were useful in opening up new districts and making the old more navigable. Lighting was improved, and at last gas made its belated entry into many parts of Paris, though not yet into the houses. Trees were planted and small parks laid out, public benches were installed, many more public water points were constructed, and the very first public urinals appeared. Some attempt – though not a very coherent one – was made to deal with Paris's famous lack of proper drains either for sewage or for surface water, and the accompanying smell of rotting cabbage 'by which the Parisian, returning from a journey, recognises his city', as Rambuteau himself nostalgically remarked.

But the more that was done to air and beautify the

Right Bank, particularly towards the west, the more the Left Bank seemed physically and therefore socially inferior. True, two short but significant new streets had been opened, leading respectively from the Rue de la Harpe to the Sorbonne and from the Luxembourg Gardens to the Panthéon, and others had been optimistically sketched out in the suburbs further off, among market gardens, builders' yards, cow-byres, tanneries, garden-cafés, new gas-works and hospitals. But these signs of progress made the inward-looking maze of lanes between the Sorbonne and the river only seem more impenetrable and out of date. Something, it was declared, must be done, if Left Bank Paris was to keep up at all with her richer, more modern sister over the river, and that something was a prolongation eastwards of the Rue de l'Ecole de Médecine, to be generally known as the Rue des Ecoles: the street leading to the schools.

Although the Rue des Ecoles did not actually get itself built till after Napoleon's nephew had become the new Emperor in 1852 – there never seemed as much money to spend on the Left Bank as on the Right – it was planned and promoted with almost messianic zeal in the second half of the 1840s. Initially perceived just as a through route for students, cutting out tiresome detours and thus promoting 'health for studious youth', it soon began to be seen as a necessary east–west cross route for the area, doing for the Left Bank what the street named after Rambuteau himself had done for the Right in opening up the old market area. But then a new note of high-minded town planning came in – the 'slum clearance' argument, which was to become familiar in other cities far from Paris as the century went by. When at last the demolitions for the new street began, cutting across the Rue des Carmes, carrying away the Mathurins, ancient churches such as St Benoît and St Jean de Latran, lanes of old houses and tiny walled cemeteries, one ponderous advocate for this, Eugène Cramouzaud, wrote:

'The Rue des Ecoles, this "great ventilation shaft", as one illustrious man of letters has called it, thrusting before itself a great gulf, has already begun a work of restorative justice: however, the opening of this street is more than an act of justice and decent administration, it is an act of humanity.'[1]

One doubts if the tenants evicted from the houses to be pulled down saw it quite this way, particularly since no compensation was given then, or later under Haussmann, to anyone who was not actually the owner of the building. It was all very well to claim, as another contemporary pundit did, that 'this street will bring air and light into a quarter that has been neglected for a long time', but if you were someone whose dwelling was being sacrificed to create the air and light you were not likely to be grateful. There was no attempt at re-housing, and where could the dispossessed go? There were two answers to this. They could take themselves off to self-built shanties in grubby one-time villages, which an 1840s customs wall round Paris had now enclosed. Or they could crowd in ever-denser numbers into the buildings in their familiar quarter that the demolitions had left standing.

For the fact was that, though 'lined with respectable houses' and 'opening up the façades of several university buildings', the Rue des Ecoles does not seem to have raised the tone of the old district near Place Maubert through which it passed, but had rather the opposite effect. For, from then on, descriptions of Maubert and its lanes, of the Montagne Sainte Geneviève and of several other adjacent streets are always cast in a tone of disapproval – sometimes genuinely regretful that humans should be constrained to live in such slums, sometimes almost lip-smacking in condemnation. Cramouzaud (whose ideal of urban planning, by the way, was the Panthéon – 'so vast, so monumental') uttered a dire warning that, the way things were going, 'the slopes of the Montagne Sainte Geneviève will soon shelter every vagabond that the streets of Paris conceal . . . [This quarter] will be like one of those thickly wooded patches that one finds in the middle of well-cultivated country which one cannot penetrate without being hurt by brambles and thorns.' He rejected out of hand, however, the notion, already being voiced by more thoughtful commentators, that a wholly 'modern, civilised Paris' would leave nowhere for the poor to go. 'Market forces', he vaguely asserted, would take care of that.

Since, in any case, thriving cities perpetually attract more poor from the countryside and the provinces, a capital composed entirely of respectable or well-to-do areas has never been either desirable or attainable. This fact is rediscovered at long intervals: it is indeed being rediscovered in Paris today, as the traditional working population that underpin the city's services are pushed by market forces further and further out into the suburbs. But for a large part of the nineteenth and twentieth centuries the illusion prevailed that poverty itself could somehow be 'solved' by destroying the streets that harboured it. As early as the first cholera epidemic of 1832, a left-wing idealist called Perrymond was proposing the complete demolition of some of Paris's oldest quarters: the Ile de la Cité, the Ile St Louis – and a swathe of Left Bank streets near the river including the whole Place Maubert area along with the one-time medical amphitheatre, St Julien le Pauvre, the St Séverin lanes and the Rue de la Huchette.

Fortunately for the generations coming after him, only the Ile de la Cité destruction was carried out, but the mental label affixed to the most ancient part of the Left Bank long remained. Haussmann targeted it, but never quite got round to it, and nor did his successors. As late as the 1950s it was still theoretically scheduled for demolition as an 'insalubrious pocket', till fashion, rising Left Bank property values and the influence of André Malraux as Minister for Culture rescued this core of the old Latin Quarter before the bulldozers got there.

A doctor,[2] writing in the mid-nineteenth century, felt that over certain streets of the Maubert should be written, as above the Roman ghetto, 'Here Lives Poverty' – 'These hovels are the nightly refuge of all that nomadic population consisting of hawkers, pushers of hand-carts, organ grinders, acrobats, glaziers, china menders, hands from the nearby wool and cotton workshops, and, above all, rag-pickers [*chiffonniers*]. It is here that these last empty their packs, their daily haul of filth.' He noted the smell from these rubbish piles, and 'irritating dust' thought to cause lung disease, fever and rheumatism, and the fact that the ground floors of the houses were often damp with steam from washer-women plying their trade.

But hadn't Paris for centuries had hawkers, rag-pickers and washer-women? One never knows, with scandalised descriptions of poverty, whether the poverty itself had really got worse or whether a general slight rise in the living standards made the conditions in which poor families had always lived seem worse. Place Maubert had certainly gone down in the world since the days of Dante and Thomas Aquinas, and perhaps since those of Voltaire, but the rag-pickers who made their headquarters there had for centuries been an integral, if lowly, part of the urban scene.

Till well into the nineteenth century paper was commonly made from recycled cloth, and so those who scavenged this material were very necessary. Later, as cheaper paper from imported wood pulp became the norm, the *chiffonniers* diversified their efforts, and when the Second Empire came to an end in 1870 there were twelve thousand of them operating in Paris. They pushed small barrows or carried hods on their backs, into which went everything that could possibly be sorted over for reuse. Clean rags were separated from dirty ones, but so were different types of glass for re-melting, and assorted old shoes that might be conflated into 'new' ones. Bones went to make buttons and dominoes; corks went to wine merchants; orange peel to juice-makers; old bits of bread were moistened and heated for resale, or dried and then ground down to make 'coffee'; wool was unpicked to be respun into shoddy; tangled human hairs were picked out and matched for colour and length to be sold to wig-makers; cigar butts (and later cigarette ends) were unpeeled and mashed up for repackaging as 'selected' tobacco . . . Since municipal rubbish collections were unknown in Paris till Préfet Poubelle, who unwittingly gave his name to the dustbins, invented the idea in the 1880s, the *chiffonniers* were clearly as necessary to middle-class Paris as they were to those in the lowest social reaches.

Almost anything, it seems, was sellable. Some scav-engers specialised in collecting dog-dirt, which they sold by the pailful for use in the tanneries that still stood along the upper reaches of the Bièvre. There is also a record of a 'filthy drunken person who works somewhere in a hospital' selling dead foetuses round the Place Maubert to – who else? – medical students.

Such was the life sheltered now in streets such as the Rue Perdue, the Rue des Rats and the Rue des Anglais. As for the Rue des Noyers on the other side of the Place, where the de Musset house still stood, and the Rue des Carmes running up the hill behind it, now crossed at one point by the Rue des Ecoles, these had long been a cut above Maubert and remained so. The curator of the Musée Carnavalet, Georges Cain, who had been born in the still-almost-countrified district north of the Panthéon in the mid-century, wrote near the end of his life, in an utterly changed city, that the Rue des Carmes seemed to him a perfect survival of the past. It was poor, and obscure, but in the old, large doorways of one-time convents and *collèges* it still had a remnant of grandeur:

'Narrow and hump-backed, [it] climbs steeply up between shops whose coloured paintwork has been washed again and again by rains, tarnished by dust and wind, and yet this meagre street remains full of charm and poetry. It is crowned at the top by the august pile of the Panthéon while, at its foot, framed between the two rows of blackened houses, minimal hotels and *bal-musettes*, there rises against the clear sky the slim and elegant spire of Notre Dame.'[3]

We shall return to the minimal hotels of the Rue des Carmes in other seasons.

The municipal authorities were pleased with their Rue des Ecoles. There was even talk of prolonging it as far as the Jardin des Plantes and the new Gare d'Orléans which had been opened there by the river in 1840 (later re-baptised 'Gare d'Austerlitz', when Napoleonic memories came back into fashion again). Subsequent road building such as the Rue Jussieu and the Rue Monge, which carried away the walled gardens of George Sand's old convent school, overtook this idea. But in any case it was not foreseen, at the beginning of the Second Empire in 1852, that within fifteen years such new, giant carriageways would be pushed through the old fabric of the Left Bank that the Rue des Ecoles would by then be perceived as simply inadequate as a cross route for the Latin Quarter.

Perhaps that was why an odd bottleneck in it, at the junction with the Rue de l'Ecole de Médecine, was never tidied away. At the corner of the Rue de l'Ecole de Médecine and the Rue Hautefeuille stands a large, turreted dwelling, thought to have been home in the fourteenth century to a prominent Parisian, Pierre Sarrazin. The late-eighteenth-century designers of what is still the core of the medical schools had no plans to demolish this: the erstwhile Rue des Cordeliers remained narrow for its entire length. Not till the end of the nine-teenth century did rebuilding change the façade of the medical schools, and this was when most of the Rue de l'Ecole de Médecine was widened to its present dimen-sions. But by this time some respect for antiquity had set in and no one liked to suggest demolishing the Hôtel Sarrazin, any more than they suggested demolishing another turreted mansion a few doors down the Rue Hautefeuille, next to where the long-established Baillière book-dealers now had their shop. Rue Hautefeuille, running as it did through one of the more prestigious parts of the Latin Quarter, had now been accorded a degree of status as 'one of Paris's oldest streets'. It was visible, in the way that the equally old but unregarded Maubert district was not, and its ancient vestiges, unlike those of Maubert, made apparent their aristocratic connections.

So the Hôtel Sarrazin stands to this day, nicely cleaned up, with the outline of some long-ago arched windows picked out in the stonework, effectively confining the last stretch of the Rue de l'Ecole de Médecine to its medieval dimensions. But didn't some brisk prefectorial official decide to widen the street a little by demolishing buildings on its other side? Again, no. For on that side stood the elegant amphitheatre of the Royal School of Surgery, built under Louis XIV and later turned into the Royal School of Design. Evidently no one quite had the nerve to pull that down either. In any case, these prem-ises were by then housing the Musée Dupuytren, much cherished by the powerful medical lobby in the street. Then, and for over a century, into the 1960s, murky windows displaying pickled dead babies, deformed spleens and unusual brain tumours enlivened the walk down that anomalous, narrow hundred metres, which has remained as it was in defiance of all town planning principles.

Still, today, buses number 63, 86 and 87, travelling

west across the Boulevard St Michel, which has replaced the old Rue de la Harpe, have to squeeze their way at walking pace between the amphitheatre and the Hôtel Sarrazin. There is barely room for pedestrians on either side, and at the tightest point the buses give the impression of sucking in their sides and effecting a sideways shuffle, before letting their breath out again in the relatively spacious section alongside the medical schools.

Did Arthur Jacob, well on in life, visit his old and still entirely recognisable haunts, keeping in contact with the Baillières, and so have a chance to gaze on the new, hygienic Rue des Ecoles stretching eastwards? There are indications that he made a number of visits to France, once the steamships and the trains had transformed the old journey utterly. He was apparently in Paris several times during the early 1850s, for the well-used guidebook that survives in his book collection is of that period.

Since his youth there kings had risen and fallen again, two more revolutions had swept Paris, and now a new emperor was in place. But the greater transformation of the Latin Quarter was still to come. Let us hope that Arthur, given his advancing age and his retreat, in widowerhood, from such frivolities as travel, was spared that. In 1860 he was seventy, an age at which the landscapes of youth, and their association with a simpler, freer life, are so deeply internalised that their image cannot be modified, only destroyed. Evidence of the way the urban upheaval of the Second Empire brutalised the perceptions of the ordinary Parisians in the name of Progress was given a coherent voice by several writers of the time. Victor Hugo and Baudelaire, both younger than Arthur but old enough to belong to his world, deplored the march of the new, regimented highways and the fragmentation of a streetscape that was integral to their own experiences and memories. 'Ce vieux Paris n'est plus qu'une rue éternelle...' lamented Hugo.

The Goncourt brothers, rather younger again, complained that the Paris Balzac had immortalised was disappearing before their eyes.

Under the Emperor Louis-Napoléon's extraordinarily determined and powerful Préfet, Georges-Eugène Haussmann, Paris acquired her present layout and her comprehensive road system, though much of the planning instigated then was not actually carried out till the Third Republic of the 1870s. It has been estimated that the demolitions undertaken to this end, during Haussmann's rule alone, removed over seventeen thousand families from their homes. Almost by definition, these tended to be poor people who reaped no benefit from the extraordinary speculation in land and property that accompanied the Haussmann compulsory purchases, nor could they flock to inhabit the grandiose apartment blocks that lined every new street that was opened. Haussmann might well claim that he had demolished twelve thousand-odd buildings but had built five times that number: the majority of those blocks, with their ponderous street doorways, tiers of balconies and plaster decorations, were in entirely new areas. For the first time, a degree of social segregation was creeping into Paris. The old, vertical stratification, which had had a social mix of grand families on the first floor, modestly respectable ones on the upper floors and the poor in the attics, was replaced in the newer quarters by buildings inhabited solely by the middle and upper classes with their own servants lodged at the top.

Because of this, Haussmann's works have sometimes been written about as if he had a particular mission to drive out of Paris the less respectable classes. There is an accompanying myth that his broad new boulevards were designed that way in order that a cannon might shoot straight down them at a rioting mob. This hindsight misperception, however, confuses effect with intention.

In the heady 1850s and '60s, neither Haussmann nor his Emperor foresaw the outbreak of the Franco-Prussian War in 1870, still less the brief and bloody civil War in Paris ('the Commune') which followed it. To the moment of his own downfall in 1869, when he was publicly accused by Jules Ferry[4] of 'fantasy accounting' and personal profiteering, Haussmann himself believed that he had decades ahead of him to continue his schemes. Till his death, felled by a sudden stroke, in 1891, he maintained that he had been sacrificed by Louis-Napoléon who was attempting to salvage his own role as Emperor.

Unlike the town planners of Louis-Philippe's reign, or those of a hundred-odd years later, Haussmann's huge schemes were not driven by benign views on urbanism or by the desire to launch a new social order, but by the simpler aim of creating a visibly wealthier and grander Paris and to 'create wealth' in so doing. He never appeared interested, either for good or ill, in the ancient patterns of streets through which he scythed his new boulevards, which is why many of them remained in place – truncated and dislocated, perhaps, but not eradicated. Quite often, only a portion of an old block of houses would be sliced off, leaving the rest intact, looming like a crippled grandfather over the new street alongside. Ironically, had Haussmann's vision been of a more high-minded, socially aware variety, the resulting loss to Paris would probably have been far greater.

His grand plans for Paris did not – unlike the far less conspicuous plans then being carried out in London – include a comprehensive sewage system. He was against a main drainage scheme, maintaining that it would simply lead to all the filth ending up in the Seine. He had a point there, since, before Bazalgette designed his massive, coherent solution to London's problem, London's sewers had indeed been disgorging all along the Thames with disastrous effects on the water supply. But Haussmann, ever one for profits, also seems to have been influenced by the money in old-style latrines: for a long time, the pumped-out contents of Paris's innumerable, individual house-privies had been spread out to dry, powdered and then sold for handsome sums as fertiliser. Indeed, the system continued in some antiquated districts well into the twentieth century. It is significant that at Haussmann's fall, followed shortly by that of the Second Empire, very few working-class homes had yet acquired any source of running water at all. Many respectable blocks only had it in a ground-floor hallway tap or courtyard pump, and the water-carriers were still in business.

Another, very modern proposal, for an underground railway like the one being built in London at the beginning of the 1860s, was also rejected out of hand by Haussmann. He was not interested in how the ordinary workers, whom he had displaced from many old areas of Paris to the expanding suburbs, would now get about. It was to be almost another forty years before the Paris administration came to see that the Haussmann boulevards in fact provided the ideal conditions to build a 'cut-and-cover' subway system not far below street level.

Relatively, Haussmann had less effect on the Left Bank than on the Right, partly because he turned his attention to it later and did not complete so much there, but he changed the Latin Quarter for ever, all the same. He sliced the Boulevard St Michel through it from north to south as a prolongation of the boulevard he had already created on the Right Bank – in fact, Boulevard St Michel first appears on maps as 'Boulevard Sébastopol, Left Bank'. This swallowed much of the old Rue de la Harpe, and just shaved past the ruined Roman baths under the Hôtel de Cluny – which antiquarians had to fight to preserve. How many Sorbonne students of today realise that their Boul' Mich', which they take to be the natural main artery of the Latin Quarter, is actually a late imposition, unrelated to most of the surrounding streets? Similarly, a few years later, the Boulevard St Germain swept through from west to east, turning the old route through St André des Arts into a backwater, destroying the intricate geography between St Germain des Prés and the Ecoles de Médecine, and reducing Place Maubert to a segment of its former self. A little later again the broad Rue de Rennes, running down from the new railway station at Montparnasse, cut across what remained of the old Abbey buildings on the south side to form the Place St Germain des Prés. There, it stopped short – though a high, blank wall left by demolition at the top of the narrow Rue Bonaparte remains like a tide-mark of its intentions. Initially, the idea had been to carry the Rue de Rennes right down to the Seine.

A minor poet, Charles Cros, absinthe-drinker, friend of Verlaine and Rimbaud but more enduringly known as an early pioneer of sound recording, which he named 'the voice of the past', left a piece of plangent light verse:

> La maison est démolie,
> Le petit nid en l'air
> Où j'eusse ton cœur, et ta chair,
> Ma maîtresse si jolie!
> . . . Tombez pierres, ciment, fer,
> L'amour jamais ne s'oublie.

(The house is torn down, and with it the airy nest
Where I possessed you, my pretty mistress, heart and
   flesh!
. . . Stones, cement and iron may fall, but love does not
   forget.)

A lost building, a lost love, both equally preserved in memory – a classic Latin Quarter lament. Student affairs with Left Bank working-class girls must have occurred long before nineteenth-century writers made them into the stuff of Romance. But more down-to-earth evidence of the effect of Haussmannisation in the Latin Quarter comes from a water-carrier and his family, who were interviewed by a journalist in 1869, the very year when Jules Ferry made his accusations about the Préfet enriching himself and his kind at the expense of the people of Paris.

Gérard and his wife both came from the Auvergne and had three surviving children. Gérard habitually collected his water in forty-litre loads, at the venerable fountain of St Michel at the top of the Rue de la Harpe near the Luxembourg Gardens. This fountain, and the space in which it stood, had by then given its name to the Boulevard St Michel, which confusingly was to beget a different Place St Michel several hundred metres north where the new boulevard met the river. Here, typifying the flamboyant spirit of the times, a grand new fountain was placed, ornamental rather than useful, complete with a Greek god, rocks, winged lions, and water apparently cascading directly out of the new baroque apartment block occupying one of those wedge-shaped spaces that the new road systems were everywhere creating.

But in 1869 the old fountain by the Luxembourg Gardens was still in place, and this was where Gérard and his kind congregated. By dint of his incessant labour, his 'very robust' constitution, and his wife's home-work in the leather industry, the couple were able to live in 'a very modest comfort'. Their near-illiteracy had put paid to their one attempt to branch out into the other traditional Auvergnat trade, that of supplying customers with wood and coal. Their housekeeping was rough and ready, but they ate decently of meat, vegetables and bread, some cider but 'hardly any wine'. Understanding the usefulness of being able to read and write, they sent their children to one of the free schools by then established in Paris. They were lucky enough to rent, for one hundred and eighty francs a year (between £7 and £8), two rooms on the fifth floor of an old building. This lodging, though a tight fit, was 'fairly healthy, being high up and south-facing, which allows for them to get air and sun'. The journalist added, however, a few lines later:

> 'Lying right in the line of one of the large new arteries of communication now due to be built, the house is threatened with imminent compulsory purchase; one of the family's biggest worries is whether they will be able to rent anything else so convenient and so reasonably priced.'

We hear in detail about their few bits of furniture, the wife's cheerful disregard for tidiness, the family's clothes, and their rare days out together, but of news from the long future there is none. Where, when the Boulevard St Germain made its inexorable way across their house, did they go? What, in any case, happened to Gérard, all the Gérards, when the Third Republic at last introduced modernity, and the long history of water-carriers in the French capital came to an obscure end?

Paris was, in any case, transformed out of all recognition, not only in aspect and architecture but also in extent. From a population of just over half a million in 1800, it had getting on for three-quarters of a million in the early years of the Restoration and over one million by the mid-century. But under the Second Empire, the surrounding lands and villages that had all been summarily enclosed by the customs wall of the 1840s now filled up like a reservoir with people, housing and small-scale industries. Skilled and semi-skilled men, drawn initially to Paris from central France to work on the acres of building sites, stayed on, and now that the railways were established their wives came to join them. The itinerant labourers, who for generations had crossed France on their biannual migrations, like swallows in their white smocks, turned into Paris citizens. It was this much enlarged Paris of twenty *arrondissements* that clocked up a population of nearly two million by the early 1870s, and two and a half million by the mid-1890s. In this lighted, drained metropolis, a place of trams and gaslight and a network of rapid post tunnels that conveyed notes through pneumatic tubes, what did simple men do, men who had nothing but their manual strength to offer? It is much to be hoped that Gérard's education of his children paid off, that they got respectable jobs, and were able to make room in their homes for their old peasant of a father.

Chapter X

'A Country in the Département of the Seine'

Under the Second Empire rents rose, as so many of the old tenements where the poor traditionally roosted were knocked down. Many working-class incomes also declined, relative to the booming cost of living that was driven by the wealth of the property-owning classes. There were pockets of abject poverty in central Paris in the late nineteenth century, left there like detritus by a moving tide.

Needless to say, the arrival of the Boulevard St Germain across the centuries-old Place Maubert did nothing to 'improve' the huddle of ancient streets between it and the river. Apart from one other piece of road building there – the Rue Lagrange, a prolongation of the Rue Monge – the old lanes were left much to their own devices. Now running at a different level from the alien, raised-up boulevard, the Rues Perdue, Maître Albert, Bièvre, Galande and the like retreated into themselves, sheltering a still poorer and more obscure life than they had a generation before. The small, old church of St Julien le Pauvre was by then semi-ruinous. Having been a morgue for the Hôtel Dieu, it was now the place to which were brought vagrants who died in the street or unidentified bodies from traffic accidents. Its one-time churchyard resembled a neglected farmyard, with rubbish, a well, vegetation and pecking chickens. At least it was a quiet spot.

Other streets nearby were home to a more urban degradation. According to Georges Cain, the curator of the Musée Carnavalet, they reeked of the cheapest sort of wine, and of more dubious 'cognacs' made in home distilleries with wood alcohol, molasses and caramel colouring to give tint and flavour. Drunks lay about at street corners and the police were often seen knocking on doors. There was a particularly notorious establishment in the Rue Galande, occupying the half-ruined premises of what had, four centuries before, been a grand house, reputedly the home of Gabrielle d'Estrées, the mistress of Henri IV. With hazy reference to popular revolutionary notions, with which the outcasts of society might fortify their self-esteem, this was called Le Château Rouge, The Red Castle – aka The Guillotine. There had been some attempt, earlier in the century, to turn its large rooms and courtyard into some sort of *bal musette*, with greenery, shooting galleries and musical entertainment, but by 1890 it was the resort of prostitutes of both sexes and of criminals. The novelist J.K. Huysmans frequented the place, initially to gather material for a book but by and by because he enjoyed the feeling of having an entrée into an underworld of danger. He made colourful acquaintances there and told stories to his friends about having narrowly escaped a plot against his own life – a tale which, like many of Huysmans', was probably without much foundation.

Another wine merchant created a dance-hall in his cellar – a forerunner of the many Latin Quarter 'jazz-cellars' of fifty years later. Huge cellars, probably older even than the ancient houses, ran and still run under the narrow streets of the Maub', linking with those of the houses opposite as in a giant rabbit warren. This particular cellar, reached by a spiral iron staircase behind the bar, was large but so low-ceilinged that the double bass in the three-piece orchestra had to hold his instrument sideways. A more squalid retreat, in the old Rue des Lavandières that was soon to disappear, was Chez le Père Lunette, which offered no entertainment but the chance to get drunk cheaply in intimate company. Nearby in the Rue Maître Albert there were some of the cheapest lodging houses in all Paris, including an infamous one where it was said that, for a tiny sum, you could slumber on a hard bench all night with your head and arms resting on a rope. In the morning, the lodging-house keeper simply released the rope to precipitate his tenants out of sleep and onto the floor. Or did he? The story is often told but already, by the 1870s, an investigator into Parisian poverty[1] maintained that, though he had seen such a place as a child in the 1840s, it no longer existed.

The detail is a telling one. So is Huysmans' pre-occupation with the underworld. So too is the fact that, by the 1890s, out-of-work men had taken to hanging round the gate of the Château Rouge and other dives offering to escort inside members of the bourgeoisie and foreigners in search of local colour. They also volunteered, on advance payment of a decent sum, to act as 'guardian angels' to see their probably drunk clients home at the end of the night. Poverty and squalor themselves were being commodified, a process which in the end extinguishes them in that particular place – just as all forms of tourism, in the long run, destroy the distinctive quality that is being sought. Two or three decades on, and journalists from across the Channel, or the Atlantic, would be writing books called *How to Find Old Paris*, recommending one-time medieval dungeons with names like 'Le Caveau des Oubliettes Rouges' (opposite St Julien), or warning '. . . in the summer of 1927 [the place] had become a little grasping and the air of spontaneity was lacking.

I'm afraid it is becoming commercialised like the rest of the Parisian resorts.'

The same commodification had happened, in the course of the nineteenth century, to the long-established idyll of Latin Quarter life as something outside the constraints, the class structures and the family ties of the rest of Parisian and French society. For centuries before Balzac and Flaubert made the arrival of an innocent in Paris the emblematic theme of novels, young men of the provincial bourgeoisie were sent to study in Paris. But this period represented far more – or sometimes less – than the chance to acquire a professional qualification as doctor, lawyer or administrator. It was a *rite de passage*, a break from the heavy embrace of the French family and the scenes of childhood, a time for the sowing of wild oats before the serious business of adulthood had to be undertaken. Sometimes, if the student was very able or had a creative talent, this period of licensed freedom might be transformed into the stuff of a real-life career. Stendhal claimed that everyone who had ever achieved anything in the capital had arrived there from elsewhere at the age of seventeen. Victor Hugo said, 'He who calls himself a student is also calling himself a Parisian. To study in Paris is to be born there' – born into a new identity, it is implied.

But for the great mass of students the new identity was not really a long-term prospect. Some, becoming addicted to the student life rather than to studying, began turning the sheer mechanism of daily life on meagre funds into a full-time occupation. Many took to painting, with or without talent, as a pretext for staying where they were, and so the world of the student blurred into that of the 'artist'. Poverty and art, the two great nineteenth-century icons of unworldliness, gave disordered lives a gloss of morality and romance, and indeed of the Romantic Movement. By the time of the Restoration a general reaction was taking place against the Enlightenment of the previous century. Imagination and feeling were now being prized above rationality; exaltation and excess above calm, order and even honesty. An awakening interest in the distant, medieval past, in Gothic architecture, folk tales and legends, provided in the 1830s a distinctive male style for those who wished to advertise their Romantic credentials. Long hair, wide-brimmed felt hats, velvet coats, floppy bows instead of high neck-cloths, were first nonconformist but eventually, as the years passed, fossilised into an artistic convention in themselves.

Guizot, Louis-Philippe's austere Minister of Education, was under no illusions as to the physical and moral squalor into which some of the young men of the Latin Quarter descended once they were cut off from home influences for many months at a time. He attributed this degeneration partly to the fact that these *enfants de la bourgeoisie* took minimal lodgings in tenements alongside the poor and the rough, including, of course, working-class girls . . . Guizot's dream, never realised, was to remove the Sorbonne to some quite other French town, far from the distractions and temptations of a metropolis, on the model of Oxford and Cambridge.

Most students, in practice, survived their time in the Latin Quarter unscathed. Henry Murger, author of *Scènes de la Vie de Bohème* which was first published in parts in the late 1840s, wrote, of the mass of young men from the provinces, that, though 'they turn their backs abruptly on a decent living to chase after the adventures of a hazardous existence', most of them were put off as soon as they began to experience the realities of cold and hunger. 'They make haste to get out of this situation, setting off on foot for home and good roast meat. They abandon their large ideas also, settle down in marriage with the little cousin and become lawyers in medium-sized towns. In the evening, by the fireside, they enjoy talking about the poverty they lived in when they were penniless artists, rather as a traveller enjoys talking about the tiger-hunts he has been on.'

Clearly, by the mid-century, the *vie de bohème* itself, that gift package of student-artist life rolled into one (and tied with a rather grubby, floppy bow), had become a recognised cliché. But had Murger created it? He was the first person to use 'Bohemians' as a general term for those leading an urban-gipsy way of life. His magazine series of the late 1840s, drawn at least in part from his own experiences, at first aroused not much interest. Only when the series was turned into a play in 1849, just when Paris was in the throes of yet another romanticised popular uprising, did the concept of a country of the heart called 'Bohemia' enter mass consciousness. Murger wrote: 'Bohemia is a country in the Département of the Seine. It is bordered on the north by cold, on the west by hunger, on the south by love and on the east by hope.' But he produced variant, less optimistic versions of the same geography. And only two or three years later his contemporary, lawyer and writer Alphonse de Calonne, wrote: 'Bohemia is a sad country. It is bordered on the north by need, on the south by poverty, on the east by illusion and on the west by the infirmary.'

Our present view of Murger's invented country as hyper-romantic derives from the version of it in Puccini's opera *La Bohème*, which was not to make its appearance for another half-century. Murger himself, the son of a tailor and a concierge, had fewer illusions, as he eked out a living in a Left Bank garret with a handful of friends and a communal purse. 'The Water-drinkers' they called themselves. Ironically, he would have liked a more bourgeois lifestyle, but had no means of attaining it. His Mimi, long before the operatic frozen hand, was already a somewhat sentimentalised version of the original – or rather, two originals. One, a 'platonic' love, was the wife of a petty crook; she later became a rather successful prostitute. The other, like the fictional Mimi, was a maker of artificial flowers, who had left her cobbler husband for life in the Latin Quarter. She eventually left Murger too, for a soldier. He only caught up with her much later, when she was dying of tuberculosis in the Hôpital de la Pitié. He did not often visit her there, on the grounds that he had no money to bring her anything nice. When she died, her unclaimed body went, like so many others before, into the dissection halls.

Shortly afterwards, the play was produced, made money, and Murger's work became well known. He found a new love, moved to the Right Bank and died twelve years later, probably of syphilis. He was only thirty-nine.

Yet the imaginary Mimi was not all Murger's invention. Alfred de Musset, twelve years older, a dweller in the Latin Quarter from childhood and a student who had given up first on law and then on medicine, was a well-established writer and poet by the 1840s. In 1845 he published a short story called *Mimi Pinson*, and the Mimi poem included in it was set to music the year after by Frédéric Bérat. De Musset's Mimi has only one dress and one bonnet to her name and likes to sing when a little tipsy after 'a nice supper', but she means to remain virginal and is quick to reprimand students who hope to take liberties with her. She serves in a café, but can also rely on her needle for an honest living. In other words, she is that classic Left Bank figure, the working-class *grisette*, named after the simple grey stuff of her dress, in those days before the mass production of brighter materials. Since sewing machines had not yet been invented either, she was usually a seamstress, for whom there was an almost inexhaustible demand, but the romantic eye transformed this grinding, ill-paid work into a pretty, dainty occupation, especially when conducted in an attic among students and tame sparrows. In real life, the *grisette* was not virginal; she offered love, or at any rate sex, to a jolly young student – just one at a time – in return for suppers and fun. Predictably, he abandoned her after a while to return to his own class (the paternal roast joints, the marriage with the *petite cousine*). At this point the *grisette*, it was hoped, did not die tragically of tuberculosis and a broken heart, but settled down herself with a local grocer.

The huge and rather pompous *Tableau de Paris*, compiled by Edmond Texier in the mid-1850s, described *grisettes* as belonging to what were by then being regarded as the Good Old Days, probably shortly after the Restoration, rather than to the time when he was writing – 'Where are they now, Lisette[2] and Mimi Pinson? Where are these excellent girls, so courageous in the face of work and poverty, always with love in their hearts, a joyful word on their lips and the frank smile which creates a pretty dimple in the cheek? You might as well ask, with the old French poet [Villon is meant] Where are the snows of yesteryear? . . . The old Latin Quarter is no more.'

Texier went on to evoke the simple pleasures of Sunday trips to the country, or to carnivals and to the small suburban pleasure gardens that were called *guinguettes*, a time of innocence when vulgar dances such as the cancan had not yet been invented. Modern *grisettes*, according to him, had 'lost their most precious attribute – their selflessness'. They only entered relationships with students for what they could get: in short, they had become prostitutes.

Whether in fact the fabulous, loyal, golden-hearted but unencumbering Mimis had ever existed in old Paris, like unicorns they entered the public consciousness and remained there. Right at the end of the nineteenth century a Conservatoire Mimi Pinson was formed: its aim was to teach deserving working-class girls to play musical instruments.

The famed stereotype also crossed the Channel. The Anglo-Irish writer George Moore, from a well-to-do family in County Mayo (the same social world, that is, as the Jacob clan), came to Paris aged twenty-one in 1873, initially with the aim of becoming an artist. His notoriously 'Bohemian' novel, *A Modern Lover* (1883), was the eventual result, but during his seven-year stay he seems to have made few contacts with real-life artists or writers. He lived in relative comfort, first in the Hôtel Voltaire, on the quay opposite the Louvre, which was a big, respectable 'family' hotel (meals included), and later abandoned the Left Bank altogether for a hotel near the new Opera House. Back in Britain, he eventually achieved some success with *Esther Waters*, a novel about unmarried motherhood, but it was left to another writer in English, George du Maurier, to bring the classic country of Bohemia into more limpid focus for an Anglo-Saxon public. This was with his novel *Trilby* (1894), which took England by storm.

Du Maurier's mother was English, but his grandfather had been a French émigré from the Revolution. His father had passed most of his childhood in England before 1814, after which the family moved back and forth between the two countries. There was a period spent on the western edge of Paris, near the then-wild Bois de Boulogne and its marshy, duck-haunted lake, and, later, several years in the Rue du Bac. Du Maurier returned to the Left Bank as a young art student in the 1850s, which is the time evoked in *Trilby*. He lived with two congenial British friends in a large, dilapidated old hotel between the Odéon theatre and the Luxembourg Gardens, frequented circles where people 'were always talking about "art"' but only ever seemed to draw on restaurant paper tablecloths, and where 'there was too much singing and playing, too much fencing and boxing and idle and pleasant chatter'. His friends, like him, were busy escaping from conventional careers at home, and one has the impression that for them life in Paris was already being lived as a literary artefact, at one remove from reality. Certainly, any Bohemian poverty was only notional and relative: a sumptuous Christmas hamper of turkey, beef, mince pies, cheese and pudding was conveniently sent over by 'friends in London'.

All this, many decades later, du Maurier placed at one further remove from real life by putting it into *Trilby*. He transformed himself and his friends into 'three musketeers of the brush', and added the imaginary Trilby herself – another golden-hearted, blade-straight girl, product of a Scottish-French union but an undoubted citizen of the land of Bohemia. Under the influence of the middle-aged Svengali (Jewish, a hypnotist, and conventionally sinister), Trilby, a tone-deaf artists' model, becomes a famous singer – which one may regard as a sanitised version of becoming a famous courtesan. 'Little Billie', the du Maurier alter ego in the novel, gets brain fever from unrequited love of Trilby and nearly dies, but recovers and becomes a famous painter. Trilby herself eventually dies of 'weakness', is forgiven on her deathbed by Little Billie's mother and is buried in Kensal Green Cemetery. The surviving friends meet in Paris many years later for a nostalgic middle-aged reunion.

This romantic fantasy enjoyed huge popularity in its time, and is now all but forgotten. Apparently very many people yearned to have a taste of Trilby's world: 'Trilby-style' girls were soon to be seen in arty London circles. But, beyond that, the book crystallised for an English-speaking readership the idea of Paris as a place not just of romance and freedom from convention but as the location of a whole possible parallel life, an exciting alternative identity. (In fact George du Maurier's younger brother, from the same cosmopolitan and bilingual upbringing, carried this potential to a self-defeating extreme by turning himself into a French army trooper.)

Written so long after the experiences that inspired it,

Trilby's overblown drama is redeemed to some extent by its perception of the ineradicable trace left on an individual's life by intense feeling, and the conflict between this and the inevitable transience of life. Immortality, George du Maurier's similarly gifted granddaughter, Daphne, was to write long after his death, is probably a myth, but 'when we die, we leave something of ourselves, like the wake of a vessel, as a reminder that we passed this way. There are footprints in the sand, and the mark of a hand upon a wall . . .'[3]

George du Maurier died less than two years after his book's success, his own footprint – and the family fortunes – now secure. The country of Bohemia in the Département of the Seine continued its posthumous existence in the Anglo-Saxon consciousness, surfacing again near the end of the 1920s in a coarsened version in Ernest Hemingway's *The Sun Also Rises*.[4] The American expatriates who populate the early chapters of this novel, with their unhurried days spent writing in comfortable cafés, their 'modest' meals of oysters, their trips to bet at the fashionable race-course and their drunken evenings, seem very far from the Water-drinkers, and Murger's own experience of trying to live on forty francs a month by pawning his clothes. The same sort of café society, accompanied by the same claims of 'poverty', reappears in Hemingway's much later memoir, *A Moveable Feast*. The fact that almost the only French citizens visible in either his novel or his memoir are waiters or concierges makes one feel that the footprints in the Latin Quarter of this band of professional outsiders can have left very little trace. The *vie de bohème* was thus reduced to an exotic brand, purchasable by those with sufficient money, no longer a means of getting in touch with the discomforts and challenges of life but a means of avoiding them. George Orwell wrote a few years later, in relation to another American escapee (Henry Miller) but making a general point:

'leaving your native land . . . means transferring your roots into a shallower soil. Exile is probably more damaging to a novelist than to a painter or even a poet, for its effect is to take him out of contact with working life and narrow down his range to the streets, the café, the church, the brothel and the studio.' (*Inside the Whale*, 1940)

The streets, the café, the brothel and the studio, if not the church, have so dominated the literature of the Left Bank in the twentieth century that readers might be forgiven for thinking that was what the Latin Quarter meant – 'people drinking, talking, meditating and fornicating [rather than] working, marrying and bringing up children' (Orwell again). However, throughout the great physical upheavals and myth-making of the nineteenth and twentieth centuries in the streets between Maubert and St Germain des Prés, innumerable citizens did indeed pass their lives working, marrying and bringing up children. There was a bourgeoisie of the Left Bank who, while never participating in the high style and wealth of the great western quarters of Paris, were distinguished in their own way and tended to pride themselves on being less philistine than the inhabitants of Avenue Kléber or the Parc Monceau. Meanwhile, even in the lean decades, the Faubourg St Germain managed to retain its class and its memory of aristocratic days.

And of course there were, as there had been for hundreds and hundreds of years, the tradesmen and artisans and labourers, the clerks and piece-workers, the housewives and street-hawkers, the young and the old: generation after generation growing up, claiming the intimately known streets as their own, following the tracks of all those who had come before them, climbing up and down worn staircases, sipping coffee at zinc counters, relieving themselves over dark holes in ill-lit closets, retreating at the last into high, hidden rooms behind net curtains or at the back of courtyards, and finally going to lie under the soil of Paris up the hill in Montparnasse, or in one of the other great Parisian cities of the dead, out beyond the line of the old fortifications.

Part III

THE TWO ALBERT ALFREDS:
1830–1917

Chapter XI

THE SELF-MADE MAN

To recreate the lives of people dead long before we were born is like looking through glass into a large, dim room that is illuminated only here and there. We can see, or half see, a number of things, but as we press closely against the pane, hoping to glimpse more, our own reflection gets in the way. We knock on the glass, but it is thick; those on the far side of it will never hear us. They do not know of our existence, and their living, preoccupied minds are not likely to probe into the future so far as to imagine us or care about us, who are so distant from them in time. They are insulated from us for ever.

But across this separation they appear as our equals. They do not seem to us old people. In glimpses, the images reach us: the child in his family home, the young man making his way along the high road, the dynamic adult, the intimidating father, the man in public life – but none of these versions blots out the others. Since all belong to an era remote from our own, paradoxically they are reborn for us as if they were our contemporaries, young and vigorous. *'We meet the dead coming towards us.'*

But the images become much more confusing when the darkened glass has not always been there – when the people who are behind it are of more recent date and have once shared our own world with us. It becomes harder to see the vulnerable child, the driven young man, the shy new husband, when one version of that individual is lodged in your own memory, and he is an irascible old gentleman with a bristly moustache who was always encountered in an atmosphere faintly imbued with family tensions. Chronology is here moving in two directions at once, as in a hall of mirrors. You want to trace the stages of this person's long life in his own time-scale, beginning with his earliest years and progressing onwards, but instead you find yourself walking backwards into your own youth, which is his old age, because that is where your one authenticated image of him is to be found.

And then another paradox becomes apparent. Your own early memories may seem prosaic, yet you find that the simple passage of the decades has transformed this personal material into something more significant, concentrated and fixed as in a series of framed silhouettes. In my own childhood, people born under the reign of Queen Victoria, people who fought in the First World War, were still plentiful and unremarkable. Now, my commonplace recollections of these elders have become fabulous, even to me. Did I once really know, as part of my everyday life, people who had grown to adulthood before the nineteenth century ended, and some who would, if living today, be one hundred and fifty years old? Imagine having them back for a day to talk to, now. It seems extraordinary, the richness that was there and that has now just ebbed away, leaving only a silence and unanswered questions.

And yet, with another shift of view, I realise that some of these figures from my childhood are still as real and familiar to me today as they ever were. For a few moments it seems almost unbelievable that, to subsequent generations, they are but names on a family tree, known names perhaps but essentially and for ever strangers behind the glass.

In my childhood, occasional visits to the grandparents I did not know well, and was never encouraged to know better, offered to me no hint of the grandfather's past that, long after he was dead, would come to me as a gift, one piece of a complex pattern. Only when I was grown-up, and he was in his eighties, did he once, uncharacteristically, write to me in Paris: 'How sensible of you to pick a *petit quartier* to stay in. As a young man, I lived on the Left Bank for a year, and worked in the same street where you are now. I wonder if there is still a tramway terminus in the Place St Germain?'

That was at the beginning of 1960. The trams had long gone, and St Germain des Prés, for that matter, had known the passage of Sartre and de Beauvoir and the caravanserai that followed them, and was no longer a district devoted to modest commerce. But, even in my youthful self-centredness, I must have been touched by this image of a young man in Paris I had never known existed, and this unsuspected precise link between us, across sixty-five years, as we trod the very same street . . . Certainly his letter, long lost now as a physical object, stayed in my mind.

But to find him properly I must go further back. Back to a picture or two in that classic window on the past: a gilt-clasped, late nineteenth-century photo album. The cover is ornate and leathery, the thick, double-cardboard pages each form two ready-made frames, but the total content of information is, for such a heavy object, rather meagre. Many of the frames are unfilled, or have lost their one-time occupant, and the stoic faces looking out from others – faces held motionless for the slow cameras of the era – are unnamed and now unknowable. When these likenesses were taken, in studios off high streets furnished like make-believe drawing rooms with palms and chenille tablecloths, it must have seemed unnecessary to write names beneath. Everyone knew Mother was Mother, and naturally the girls with her were May and Maud, and as for dominating, successful Father . . . Much later, when time and war and the shortening of skirts and hair had altered for ever the late-Victorian dream, one of the family must have scented oblivion lying in wait and so had the foresight to go through the album pencilling 'Sophie T' and 'M' and 'B' and 'Grandma S' beneath some of the photos; but even she (it is nearly always women who take on such tasks) did not foresee the need to be more explicit. Nor did she identify some of the faces at all, those that had perhaps already passed into the ranks of distant, dead cousinhood.

'B' is there, in several incarnations, but most evidently as a little boy of about seven wearing a Norfolk suit, a straw hat with a round brim like a halo, and a solemn, slightly apprehensive expression. In his hands he holds, but loosely, as if paying more attention to the camera, a toy steam engine – a delectable, long-funnelled antique with brass trim that would now change hands for hundreds of pounds. The front of the engine points downwards, as if rehearsing the angle of that famous engine that would, a dozen years later, burst through the buffers of the Gare Montparnasse on the Left Bank and hang perilously over the street below, billowing steam. This, the young man to be, would see for himself.

There is another photo, clearly taken the same day in the same studio, in which B holds a toy sailing boat. His inattention to this, too, makes me think that these were studio toys provided by the photographer, and that the little boy was by then already more interested in pictures, in buildings, in gardens, in sketching – the passions that were to illuminate his adult life.

This child, christened Albert Alfred like his father before him but always known as Bertie, lived in St John's parish,

Lewisham, then a new and highly respectable suburb. Home was first a stuccoed, semi-detached villa and then, as both the family and its prosperity increased, a larger and more imposing detached one. (Devotees of E. Nesbit's Bastable family may recall that they live in a similar quarter of Lewisham at the same period.) In the 1880s, while Bertie was growing up, country fields still opened out at the end of the road. His father was a successful publisher and bookseller dealing principally with medical works. His mother was the daughter of a long-established Lewisham family, the Simsons, who had originally made their money in ship-building, then in timber. Her father, the maternal grandfather, was Master of a City livery company. Bertie had two sisters and a younger brother. The family went on long seaside summer holidays: by and by Bertie would be sent to a little boys' boarding school and later to Charterhouse. A classic start in life in the comfortably-off upper reaches of the middle class who set the tone for England.

But where had the first Albert Alfred started? Where did his origins lie? The information is surprisingly sparse, but that fact in itself tells a story.

Stephen Tendall or Tindall, the young man who was driving a coach regularly between London and Dover in 1814, when Arthur Jacob took the Dover road, can have had nothing to rely on but his wits. Probably born in a parish called Ticehurst,[1] some twenty miles from Hastings, he came of a family who from father to son had worked the land on the Kent and Sussex borders. Family mythology, by the Lewisham days, always referred to them as having been 'yeoman farmers', but the scattered evidence of later nineteenth-century Census returns for the East Sussex area suggests that many of the clan were paid farmhands rather than owning land or cattle themselves. If Stephen's father did farm in his own right, it was a modest holding, insufficient to support a family of any size.

Stephen, of the same generation as Arthur Jacob, would have grown up in the company of farm horses. Coach-driving was a logical step for such a boy, one that took him into a much more exciting world than that of the muddy lanes round Ticehurst. It was the Indian summer of the coaching era, with scores of them coming and going every day from London's inn yards. Skill, move-ment, fun, the camaraderie of the post-houses along the road, and the great and growing city itself – what more could a restless young man want?

But twenty-odd years after the Battle of Waterloo the coach business began to go into a steep decline. The railway, bringing affordable long-distance travel within reach of a mass of people for the first time, came with a roar and a gust of sulphurous iron breath and swept the coaching empires away. Where the beat of hoofs had resounded, an unnatural quietness settled on the ancient highways and on the turnpikes. Inns that had been key staging-posts, earning a fortune for their owners, shut down one after the other or sank back into being country ale-houses.

The London, Dover & Chatham Railway opened its first section, as far as Greenwich, in 1836, and continued to push towards the coast. A rival London to Brighton line was already being built, and soon an extension of this would be planned, via Lewes, to Hastings. Shrewd men must have seen clearly what was to come, and Stephen Tindall was apparently one of them. Judging from the baptismal records of a number of his children, he had been living in the heart of Hastings, then a rela-tively small fishing port with a sprinkling of summer visitors, for the last dozen years. His occupation during this time was regularly given as 'coachman'. But in 1840, the year which is usually cited as the beginning of the end for the long-distance coach trade, his occupation was stated on an official document as 'fly driver'. A fly was a four-wheeled cab hired for short-haul journeys, in particular for conveying passengers to and from the new railways stations.

The document in question was the birth registration of his youngest son, Albert Alfred – the last child, and the only one to be officially registered according to the new regulations. According to family lore, seventeen other children had come before him. Stephen Tindall must indeed have needed his wits about him to provide for so many, even if not all survived infancy and, by 1840, the elder ones were bringing their own earnings into the family home. Stephen himself would then have been in his fifties.

The only photograph of him, taken probably a few years later, shows a thin, commanding, canny-looking man with a big nose and a bald head, clean-shaven except for a frill of beard round his chin as was fashionable towards the middle of the century. He wears a velvet-collared overcoat open over a jacket with a shadowy check pattern. His white shirt and collar are almost covered by a soft black cloth held in place with a large tie-pin. He looks like a man with a whiff of the race-course about him, a good eye for horseflesh.

Sarah, his wife, was photographed just once too, most likely on the same occasion. She must have been rather younger than her husband if she was still producing a baby in 1840, but over twenty-five years of child-bearing then lay behind her. In the photo she wears an elaborately decorated best cap with lacy lappets hanging down each side. Her grim expression is probably due not to temperament but to the fact that she has lost all her teeth. She could not read or write. This is apparent because it was she herself who registered, rather belatedly, Albert Alfred's birth, and she signed the register with a cross. One more child was probably not what this middle-aged couple needed. Indeed, having registered his presence by the new, modern method, they seem to have failed to get him baptised. They were not assiduous church-goers, for three of their previous children had been baptised all together, as if to sort out an earlier negligence.

Sixty years later, in 1901, which is the latest Census available for consultation as I write,[2] a number of Stephen's progeny and their descendants were still living in the much-expanded Hastings the railways had created. They were butchers and greengrocers; one was a baker and another a plumber and glazier, and one an insurance agent. Two others, stated to be living 'on their own means', had migrated to the more genteel part of town known as St Leonards, and another had retired along the coast to Worthing. Street directories of the same year reveal that one Miss Tindall taught in a Hastings infant school and another in a ragged school. Nothing about any of these obscurely useful lives would suggest that they had by that time a brother/cousin/uncle in an office in London's Covent Garden, editing a medical journal and employing his own staff, in a specialised publishing firm he had built up himself and which was now the largest in Britain, with links in France and Germany and contacts all over the world.

So how did this youngest of many children, son of an ageing cab driver in a small town and an illiterate mother, make his way so spectacularly in the world? How did he arrive at the big house with servants in Lewisham, the cultivated wife, the sons educated at famous public schools?

The answer lies in a central truth about the Victorian era: it was a time of unprecedented social mobility and rolling change. The notion that it was a world in which everyone 'knew their place' and that an impassable gulf separated rich from poor is a twentieth-century misperception, sentimental or accusatory according to the perspective of the viewer. We peer down history towards a period that is now fixed for us, with all outcomes known, and is therefore perceived as safe and predictable. We much underestimate the sense of turbulent material and social development in which our ancestors actually lived their lives.

By the 1840s industrial growth was transforming the whole way of life in Britain. Small country towns were growing into smoky cities. London was expanding into a megalopolis, the first one the world had known. Steam ships began to complete in a few weeks journeys that recently had taken many months, and they brought the world's goods to London and Liverpool. Railway trains started to carry people in a few hours to far corners of England. In the mid-century telegraphic cables spanned national frontiers and by and by the Atlantic, transmitting in minutes news of events a thousand miles away and thereby transforming the whole concept of news, information and opinion. Possibilities undreamed of by earlier generations seemed there for the taking, for those that had the wits, the courage and the stamina. In a prosperous place like Hastings, with its recent growth in well-to-do summer visitors indulging in the new luxury of hotels, you could not fail to be aware of the changes.

Certainly a gulf between rich and poor was there, but it appeared more bridgeable than ever before. When Albert Alfred was growing up there was much more basic education available than in previous eras, as 'National' and 'British' schools multiplied in the towns and villages, costing only a penny or two a week per pupil. Huge numbers of people still lived, as they always had, below the poverty line, in ignorance and want, but by the 1860s these 'dwellers in the abyss' were at last attracting concerned attention from journalists writing in new, popular papers – papers whose very existence, to instruct and entertain a large new literate commercial class, was a sign of social evolution.

There were chances out there to be seized, and what better field than the rapidly expanding one of paper and print? Paper, which in the past had been expensively manufactured from rags, was now, thanks to imported wood-pulp and new technology, being produced far more cheaply. People, whose immediate forebears had been content with the Bible, *Pilgrim's Progress* and a several-days-old news-sheet passed from hand to hand in the ale-house, now became voracious consumers of print. Newspapers, handbills, advertisements, headed stationery, magazines, practical and self-help manuals, part-works and books and yet more books poured from an ever-increasing number of presses. Printers and distributors turned themselves into publishers. Lending libraries and railway bookstalls spread across the land. Specialised scientific and technological periodicals appeared. In Paris, and in their expanding empire in other world capitals, the Baillière family were part of the same phenomenon.

Exactly how Albert Alfred began to make his way in this field, after what can have been little more than a basic education in the 3 Rs, I do not know. Typically, working-class origins leave scant record, since there has usually been no one on hand with the inclination or the leisure to value the family history. Photographs, letters and legal documents have been few or non-existent; oblivion soon closes over departed names. And, ironically, the fact of a man doing well in later life has usually served, in the socially sensitive past, not to illuminate his origins but to obscure them further.

It seems that, in his teens, Albert Alfred took the train up from the coast to London to seek his fortune. Or perhaps he was sent up by his father, who knew a likely lad when he saw one. There is no tradition that another family member, such as an elder brother, paved the way for Albert Alfred; though marriage records, for the Hastings church which many of the Tindalls attended, do indicate a possible cousin who worked on the local news-sheet. I am fairly sure that Albert Alfred did not serve a traditional apprenticeship to become a Master Printer as, had he done so, that reassuringly solid credential would have been incorporated into the brief family lore on him. The old, decorous system of seven years' formal learning was often bypassed now in this most modern of trades, as clever youngsters learnt their skills on the job and then hastened to set up on their own.[3]

Albert Alfred's eventual obituaries, as a well-known figure in the book trade, spoke vaguely of him having found employment, as a young man, 'in a commercial firm'. One may be fairly sure that this was to do either with paper or with print. Here, no doubt, he picked up the working knowledge of printing and costs that a more liberally educated young man 'going into publishing' typically lacked. He must also have acquired the rudiments of book-keeping, though, for many years, his own firm seems to have run successfully with none of the careful accounting that would later become standard. Such was the nature of Victorian entrepreneurship, and in the twelve-hour days that were commonplace then in offices huge amounts of work were summarily got through. Under the obituarists' evasive fictions about Albert Alfred's childhood – 'yeoman farmer', 'educated privately', fictions which he himself had no doubt encouraged – are buried what must have been many subsequent years of passionate energy and ruthless endeavour, self-confidence and sheer nerve.

Long after he was dead, his grandson was to remark that he had always felt the founder of the family firm to be 'a bit of a rogue', but perhaps, in the world in which he had made his way, that had been necessary.

It was in the mid-1860s that Albert Alfred, then about twenty-five, was thinking of branching out on his own. My guess is that he sought work as a 'jobber', a broker who undertook to organise the printing and distribution of writings by individual customers. By then he had managed to get acquainted with some doctors, probably because Fleet Street and the Strand, then the centre of the paper and print trade, was also the area of King's

College Medical School, Charing Cross Hospital and, at that time, the British Medical Association. Born into a different class, would he have liked to become a doctor himself? Certainly he was later to acquire a great deal of heterogeneous medical knowledge. He apparently had some hand in the marketing of a medical paper edited by a successful surgeon who practised near Piccadilly. This surgeon, said to be 'original in his views and bold in expressing his opinions', took to young Albert Alfred Tindall. When two other surgeons with whom he was in touch, similarly proprietors of a medical journal and also well known for forthright views, were in difficulty with their printing arrangements, Tindall was suggested as a useful fellow to come and look into the problem. These Dublin surgeons were, of course, Arthur Jacob and his son Archibald.

Arthur had, in theory, relinquished editorship of *The Medical Press* to Archibald several years before, but was still very much a presence. Archibald was a man given to enthusiastic building schemes that were not always practical. (After his father's final retirement, when Archibald took possession of the house in Ely Place, he tried to construct a wholly unsuccessful conservatory on a sunless back roof.) He conceived the idea of printing *The Medical Press* himself at the small Dublin office from which it was run. He imported a printing press, which almost at once threatened to fall through the joists of the upper floor on which it had unwisely been placed. At this point, useful young Tindall was summoned from London to catch the night packet.

It was his first big chance, and he seized it. In no time, he had assessed the problem, and the Jacobs. He suggested to them that he himself was the man to take on the printing and the distribution of the journal in London, particularly since the London surgeon was thinking of retirement and the two journals might be amalgamated to reach a far larger joint readership.

And so it happened. Soon, Albert Alfred Tindall became much more than just a production manager for the enlarged journal: he was eventually, for many years, its sole editor. Long after, his granddaughter wrote of his first appearance in Dublin, 'he had no social standing, but he was good-looking and had charm.' (So, an honorary Irishman, perhaps?) 'He also had a fine baritone voice, and the Jacobs loved singing. By degrees, they domesticated him.' One might rather say that he possessed the natural skill to tame *them*, and to make himself indispensable to them and their journal.

He had, as yet, no office of his own. He quickly rented a room just off the Strand from a bearded, food-stained middle-aged man named Cox, who lacked his dynamism but had inherited a small publishing concern. Religious periodicals were Cox's speciality, in that era when religious convictions were a middle-class passion. He also, in an odd pairing, published books on 'artistic anatomy'. Exactly how Albert Alfred lived and built up some capital during the later 1860s it is hard to tell, but by 1870 he had had the inspired idea of commissioning and publishing himself the first of a series of Student Aid booklets, designed to help medical students pass exams. *Aids to Surgery*, price one shilling, sold and sold. General practitioners kept copies by them for decades: you never knew, in those days, when you might be called on to remove an appendix or perform a hasty Caesarean by oil lamp in some remote house. *Aids to Anatomy* was for years marketed as 'A pocket version of Gray's', till the publishers of the famous *Gray's Anatomy* itself finally complained. *Aids to Anatomy* even featured in a music hall song, 'My Little Pocket Gray'.

At about the same time as the first *Aid* booklets appeared, a second big chance came Albert Alfred's way. With the recommendation of the Jacobs, he had got onto terms with the London office of Baillière. The proprietor, Hippolyte Baillière, Jean-Baptiste's younger brother, died in 1867. His sons were already established in the family interest in New York and Melbourne. His widow tried to carry on the London firm but without success; debts mounted. She had been born in England, where her royalist Continental family seem to have taken refuge from the first Napoleon. She did not want to settle in France, where his nephew, the Emperor Napoleon III, still held sway. She had plans to go and live with a relative who had married into an Anglo-Irish family and was currently settled in a seaside suburb of Dublin – not far up the railway line from where Archibald Jacob had bought a holiday home for his growing family. I think it was the Jacobs who suggested that, once again, the energetic young Mr Tindall might be the man to come to the rescue.

The later family story was that Madame Baillière sold all the assets of the firm in 1870 to Tindall and Cox, who had clubbed together, and that they thereafter ran it as the soon to be renowned medical publishers under the name Baillière, Tindall & Cox. Several early letter-copy books, however, which happen to have survived against time and chance when all other material has gone, and have come to rest in a university archive,[4] suggest a rather different story. Baillière's was as much a book-dealer as it was a publisher, obtaining and despatching books all over the world. The bulk of the London trade involved deliveries of books from Paris. Although these were not all medical books, works in French did then still predominate in medical literature. By gravitating towards doctors, Albert Alfred was now encountering a foreign culture and a language in which he could have had no previous grounding. Paris was beckoning him. But he was not yet quite up to confronting it.

The letter books suggest that in the early 1870s two men of French origin continued to run the day-to-day business. The firm went on trading as 'Baillière and Co.' (or Baillière et Cie, according to which language a letter was written in) for another half-dozen years, before all formal connection with the original firm was severed. No doubt Albert Alfred, striding about the Strand district making useful contacts, thinking up his *Aid* series and perfecting his air of a successful businessman, gave the impression that he owned the reborn firm, as eventually he did. But letters of that time still refer to him not as 'the Chief' but as 'our Mr Tindall'.

Business was rapidly building and his bright ideas continued. In March 1874 he wrote a letter in his own clear hand – everything was handwritten: the typewriter, like the telephone, would not make a general appearance in offices for another thirty years – to the private secretary of the Princess Royal. This was Queen Victoria's eldest daughter, born the same year as Albert Alfred himself. She had married Prince Friedrich Wilhelm of Prussia at seventeen and by 1874 had eight children. Albert Alfred was asking if the firm might dedicate to her the translation of a book to be called in English *The Young Mother's Guide* – 'the author is one of the most accomplished French physicians, director General of Nurses and Crèches . . . The work has done an incalculable amount of good in France and will, we are convinced, be the means in this country of rescuing many little lives from a premature grave . . .' The compliment was graciously accepted.

Behind this canny idea was some personal emotion. For Albert Alfred himself was soon to become a father for the first time: his daughter May was born in the month of that name. Aged thirty-three, he had married Sophia Simson the summer before. For a man from nowhere it was a remarkably good match. My guess is that Albert Alfred had already been living in Lewisham, and that they met at their local church, St John's. Sophia had been teaching Sunday school there and was involved in other classic good works of Victorian womanhood such as the Dorcas Society (bedlinen for poor mothers).

A young man met under the auspices of the Church of England in a fashionable parish was bound to have an aura of reassuring respectability about him, however nebulous his family. Charm and general conviviality no doubt helped, and there was Albert's fine baritone voice: he joined the Church choir and was one of the founders of a local choral society. By this time he could afford to dress with the elegance that shows in later photographs of him. He would also by then have shed the remains of whatever rural accent he had carried from his Kent childhood. His grandson recalled, many years after his death, that 'he sounded as you would expect: like a Victorian gentleman.'

Sophia was slim, dark, rather good-looking by the standards of today but not pretty by those of her own time, which favoured a plumper face and a 'rosebud mouth'. She is said to have been gentle and retiring: in the few surviving photos she looks nervous. A faint echo from voices now long dead categorises her as 'over-educated': in secret, she wrote poetry. She does not sound to have been well suited to the animal vitality of Albert Alfred but, given her financially and socially solid background, she was clearly a prize he was not going to miss. No doubt she brought a marriage settlement with her. She was already twenty-nine. Whatever reservations the Simsons may have had, it was time that dear Sophie fulfilled a woman's destiny in a home of her own ... After all, Albert Alfred was doing so well. And in these changing, modern days ...

Further rumours from the past suggest that after marriage Albert took to jeering at Sophia's cultural tastes and complained that she did not darn his socks as he wanted. Perhaps he was jealous of her superior education, or merely wished to assure himself and everyone else that education was not everything. And perhaps too, in his concept of how the married should treat one another alone at home, which was not something you could learn by observation or from an etiquette book, he had reverted to the manners of his own parents. Years later, for his second wife, he chose a well-born but easy-going woman who quite liked darning, had no intellectual pretensions and knew better than to argue with him.

He is also alleged to have found Sophia's diary and read it aloud, with comments. But then everything remembered about Sophia is tinted by the fact that she died before her time. To such a one, the role of blameless victim is readily awarded.

Bertie was born early in 1876, less than two years after May. Another girl, Maud, followed in 1879. Then there was a longer pause until the birth of a second son, Howard, in 1884.

In time to come Albert Alfred's grandchildren rather liked the Old Man, as he was known in the family. He was fun. He entered into their world, conspired with them to break rules about sweets and bedtime, and even once egged on his granddaughter to pick some daffodils from a private property as a present for her mother – a gift that was not well received, and indeed gives one further pause for thought about the Old Man's probity. Once, rather too late in their childhood, he took them for a blustery trip on a Brighton pleasure steamer and a meal of fish and chips in a cheap café. He relished the outing more than they did, since by then their tastes were reflecting their more refined upbringing. Perhaps he had missed out on such things in his own unmentioned youth. With his own children, relations were not always easy. May grew up large, handsome and as assertive as he was, and was able to stand up to him, but the younger children are said to have taken after their mother and 'he scolded and abused them and pried into their private lives so that they became shy and secretive.'[5] Bertie's diary, however, that he kept during his own year in Paris, gives a more complex picture.

Bertie was thirteen when he lost his mother. Afterwards, he became a great keeper of photographs, programmes, newspaper cuttings and Christmas cards. The first items in the album into which he pasted his collection are the local-paper reports of Sophia's funeral and of the stained-glass window that was erected a few months later to commemorate her. There is also a folded sheet of cream writing paper, on which are carefully noted down the various illnesses of the three eldest children. In January 1878, for instance, May had had chicken pox, and by February Bertie, just two, had caught it. By the end of the following year, rising four, he had had scarlet fever and passed it on to May. By 1882 Maud had joined the family and all three children had had measles. Oddly, Maud was thought to have had measles again, in 1887. She was evidently considered a delicate child, for she had some other illness, unnoted, in the spring of 1889, which started a fatal train of events. There seems a peculiar poignancy in the fact that this anxious little *aide-mémoire* on nursery ailments is the one piece of his mother's handwriting that Bertie managed to preserve.

Some mild contact with the family in Kent had evidently been maintained. The old fly-driver and his wife eventually retired to Brede, a village some seven miles from Hastings. They were surely dead by the 1880s, but in adult life Bertie had a vague memory of a 'holiday on a farm' when he had been quite small, and of references to 'the Brede people'. Presumably these were some younger Tindall relatives who had remained conveniently on the land. Farm holidays were one of those things, like flannel next to the skin and regular 'doses', that were thought to be good for children, especially London ones, and any social mismatch might be tactfully put down to the difference between urban and rural ways.

Spells at the seaside, breathing 'ozone', were also held to be highly restorative for children who were sickly, and given the soot-laden air of the whole of London by the late nineteenth century this was no doubt valid. Hastings was now a well-established seaside resort, a hilly, healthy place, and so it was to some relatives in Hastings, living in the picturesque Old Town, that little Maud, aged nine and a half, was despatched. Old enough to manage as a guest on her own, but too young, it was no doubt thought, to be fussy . . . And there may have been other children on hand to play with.

In Hastings, however, Maud contracted typhoid fever, which is a severe and potentially fatal form of gastro-enteritis. In previous eras it had been endemic in Britain, and indeed it was probably the cause of Prince Albert's untimely death in 1861, which does not say a great deal for the water supply at Windsor. But nearly thirty years later, with the huge drainage works that had been carried out in London and in most other towns, it was very much in retreat. Middle-class families living in suburban comfort did not expect to encounter typhoid. It had become a working-class ailment, associated with primi-tive plumbing and unhygienic habits.

Telegrams went back and forth. Sophia went down to Hastings to nurse her daughter, who gradually recov-ered. It was Sophia who died. She was forty-four. The death was registered by one of the St Leonards relatives, though it took place, for reasons one can imagine, in rented lodgings facing Hastings' sea-front. The cause of death was testified by the doctor in attendance as 'Double pneumonia, fifteen days' with an extra (and surely irrele-vant) mention of arthritis. But typhoid is what she was always said, in the family, to have contracted, tending Maud.

After this tragedy there seems, for reasons one can understand too well, to have been very little further contact with Hastings. Much later in life Bertie, according to his own son, gave the impression of knowing nothing at all about his father's side of the family. Left an emotional waif by the sudden loss of the mother who understood his reticences and sympathised with his developing artistic interests, he now had only his overbearing father as an adult in the forefront of his life. The words of the Bastable children, also of Lewisham, echo in the mind: 'Our Mother is dead, and if you think we don't care because I don't tell you much about her you only show that you do not understand people at all . . . Most of our things are black or grey since Mother died.'

Unlike the fictional Bastables, the Tindall children were too disparate in sex and age to form a cohesive front to keep grief at bay. May mounted something of a campaign against the new stepmother, when she appeared, and induced the five-years-younger Maud to follow her, but Bertie was a boy on his own, as was Howard, who was separated from Bertie by being eight years younger. Now, more than ever, Albert Alfred Tindall must have seemed like a force of nature, blotting out everyone else around him.

Chapter XII

Business in Gay Paree

Just as Albert Alfred Tindall entered the Baillière orbit, Paris was plunged into the unexpectedly disastrous Franco-Prussian War and the abrupt end of the Second Empire.

It had all been going so well – well, that is, if you were in a position to enjoy the extravagantly consumerist society that Napoleon III had fostered, and admired the new Paris evolving in a golden web from Baron Haussmann's fingers. As well as the evisceration of many old districts and the destruction of thousands of solid old houses, whole new quarters had been built. Huge new department stores, gas-lit, with plate-glass windows and grandiose wrought-iron staircases, were replacing the old shops of individual drapers, hatters and glovers in covered passages such as the Cour de Commerce St André. Charles Garnier's new and very ornate Opera House, with its own avenue leading to it, was being built in Paris's new, western heart. A couple of kilometres further out, what had been the isolated rural village of Monceau at the Restoration, a place of wet nurses and milkmaids, was now bordered by a park lined with the enormous houses of those to whom speculation in property had brought unprecedented wealth. The whole ring of suburban villages – Grenelle, Vaugirard, Ivry, Montmartre, Belleville and the rest – that had been included within the customs wall of the 1840s were, from 1860, incorporated into the new, enlarged Paris of twenty *arrondissements*.

Plenty of people deplored what Paris had become, from exiled French nationals plotting in the back rooms of restaurants in London's Soho, to the young Emile Zola who was then working in Paris's most successful bookshop. He had just completed his schema for a huge novel sequence set in Paris and elsewhere under the Second Empire, when the Empire itself collapsed with spectacular suddenness. No one, including Zola, had foreseen this in the first half of 1870, least of all the Emperor Napoleon III himself. He had made some recent liberalising gestures. Surely that should keep everyone content, even the muttering republicans? He had sought war with the Prussians under the impression that victory would follow and that this would further extend France's landmass and her world status. Yet by the early autumn those of the French regular army who had not already been killed were trapped in the fortress of Metz, the Emperor himself was a prisoner of War and the Prussian forces were marching on Paris. The thirty-three-kilometre customs wall round Paris was hastily strengthened and fortified. Behind this barrier, the capital would spend the winter of 1870–71 under siege – more literally, a blockade – a strangely medieval experience for a huge modern city. Cold and hunger increased as the winter went by, and so did civil unrest, as different factions of nationalists and republicans each strove to drag the events their way and to save France's bedraggled 'honour' according to their own ideology.

Across the Channel (where Napoleon III was eventually allowed to seek refuge, as repeated waves of French exiles had before him) only qualified sympathy was expressed. The French, it was felt, were always revolting against their leaders: it was a stupid Gallic habit. And why had they made War on the Prussians anyway?

In Britain, at that date, the German provinces still figured as a benign source of learning and culture – and, indeed, as the source of the Royal Family, given Victoria's Hanoverian origin and the late Prince Albert's more obviously Germanic one. Although France had been an ally in the unsatisfactory Crimean War, she still figured in the popular British mind as the traditional, centuries-old enemy, and there was a vague, general feeling that she had got her comeuppance. Besides, the urban French ate horseflesh, something to which the horsey British had never knowingly stooped. At tea tables in Kensington and Lewisham, where 'French novels' denoted something exciting but essentially indecent, there were jokes about how the Parisians were now eating rats – 'A change from frogs, doncha know?'

In fact they were reduced, before the Siege was over, to eating nearly all the animals in the Jardin des Plantes, including the beloved elephant and giraffe. Not quite all, however. The monkeys were spared. Darwin's *Origin of Species* had been published ten years previously, and a general notion of its ideas had entered the European thought stream. Might eating monkeys, particularly the larger apes, be all too near to eating one's own distant relations? Evidently even the most fervently Catholic French, whose piety had been encouraged again under the Second Empire, had been made uneasy by the thought.

How Arthur Jacob, close observer of the animal world, friend to bear and monkey, one-time Paris inhabitant and almost certainly an unbeliever, viewed all this from his retirement in Cumbria, I can only guess. His capacity for wintry amusement, no doubt, did not desert him.

Intimations of the troubles in France crop up in the earliest surviving letter books of what was still Baillière, London, as a series of tiresome but minor impediments to the real business of life, which was the book trade:

8th October 1870, to someone in the Cambridge University Library: 'We are much obliged for your note and will pursue the livraison of [illegible] as soon as ever communication with France is restored . . .' This, with its rogue French term for 'delivery', was signed by a W. Galette who, however, seems to have made his way to Paris before the Siege closed in completely, since by 7th February a colleague was writing to him there, in French, with a grateful mention of his *zèle et exactitude*. Evidently some mail was getting through, probably couriered by English nationals with passports that allowed them to come and go, but, as the Siege was overtaken by the brief and disastrous uprising known as the Commune, trade through Paris became increasingly difficult. There is a reference at one point to a whole package of books having been detained by a *commissaire-priseur* (a customs valuer) and, in May, at the peak of the Commune, to two previous letters having been stolen by 'a thief'. By later in the summer, however, the Commune and its brutal suppression were but another bloody French memory and a series of burnt-out buildings (including the Paris Town Hall and all its stored records). It also left, among the bourgeoisie, a fear of insurrection, and, on the Left, a bitterness, that were collectively to haunt French society for generations to come.

Galette seems to have remained in Paris, and was for some years the main contact and book-finder there for the reconstituted London firm. The formal link with the French Baillière enterprise was severed, but for many years the shop and head office in the Rue Hautefeuille remained an important source of books for England, as well as a distributor for London-produced wares – including the increasingly successful *Medical Press*. By 1874 Galette had been replaced by another representative, one Lemoigne, who had his own shop and book-dealing business in the Rue Bonaparte which runs down from the Place St Germain to the river. We shall hear of him again.

Once peace was restored, the passage of *ballots* (small crates) of books to and fro across the Channel seems to have been extraordinarily rapid and efficient by the standards of later eras. On the occasions when it was less so, the firm in London did not hesitate to complain in intemperate terms that would hardly have been considered appropriate in later days either:

'Nous avons vainement attendu depuis lundi le paquet que vous devriez nous envoyer, ce retard nous a été très désagréable et nous vous prions de bien vouloir nous en dire le motif...' ('Since Monday, we have been waiting in vain for the package you were supposed to send us, this delay has been most unpleasant for us and we would ask you to be so good as to tell us the reason ...')

'... We are much surprised and annoyed that you have not sent the Instructions Generales Anthropologique nor any letter to explain why it is not sent, our client applies for it every day, some days *twice*, and we cannot give any explanation. You must know that this is very serious for us, and that we cannot do business in this manner ...'

'... As to the "Instructions Générales pour les recherches anthropologique", which you report *"est complètement épuisé"* [completely out of print] our customer wrote to Paris and by return of post received it in the enclosed wrapper from M. Masson – you must know that such a case is calculated to do us serious mischief. Of course we do not require a copy now.'

Such explosions punctuate for years correspondence which otherwise consists of great lists of books, increasingly medical, which were apparently received safely, but the peremptory refrain 'Send the books by return or let us know the reason why' is often employed. One begins to feel extremely sorry for Monsieur Lemoigne, particularly when, in 1879, a crisis point seems to have been reached. By this time the London firm had constituted itself Baillière, Tindall & Cox, and it was George Cox, he of the food-stained waistcoats and the artistic anatomy books, who wrote the following:

'We have suffered inconvenience and serious losses from neglect of apparently simple matters . . . delay in obtaining settlement of our accounts, that we hoped you would endeavour to rectify the fault complained of – but without effect.

'I enclose a postcard from MM. J-B Baillière et Fils which discloses an omission which cannot be overlooked. [Apparently this was a lost parcel.]

'Under these circumstances you will not be surprised that we have decided to make an alteration. I expect to be in Paris next month and will then wind up our accounts.

'I write this with great regret but if we are to retain any part of our French trade no other course is open to us . . .'

As Cox wrote this in English, and there is no evidence that Lemoigne spoke or wrote anything but French, one wonders rather how their encounter in Paris progressed. Particularly as, four years later, a letter in correct French formally engaged – or re-engaged – Lemoigne as Paris representative. In the mean time, 'our Mr Tindall' had also been in Paris on the firm's business, apparently on several occasions.

It is hardly to be expected that Albert Alfred spoke much French either. His scant education would not have endowed him with any, and his son Bertie was to comment later, in the privacy of his diary, on his father's 'stumbling attempts to speak the language'. But in these circumstances it seems impressive that he attempted to speak it at all. Had he, perhaps, made a number of visits to France, to that Gay Paree that, by the 1860s, was taking such a distinctive shape in the English consciousness?

Co-existent with the image of Bohemia, but a far cry from the romanticised simplicities of that country of the mind, Gay Paree is traditionally regarded as a classic Second Empire product. While the Imperial court and the newly opulent layers of *le tout Paris* set the pace by indulging in extravagant balls and masques, more ordinary crowds flocked to the café-concerts. Towards the end of the Empire the rules regulating these were relaxed, allowing costumed shows as well as music and songs and permitting customers to dance as well. After that, Parisian nightlife entered a new phase, and at the same period coffee shops emerged from behind four walls to become the terrace cafés now so identified with Paris.

The Folies Bergère was founded, just north of the Grands Boulevards, unpropitiously in 1870, shortly before the Franco-Prussian War cut across the festivities. But a year later the music was playing again, and the frills, feathers and bosoms were being flourished as if nothing had happened in between. The Moulin de la Galette, a genuine mill in still semi-rural Montmartre, was transformed into a *guinguette* the same year. The raucous Moulin Rouge, also in Montmartre, which became notorious for its cancan dancers, did not open till the late 1880s, but the cancan itself was by then well established as a Parisian trademark. It had apparently started in disreputable working-class dance-halls as early as the 1830s, and gradually worked its way up into scandalous visibility. Jacques Offenbach, that emblematic Second Empire figure, endowed it with an immediately recognisable tune in his 1858 operetta *Orpheus in the Underworld*, and eight years later featured it again in his

La Vie Parisienne. In the latter opera, foreigners from 'the north' arrive at a railway station, are taken round Parisian nightlife, through experiences of drunken debauchery, but in the end find true love: a resonant theme for many visitors to the capital.

The same title, *La Vie Parisienne*, by then redolent of all things temptingly risqué, was later used for a long-running magazine which became one of France's most famous exports. It was really a harmlessly cheery publication much given to patriotism, but its 'saucy' covers, which could never have been used on a British magazine at the time, ensured that it acquired an exotic reputation across the Channel.

When Manet painted his intricate *Bar at the Folies Bergère* in 1881 there were beer bottles on the counter suggestive of an established British clientele. In earlier generations, English visitors to Paris had typically been rich by Parisian standards (the classic *milord anglais*), sometimes aristocratic and often intellectual, but now the frequent trains and steamers also brought over the middle classes. In Paris, they found on offer the kind of relaxation and stylish fun to which they would have had little access in the more socially and economically segregated society on their own side of the Channel. For it was remarked even by Parisians how extraordinarily mixed were the crowds at the Folies Bergère, not only in income but in degrees of respectability. Fathers of families took their wives there for an evening out, but at the same time the huge glassed-in *jardin d'hiver* at the back, full of plants and mirrors and dim lights, was regularly frequented by 'women of small virtue' and men on the lookout for them. In London at that date the ordinary businessman would find little to fill the gap between the frankly working-class lowlife of the music halls and the unreachably discreet, expensive pleasures enjoyed by some of high society. To such men, Paris readily became a Secret Garden to which they had discovered the key.

It has been suggested that the whole concept of Gay Paree, as a place of liberation and fulfilment, developed as a response to Victorian repression on the other side of the Channel. But this ignores the realities underpinning French gaiety. It is true that the very name Gay Paree mimicked English pronunciation at a time when the word 'gay' in covert English slang (though not in French) indicated female prostitution. But, unlike England, France had developed its own repression in the form of a comprehensive system of 'Morality Police', with legalised brothels and girls subject to regular medical inspections. Perhaps this made the whole enterprise feel more respectable, and therefore more moral, to some of the English visitors.

But if those of more romantic cast quailed at ringing a labelled bell beside frosted-glass windows and being welcomed by a smiling Madame into a plush-hung interior, there was no shortage in Paris's now well-lit streets of other women looking to oblige. Late in the century, one survey put the number of clandestine, unlicensed prostitutes in the capital at sixty thousand, though it is difficult to see how even this conjectural figure was reached. The women in question ranged from drunken old biddies accommodating passing soldiers and vagrants on the grassy slopes of the fortifications, through under-age girls tugging at gentlemen's sleeves in the street, all the way to relatively genteel widows or girls dressed soberly as ladies. Apparently these last, with a veiled glance, would allow a respectable-looking stranger to follow them into their home courtyard and hence to their apartment.

Like the nightlife, in Paris the oldest profession was more socially mixed and inclusive than its equivalent in London. The image of the irrevocably Fallen Woman was not part of the French construct. Many girls who profited commercially from youth and freedom disappeared into more or less respectable marriage once they had saved up a dowry. This was particularly true of the Left Bank, where de facto prostitution was recognised as being a fresher, younger, more innocent trade than on the money-centred Right Bank. *Grisette*-style girls were still keeping students company, and there were also several renowned Brasseries de Femmes in the Rue Monsieur le Prince and the Boulevard St Michel. In these big cafés, pretty local girls were given free meals if they talked to customers and encouraged them to buy more drinks. What other arrangements they made with the customers was their own affair.

It is hard to believe that the dynamic Albert Alfred, who worked in the Strand-Covent Garden area which was then the epicentre of London prostitution, passed through his visits to Paris with total disregard for the more attractive and classless opportunities it offered.

Long afterwards, when he was an old man, and the business venture he had founded with George Cox of the artistic anatomy had become a widely respected firm of medical publishers, Albert Alfred embarrassed his grandchildren terribly on the memorable day out in Brighton – 'Granpa had an eye for a pretty woman of the Rubensesque type and commented in the loud voice of the chronically deaf on the charms of our fellow promenaders, especially their legs. In despair, Tom and I expressed a passionate desire to visit the aquarium, where few of the pretty ladies went and their beauty was hidden in semi-darkness . . .'[1]

In his second marriage, by which time he was in a position to follow his own tastes rather than monetary considerations, he chose a woman of some beauty and generous proportions. She was the daughter of a baronet, though illegitimate because she was one of a brood of children born of a bigamous second marriage. Not till many years later did a landmark court case award any legal inheritance to her. On marriage, Albert Alfred apparently confided in his son Bertie, then aged fifteen,

'I'll give her one child, to keep her happy.' He did just that: one further daughter was born in the Lewisham house and no more. His remark gives one pause for thought on two counts. It clearly indicates (as do the birth rates of the time) that by the 1890s some form of contraception was widely practised among the more aware sections of the population. It also suggests that his relationship with his elder son was not quite as oppressive as some younger members of the family later suggested, though what the shy and certainly virginal Bertie made of his father's man-to-man confidence it is hard to imagine.

By the late nineteenth century to have been at public school was the hallmark of an English gentleman, an essential rite of passage for Albert Alfred's sons. Bertie was duly sent to boarding prep school and then to Charterhouse, the long-established City school which had fairly recently moved into grandiose new buildings outside London to accommodate the rising demand for places. He was not, however, to continue on to Oxford or Cambridge as he might reasonably have expected to do and as his studious tastes would have warranted. The official reason was that Albert Alfred could not afford to spend any more on his eldest son. Albert Alfred, however, lived in an increasingly affluent style in the years that followed, presently moving to a substantial house in Kent, near Maidstone. Here, in true country-gentleman style, he cultivated a fine garden, before moving on again to a still larger and brand-new house in Sussex with a billiard room, conservatories and stables. Some of his wife's grand if irregularly born family lived in the area. Contrary to what one might imagine, he seems to have taken active interest and pleasure in his herbaceous borders, lawns, fruit trees and vegetable gardens, becoming a pillar of local flower shows. Evidently the genes of his lost rural ancestors were still alive within him.

When the time came, the much younger Howard was allowed to read History at Cambridge. The real reason for Albert Alfred's parsimony over university for Bertie was probably that he did not want his eldest, the heir to the family business, cultivating academic interests that might carry him in a different direction. Signs from Bertie's later life suggest that he might have chosen, rather, a career in architecture or museum-curating. It may also have been that Albert Alfred felt obscurely jealous of his children, whose upbringing he must have perceived as luxurious compared with his own.

But, in fairness, he did his best to equip his eldest well for a role in the international book trade, sending him first to stay with a contact in Germany for six months, and then to Paris for almost the whole of 1895. And Bertie was grateful, partly, no doubt, because he was told he should be and, as a Victorian son, it did not yet occur to him to think otherwise, and partly because his affectionate nature inclined him to love those around him. 'Dear old Father,' he wrote in his diary in Paris when he had just seen the Old Man off at the Gare du Nord, 'he has been good to me, not many fellows can boast of such an education as I have had.'

How was this education going to be pursued? Why, of course – by work experience at the premises of Monsieur Lemoigne, the vital Parisian contact whose past relations with Baillière, Tindall & Cox had been so chequered. Bertie does not appear to have known that, and probably did not suspect that his presence at Lemoigne's was not merely for his own benefit but was designed to bind Lemoigne more firmly to the London interest. For good measure, he was also to be a paying guest at the Lemoigne home, not far from the shop in 12 Rue Bonaparte. He was to have two attic rooms, with a breakfast of coffee and rolls brought up to him every morning, and to share the Lemoignes' table at lunch and dinner. Monsieur and Madame Lemoigne had teenage sons themselves. It must have seemed an ideal arrangement.

The Lemoigne apartment was in a handsome, stone-fronted house in the Rue de l'Abbaye, immediately behind the surviving church of the Abbey St Germain and over-looking its northern wall. The street had been laid out in 1800, after the Revolution and the saltpetre-store explosion had reduced many of the Abbey buildings to ruins. Beneath the cobbles of the Rue de l'Abbaye and its single row of houses lay (and lie today) the foundations of the once-beautiful Chapel of the Virgin and the monks' library and cloister. The skeleton of a perpendicular-Gothic window is still to be seen in a hallway on the wall that divides one house from the next. Immediately behind the street the tiny Place Furstemberg, with its central ornate lamp standard, preserves the footprint of the one-time Abbey stable yard.

Bertie, in spite of an already passionate interest in old stones, does not seem to have known that he was occu-pying such hallowed ground. A pity, since, had he realised, he might have been just a little happier. In other respects, the area that was to become so celebrated in the twen-tieth century as St Germain des Prés was at that period an unassuming district. As to the accommodation offered to him, Bertie's initial reaction was that of generations of English visitors used to the more spacious and comfort-able homes of England:

'We drove straight to Lemoigne's place [from the Gare du Nord] and he showed me my rooms, which are as pokey as his own flat, consisting of a room with a small cupboard and stand to work in and a sitting room with a bedstead with a nice look out on chimneys, with a horrible bed, a rickety table, two chairs and a washboard-stand and nothing more, they are very small and uncomfortable. We had dinner with Lemoigne's whole family of four and a wife and left them for the night at 10, Father having found lodgings in a small hotel about a few minutes' walk away.'

Bertie wrote this, and all the other entries recounting his Paris year, in a Letts one-page-a-day pocket diary designed, rather, to record daily expenses. He did record these faithfully, like many of his generation – and was to do so for the rest of his long life – but as he also used the book to describe what he had done on most days, and often what he had felt too, he sometimes had to resort to minute writing to cram everything in. As well as this, he had the habit, common among nineteenth-century letter-writers, of using every bit of remaining space once he had reached the bottom of the page by doubling back and writing between the lines. Only once I had realised this did some of his more apparently incoherent entries make sense, though I feel there are some, including the above, where Bertie himself got slightly lost in the verbal maze he had created.

The Paris that Bertie discovered in 1895 was superficially very different from that of earlier generations. Arthur Jacob would only have recognised disjointed bits of it submerged in the greater mass. The population was now about two and a half million. Close-built urban landscape extended right up to the fortifications – *les fortifs*' in Paris slang.[2] Although the land on the far side of these grassy ramparts was supposed to be kept clear as a zone of fire, with a network of forts along it, in practice, since the customs gates themselves had been abolished, it had filled up with illicitly constructed shanties and summer houses, vegetable patches, grazing donkeys, gipsy caravans, the yards of small industries, rag-pickers' dumps and impromptu summertime cafés under awnings. Big flea markets were held every week, one just outside the northern exit from Paris, the Porte de Clignancourt, and another in the south-west just inside the Porte de Vanves. Part rural idyll for the poor escaping from the streets of inner Paris, part slum for the marginal members of society, the Zone, as it came to be universally called, persisted into the second half of the twentieth century, long after the spread of Paris had leapfrogged over it and created new and more permanent suburbs much further out.

Already, when Bertie arrived in Paris, tramlines were carrying Parisians well beyond the Zone to these future suburbs, then still charming villages. From the tram terminus on the Place St Germain almost outside their door, the Lemoignes could get all the way to Châtillon where they had a country retreat. They could also get westwards to the Bois de Boulogne and eastwards to the Bois de Vincennes. Both these originally private and royal hunting grounds had been given to the municipality of Paris by the Emperor Napoleon III. During his earlier enforced exile in England while kings were back on the French throne, he had been impressed by the London parks. Both wild woods had been landscaped and prettified. In the Bois de Boulogne, where George du Maurier nostalgically recalled duck-shooting in boyhood on a remote mere, two lakes and an artificial waterfall were made.

But Paris was not yet punctuated by Metro stations, those Art Nouveau erections of wrought-iron tulips and lilies that have come to epitomise for us the *fin de siècle*. A protracted debate about whether the trains should run underground, as in London, or on iron structures overhead, as in New York, was only just being settled in favour of digging down. The work had yet to begin, and it would be 1900 before the first line was opened between the Etoile and the site of the Bastille. Nor, in 1895, had the wrought-iron *pissoirs*, that were destined for the next two generations to be such a ubiquitous feature of the Paris streets, quite made their appearance. The 1890s did, however, see a rush of statues onto the streets: two Joans of Arc on the Right Bank, Danton at the junction of the Rue de l'Ecole de Médecine and the Boulevard St Germain, Louis Blanc and Voltaire on the far side of the Latin Quarter in the Rue Monge, Jean-Jacques Rousseau in front of the Panthéon, a lion up the hill on the site of the old Porte Denfert growling eastwards towards the lands that had been lost to the Prussians in 1870. Henry Murger would get a bust in the Luxembourg Gardens in 1895.

Later in the decade more would be erected, including one commemorating Etienne Dolet at Place Maubert, his place of execution. This statue was generally despised by the artistic taste of the Left Bank as being of poor quality[3] and damaging further the proportions of what was left of the Maub'. While the Parisian municipality were at it, they demolished yet a few more ancient houses there and in the Rue Galande, and added one of the new *pissoirs* to the Place for further embellishment.

But this, in 1895, lay a few years in the future. The Place Maubert that Bertie passed through as he strode off to inspect St Julien le Pauvre, St Séverin or St Etienne du Mont was essentially still the battered remnant of what had been there for centuries. The Rue des Noyers, with de Musset's family home, still stood on the far side of the Boulevard, so did the Marché des Carmes, so did all the top-heavy old houses in the narrow, steep Rue des Carmes, which would not be widened till the 1920s. Indeed, across most of the Latin Quarter, the works of Haussmann had laid only a light veil over a townscape that still had much of its dense, original texture. The buildings still looked like fortresses; narrow doors and passageways still led to labyrinthian hidden courtyards. Off the Rue des Carmes, up a flight of darkly enticing steps, the twelfth-century Clos Bruneau survived as a cul-de-sac. In the early mornings, which were scented with fresh coffee and stale tobacco, street sweepers manipulated rolls of sacking in the gutters to direct the copious streams of water in sluicing away the detritus of the horse-drawn city, just as their predecessors had done for generations with the open central ditches.

Today the horses have all gone. But entrenched Parisian habits die hard. Water still gushes in profusion at the pavement edges. Medieval houses still loom over cobbled byways. Beggars still accost one. Tramps have never been entirely banished from the streets. Waiters still wear black waistcoats and long white aprons. If Bertie could return today to the Paris he first discovered over a hundred years ago, trams or no trams, he would find much of it entirely recognisable.

Chapter XIII

BERTIE ALONE

Two things emerge clearly from the daily record Bertie kept for much of his Parisian year. One is that, whatever dutiful gratitude he might feel, he would really rather have been in Lewisham with his sisters. There was a little sister now too, baby Doris, the one child of 'Mothery', the second Mrs Tindall, and there was young Howard also in the holidays from prep school. Then there was his prized bike: one of the modern chain-driven models that had replaced the hazardous penny-farthings. Through bicycling, the young of both sexes were discovering a freedom of movement unknown to earlier generations.

There was also someone called Adela, who was staying with the family in mid-January when Bertie took his leave. He recorded:

> 'I was down and so was Adela a good time before eight and when everything was finished we sat chatting together until the others came down. I think I said goodbye to that dear little girl with more reluctance than [to] anybody except May as she has done so much to make me feel at home and comfortable during her short stay.'

It seems an odd phrase to use, since the Lewisham home was Bertie's own, but a clue to what his experience of childhood had been is provided by an entry in Paris two weeks later, on 5 February: 'It was my birthday . . . It is now the ninth birthday I have spent away from home.'

Since he was then turning nineteen, he had evidently been at boarding school since the age of ten: that is, since then he had been away for three-quarters of each year. He would have been alone at school when he was told the news of his mother's death, and also, several years later, that of the new baby's birth. This exile was the standard practice for English boys of Bertie's class, then and for another half-century; some, no doubt, were less affected by it than others.

'. . . I did not get anything or hear a word from anybody the whole day long . . . Father had left with M. Lemoigne a beautiful diamond tie pin to be given to me on the 5th and also from Mothery 3 shirt studs, and that was the only recognition of its being my birthday and that did not come direct from home.'

As if to console himself that day, he bought ten centimes' worth of hot chestnuts from a street-seller, a 'Japanese ashtray' for fifty centimes (the cost of two stamps for England) and 'two saucers for plants'. On the following day – 'Directly after dejeuner I went out to the Louvre and spent some two hours and a half there, among the sketches and designs, Phoenician and Assyrian halls and Middle Age pottery. Then I went into the chief room of pictures . . .' Not much real consolation there, one would think, but – 'On arriving home at 4.30 the Concierge's wife handed me a packet from home, at last, a day and three-quarters late. There was a long letter from May and a BBB silver mounted pipe, a letter and tie from Adela and a tie from Maud and Howard, and lastly a note from Mother and Father and three tins of cocoa. On the strength of that I sat down to my letters with a pipe and a cup of cocoa and did not budge until dinner time.' Pipes and cocoa were not then the accoutrements of middle age, but of grown-up bachelor life; in the same way that words such as 'most enjoyable' and 'exceedingly', which would now be used only by the very old, were then fresh and vigorous.

The other theme that emerges strongly from the diary was that he was determined to see as much of the treasures of Paris as he could in the time that was accorded to him to improve his French before starting full-time work in the Rue Bonaparte. But this was far more than the earnest resolve of someone consciously imbibing 'culture'. It is clear that Bertie derived sensory satisfaction and interest from art and architecture to a level unusual in a nineteen-year-old boy in that or any other era. On the very day after his father left 'I went off to start my study of the Louvre' and repeat visits there pepper the diary: 'the pictures . . . always appear fresh to me.' By the weekend he was in Notre Dame for the first time, and had found his way past Maubert to St Etienne on the Montagne Sainte Geneviève – 'a very beautiful old church'. (He was to revisit it later, and found it 'even more beautiful than I thought at first'.) The following day he went to morning service at the British Embassy church, then 'walked the length of the Bois, then home to dejeuner which I had to have alone'. The day after, he went with Madame Lemoigne and her two elder boys, Paul and Emile, 'to hear the closing service of une adoration perpetuelle. I have never seen or heard such a gorgeous ceremony.' Clearly, the Victorian Anglican aversion to all things Papist was not current in the Tindall household.

Except when accompanied by one of the Lemoignes, Bertie seems to have gone everywhere on foot.

Admittedly he had only six francs per week to spend, and frequent tram-rides at between fifteen and thirty-five centimes a time would soon have consumed this, but it was rather as if it did not occur to him, in his youth and health, to do anything but walk. He set his legs in motion as naturally as Arthur Jacob had eighty years before, adding his footprints to the dense palimpsest of others throughout the Latin Quarter, discovering 'all the old narrow streets of old Paris. I went for an hour to the Cluny in the afternoon . . . It is a strange feeling, knowing that you are walking on the same pavement under the same roof as the Romans.' By and by he penetrated behind the boulevard, wandered north of the Place Maubert by St Séverin, into the Rue de la Huchette ('very poor people') and back to the St Germain territory via the Rue St André des Arts and the Rue Hautefeuille – 'narrow streets dotted here and there with some lovely old hotel of the XV or XVI'. Not till much later, exploring up the hill southwards, towards Montparnasse, did he come upon the Roman arena of Lutetia, then only partially excavated and hemmed in by houses. He was delighted to find there for himself a section of the medieval Paris wall of Philippe Auguste.

He trekked much further afield too, all over the Right Bank, discovering the secretive Ile St Louis, quartering Paris from one church or museum to another. A 'voyage of exploration' up the Boulevard Sébastopol led him to four of them. So few people then visited Paris in this way that the Sainte Chapelle on the Ile de la Cité, now a world tourist attraction, was rarely open. When, at his fifth attempt, he managed to get into it he was enchanted – 'a magnificent piece of pure Gothic work . . . the windows are lovely though the whole place is darkened by the surrounding buildings.' The as yet unfinished Sacré Cœur, however, on the heights of Montmartre, he diagnosed as 'very hideous and dark', a view widely shared since.

He went to the furthest ends of Paris as well. Hardly had he settled in when fresh snow fell in what turned out to be one of the coldest winters ever recorded.

'As I thought there might be some chance of skating, I walked directly I had had my café [breakfast coffee] and dressed to the Bois de Boulogne, getting there in ¾ of an hour, but I had to return very disappointed. I returned as I came by foot and I suppose I must have walked quite 8 miles before twelve and I did not get up till 9 o'clock. I spent an hour at the Louvre in the afternoon, and froze for the rest [of the day] as my stove positively refused to light although I laid it four different times.'

A few days later, however, he was teaching the Lemoigne boys and their teenage sister to skate in the Bois de Vincennes, and by mid-February reported, 'My pupils are getting on very well. Matilde skates quite respectably now though always too afraid to go alone.'

Others besides Bertie were keeping diaries that winter in the Latin Quarter. At the end of the first week in February, an elderly lawyer, a lecturer at the Sorbonne, whose family flat was high above the Boulevard St Germain overlooking the Place Maubert, wrote of having seen from his balcony 'a huge number of wild ducks passing overhead, also cormorants and other sea birds, escaping south'. Three days later, the temperature was minus fifteen centigrade. Gas meters froze, blocking the supply to the lighting on which bourgeois homes then ran. (*Gaz à tous les étages*, as it is still announced by old enamel plaques on walls.) At lower social levels people died of cold. The painter Gauguin broke a leg during that freezing winter, slipping on ice on a Left Bank quay, and swore that when it was mended he would disappear to Tahiti and never return. (He kept his vow.) Such heavy snow fell on one day that the horses could not move about the streets, bringing the traffic to a standstill. But Bertie sounds cheerful enough, writing that the Seine itself was 'frozen over hard, a thing which very rarely occurs. It is a grand sight to stand on one of the bridges and look either way . . . as far as one can see, nothing but ice.' Presumably he had by then mastered his stove.

It must also have been that week or soon after, though he does not mention it in this diary, that he painted a little watercolour with almost professional skill and great exactitude, showing the 'nice look out on chimneys' from his attic room 'for I can't see the ground in any direction'. Snow lies thick and unmelting on every roof, on distant skylights and even on the tops of brick chimney stacks where normally heat would melt it. This Latin Quarter roofscape seems a classic view from an attic in the country of Bohemia. But there is no indication in the extensive book list in his diary for 1895 (eighty books) that Bertie had read Murger, or that he saw the Puccini opera about *La Vie de Bohème* which was playing at the Odéon theatre later, in the summer. Nor, apparently, did he read du Maurier's *Trilby*, which only came out that year. His Paris was rooted in the more distant past.

He seems to have tried hard. He had enjoyed himself in Germany, learnt German quite easily and made friends. It was reasonable to hope the same might happen in Paris. An entry in mid-February, however, indicates how things were, at any rate with the Lemoignes' eldest son Paul, the nearest to him in age: 'After dinner one of Paul's friends came in and stopped until 11.30, he was very amusing, more so than Paul himself, who has scarcely a word to say at any time.'

It was not that the Lemoignes made no effort at all for their guest. There were trips to see classical plays at the Odéon theatre nearby and, later in the year when Bertie was working, to the opera. There was even an expedition with Paul to what seems to have been a grand public ball at the Hôtel de Ville, by then entirely reconstructed with lavish gilding after being burnt out during the Commune in 1871. 'I suppose there were about 20,000 people there ... the building itself is most extravagant in its magnificence of carving and decoration. We stayed to the end at 5.30. Even then there were too many people to be able to dance properly ... Omnibus to Hotel de Ville 30 cmes. Refreshments H d V 1.50. Punch and roll on way home 40 cmes.' Presumably the luxury of a bus there – buses had always been relatively expensive in Paris – was because the two young men were in evening dress. Two days before there is an item of four francs fifteen centimes noted for 'Gloves and tie for ball'. So, a relatively expensive outing.

Except at such rare events, or when the occasional and much welcomed friend from Germany visited Paris, it never seems to have occurred to Bertie in the course of his long tramps to call at a café for a reviving beer or a cup of coffee. So much for Gay Paree in the mind of this particular young Englishman, after years in the austerity of a single-sex public school, in a country where, as yet, cafés hardly existed and pubs were for the working classes. His budget, admittedly, would not readily have run to a drink in one of the now celebrated Montmartre nightspots, but he seems in any case to have had not the faintest yearning in that direction. During the year he read, among many classic French works, Zola's *L'Assommoir*, a novel whose translation had been banned in England where censorship by the biggest lending libraries still had a firm grip on what could be put down in print. But then the frightening and essentially moral *L'Assommoir* would hardly encourage one to try the absinthe for which Paris was then renowned.

In Bertie's expenses hot chestnuts often figure, as do cigarettes and tobacco, stamps, second-hand books from the quays, church collections, black ink (for sketches), hot baths (1.25 at the *Bain Douches* which were in the nearby Rue de Seine) and small sums to beggars. Once he had to spend a whole four francs (two-thirds of his weekly budget) on getting his much-used boots soled and heeled. Bootlaces figure too. I was surprised at the number of these he seemed to get through, but as they were then sold on the streets of Paris by small, poor boys trying to earn a few *sous*, it may be that Bertie, seeing in them his own young brother, regularly took pity on them.

If he ever had an encounter of a more equivocal nature, or realised he was being solicited for something other than money – unlikely in the Latin Quarter but highly likely in some of the Right Bank districts where he walked – his diary is silent on the matter. Letters arrived at intervals from Adela, each one carefully noted.

I suspect that a basic problem for Bertie in the Lemoigne household was one of slight but persistent social mismatch. France had not enjoyed Britain's huge industrial and imperial prosperity. In general the French middle classes lived more modestly than their British equivalents – a fact which remained true till after the middle of the twentieth century. One notes that the Lemoignes' flat, like most in Paris then and for decades after, had no bathroom. Paris's monolithic nineteenth-century apartment blocks, with their street entrances designed to look like carriageways and their ostentatious front balconies, actually enclose a maze of ill-lit passages and cramped bedrooms overlooking communal courtyards. There was then, and there is still today in these blocks, a necessary culture of suppression, of carefully guarded privacy, of not disturbing the ever-present neighbours or allowing them to disturb you. The elderly lawyer living on the Boulevard St Germain remarked in his own diary that year, in a footnote to a birth and a death that had taken place in the flat above unknown to most in the building: 'What an odd thing is this living together without being together, all under one roof, in these Paris dwellings.'[1]

No doubt the Lemoignes, bred to this self-sufficiency, were adept at it.

But in any case they strike one as rather a dull family. Monsieur Lemoigne may have had a top dressing of Left Bank culture derived from the book trade (he dealt in antiquarian books as well as recent ones), but there is no hint of interesting reading being done in their home or of a social life of any dynamism. The parents' silver wedding anniversary came round that year. Bertie noted, 'We could not do better than fête it, though they did not do anything to help us.' As well as the children and Bertie, only one friend was present at dinner. To Bertie's surprise, it was this elderly female who provided the dessert. It appears too that the Lemoignes had not thought of going skating till Bertie did. They seem to conform to what a contemporary commentator called 'a social class living on its savings as well as its earnings, characterised by a stiffly conventional sitting room, one long-serving maid, *lycée* for the boys however stupid . . . The key to their psychology is that their life is constantly organised according to careful accounting, which is taken very seriously.'[2] A certain amount was spent on food in such households, but almost nothing on furniture or linen, as that would have been provided once and for all by a dowry on marriage. Girls were not expected to pass exams. Travel, except within a very restricted family circuit, was unknown. Bertie remarked that once, when Matilde returned from a visit to an aunt, 'she was welcomed as if absent a whole year, by these people who have practically never left home.' In mid-March her birthday occurred:

'Bouquet of violets for Matilde – 1 franc . . . Just on sitting down to déjeuner she was kissed all round, not by me of course but by the family, and wished many happy returns of her birthday according apparently to French custom, though I don't think much of it, and nothing more was heard of her birthday until at dinner a small pastrycook cake was introduced as her birthday cake.'

That afternoon he went to the Arts et Métiers museum with Emile, the middle son, but Matilde did not accompany them. Towards the end of the month she went away again to stay at Compiègne, north of Paris.

'I suppose the house will be horribly dull now, she is the only lively figure in it except little Maurice. [Maurice, at eleven, was the same age as Bertie's brother Howard.] Paul, moody old moony philosopher, has not a word to say to anyone except "enfin, tu m'ennuies" ["You're boring me/irritating me"], although he may be clever as I don't doubt it, he keeps it all to himself and has not the slightest idea of forming part in a conversation or to make himself pleasant in the least way.'

Paul, perhaps, had been reading too much Schopenhauer, then rather fashionable, and a student boorishness was (and is) a common Left Bank affectation. The following day, however, Bertie succeeded in taking him to see the Ile St Louis, perhaps twenty minutes' walk away. 'He had never been there before.' Later, over Easter, Bertie had to make a planned outing with only Emile and young Maurice 'as Paul would not come and Matilde could not stir out of the house with me even accompanied by her two brothers without her eldest or her parents'.

This was the obverse side to Gay Paree, with its nightlife, its rowdy popular fêtes and its formal, many-course dinner parties where even respectable people indulged in risqué conversation (Bertie did attend just one of these, and was rather stunned by what he heard). Girls like Matilde, *des jeunes filles de bonnes familles*, were in reaction to these excesses kept in a state of nunnery-like segregation that would by then have been out of the question for Bertie's sisters, in the 1890s world of the New Woman across the Channel.

Towards mid-March Bertie recorded:

'I was out for 2½ [hours] in a pouring rain on an errand for M. Lemoigne or rather for Baillière, Tindall & Cox. It is the first thing of the sort I have ever done and that in French with only the smatter I have at present. But still I got through very well considering. I had to go to two publishing houses and enquire about an agent in London who had disappeared with money for some advertisements without their appearing. My attempts were however fruitless.'

Not till late April did he start working full time at the Lemoigne office, his own decision apparently:

'The hours are rather long . . . From 8.30 to 7.0 or as it sometimes is 8, with only an interval at 12 for dejeuner . . . My last free days are over and from now on I shall be at everybody's beck and call, until I work my way high enough to beck and call in my place. Anyhow I have the consolation of having made the best of my unusually long lease of freedom thanks to Father's bounty.'

As, not long before, he had recorded, 'I went for a very long walk in the afternoon all by myself as usual,' freedom had evidently had its bleak side.

However, in one respect life *chez* Lemoigne had looked up. In mid-March he had written:

'Immediately after déjeuner I went with Madame and Matilde by tram to their much talked about garden and house at Châtillon, about two miles the other side of the fortifications. The house is a very ramshackle old place and the garden is not up to much but I dare say is very nice in summer. They found a little room in the attic of a house close by which I could have from Saturday to Monday always.'

Such was to be the pattern as the days lengthened. The tramlines, which had been installed less than twenty years before, had had a transforming effect on the lives of Parisian families such as the Lemoignes, who do not ever seem to have taken *fiacres* (cabs) and would never have hired a carriage for a longer ride. The two lines that ran from the Place St Germain, out beyond the Porte de Vanves all the way to Fontenay-aux-Roses and Clamart, were still horse-drawn in 1895, though many of the trams that traversed Paris more centrally had been modernised in the previous three years, either with steam traction or with electricity. (The latter, having primitive accumulators under the wooden bench seats that gave off acid vapours, were not particularly popular.) The violet-and-yellow horse-drawn tram that deposited the Lemoignes at Châtillon therefore went slowly, at about eight to nine kilometres an hour, but it was much appreciated. Châtillon represented the unspoilt country and fresh air, an escape with a touch of magic to it, just as the country house in Normandy or on the Loire does to Parisians today. It was a way of keeping symbolic faith with the rural roots which, for most nineteenth-century Parisian families, were only a generation or two behind them.

Spring, however, was very late that year, with 'not a bud to be seen' in early April. In the Lemoigne boys' Easter holidays, shortly before Bertie was to start full-time work, he and the family spent a whole week in Châtillon. Bertie sketched, gardened and made the outing with the younger boys on which Matilde was not allowed to accompany them. There were further weekends there in May, although on the 16th: 'During the day it had the audacity to snow, at this time of year. I have never known it snow so late.'

However, at the beginning of June he wrote: 'I gardened the whole day long as hard as I could, putting all my strength and zeal into the work. There is so much to be done and so many improvements and renovations to be made.' The following day, Whit Monday: 'I worked even harder all the day than the day before and it was 4.30 before I sat down to rest abit. How I enjoy working like that. I feel a different being entirely there to what I do at Paris. How I long all the week for Saturday to come.'

The gardening gene that he seems to have inherited from the Kentish Tindalls was to blossom in adulthood. The creation of a beautiful and tree-hung garden from an empty meadow in Hertfordshire was to be the joy and pride of his adult life.

The ancient village of Châtillon occupied the site of a prehistoric hill-fort on the highest hill to the south of Paris. When Arthur Jacob was in the Latin Quarter it was a distant place, but even after the wall of the 1840s had extended the boundary of Paris over much of the countryside Châtillon still had a fine view over the meadows and windmills of Issy and Vanves. The population was then about fifteen hundred; fifty years later, at the beginning of the 1890s, it was still only a thousand more. A large number of them, according to the Census, were retired people living off property and savings. So, a genteel place of retreat. There were 339 houses, just one small workshop employing ten people, some old stone quarries, and farms nearby.

But Châtillon's country days were coming to an end. The simple charm that drew families like the Lemoignes to it would eventually be destroyed by their very presence, as the village bit by bit became a suburb. Gas street lighting had come, along with the tram, and in 1893 the local Council decided to give street numbers to the houses along the main road from Paris. For the time being, however, the grassy fortifications and the rural semi-slum at their foot still provided a barrier to Paris's slow, relentless expansion. *Les fortifs'* were demolished after the First World War, but even then the peculiar, separate identity of the Zone persisted for another generation. Other families, living in modest comfort as the Lemoignes had, still discovered in Châtillon their archetypal dream of a little house near apple blossom and birdsong within a tram-ride of the great city. We shall meet one of them.

Soon after the fourteenth of July, that watershed date which, even today, makes Parisians feel, as their great-grandparents did, that they ought to be leaving town for a summer of harvesting with country relations, Bertie left the Lemoignes for a while. He went first to the Normandy seacoast, to look at Caen, Trouville, Honfleur and Villerville, and then on the overnight boat from Le Havre to Southampton. The expedition – his first as an adult – was full of architectural delights and unusual expenses such as 'candied apple for Howard' and eight francs for a hotel room, breakfast and dinner ('splendid cooking'). At dawn, from the deck of the ship, he observed some of the British naval fleet with true-born English pride. 'Then, on landing at Southampton, train to Waterloo, then home to Lewisham.'

Home life at once reclaimed him: tennis parties, walks over the fields round Catford, much cleaning, mending and tinkering with his bicycle and the installation of 'new pneumatic tyres'. In August, the whole family took off for one of those very English nineteenth-century holidays in lodgings in what was apparently a chilly East Coast resort. Much rain fell, but 'splendid bathing trips' are nevertheless reported. The beloved bike came too: Bertie rode it from Lewisham to Liverpool Street where it accompanied him on the train. Just before departure he recorded, 'What a shame Adela isn't going to stay with us as she did two years ago. I shall miss her tremendously.' However, Adela seems to have been staying nearby, as there are frequent references to her on bathing and picnic parties. Father, meanwhile, was not a constant presence. At times the London office claimed him, and over one weekend he went off alone to the Yarmouth horse races.

By September the family were home. Bertie spent odd days at the office (now expanded into an eighteenth-century house in Covent Garden) 'helping with foreign correspondence'. Late in the month he went back to Paris. He found the Lemoignes at Châtillon in a heatwave which, in that climatically dislocated year, lasted till October. Temperatures rose to thirty-five degrees centigrade – Indian levels of heat. Days were spent indoors, avoiding the sun, and all the evening in the garden in the warm dark. 'It is really very remarkable, and will probably never happen again in my lifetime,' Bertie noted. (He lived to be ninety-six, but his prediction was correct.) 'I wrote a long letter to Adela after déjeuner, how I do love writing such letters and being able to give vent to one's feelings.'

In the first days of October, Paris reclaimed the household. Bertie's comment 'We all left Châtillon, which I shall probably never see again' seems a little sad after his selfless gardening there in the summer. 'And now I have begun again my monotonous routine of business life, coming and going to and fro and copying out the same letters, going to the same place, buying the same books . . . We are just approaching the busiest time.' In fact, for the long period in Paris when he was working in the Rue Bonaparte the days are mostly left blank, except for Saturday evenings and Sundays, his only day off. On Saturday 5th October he 'escaped from business for half an hour' to watch Pasteur's funeral cortège pass through the Place St Michel on its way to Notre Dame. On the Sunday it poured with rain as he was returning via the Grand Boulevards from Mass in a distant church – 'It was tremendously full. The music and singing were very fine indeed, still sounding in my head.' Later in the afternoon guests arrived, frustrating his attempt to give Matilde a lesson in poker-work. For Monday he wrote: '. . . We had a very fine day and abit warmer too, how I longed to be on my bicycle and away to Fontainebleau or Versailles or St Germain [en Laye] instead of being glued to my desk . . . The rain seems to have brought out the chestnuts and other trees on the Boulevards, some are in full flower again, some with flowers and no leaves.'

On the following Sunday he visited the Jardin des Plantes, then, as if tracing the pathway of Arthur Jacob long ago, found his way to Dupuytren's museum in the Rue de l'Ecole de Médecine and was rather overcome by the deformed babies in glass jars – 'To think that the human race can produce such dreadful things out of its loins is very dreadful, to think of it makes me shudder and feel quite sick.' *Loins*. Emotions less spiritual than his tenderness for Adela clearly stirred in Bertie's repressed heart.

Monsieur Lemoigne made a brief work trip to London and, in the circumstances, stayed as a guest at Lewisham. The campaign to ensure his loyalty was evidently proceeding. Shortly after he came back, Bertie made another brief escape during office hours. He raced from the Place St Germain about three-quarters of a mile up the Rue de Rennes to witness a spectacle which subsequently became enshrined in Paris iconography:

'At about four o'clock there was a terrible accident at the Gare Montparnasse, the break [*sic*] of a train refused to act and it dashed into the station at full speed, carried the buffers before it and broke its way right through the station which is high above the road, and the engine fell over into the Place de Rennes and is now hanging over the balustrade with the tender attached. The buffers saved the passengers from the telescoping of the front . . . Now the engine is in a ludicrous position upside down with crowds of sight seers around it . . . The driver and stoker jumped off.'

There had been a rumour running through the Latin Quarter that a hundred people were dead. In fact, as the carriages had just missed toppling over after the engine, most of the passengers had not even realised what had happened. Bertie knew by the evening that only one person had been killed: he thought it was the newspaper seller who had had the misfortune to be standing on the pavement exactly under the trajectory of the runaway engine. In fact it was the paper seller's wife who was crushed by it. The following day the press reported: *'Madame Héguillard, mother of two young children, had abandoned for just a few minutes her work as a seamstress to take her husband's place at the newspaper stand while he went to get the evening editions.'* The irony of her becoming the main news herself in the next day's editions was much commented on. And indeed the whole combination of circumstances – the lethally powerful steam train, the newspapers, the hustling modern world with its ready photography, the wife taking the man's place as so many women would have to twenty years later in the large-scale disaster of the First World War – was to make the event emblematic of 1890s Paris for subsequent generations.

'Sunday, 27th October. I spent a most enjoyable day with the Lemoignes under the hospitable roof of M. and Mme. Ferbin[?] at Asnières. They had given me a special invitation although I had never met them before, and they received me most kindly. I am sure that if I were asked about abit more into the society of other people instead of being continually confined to the narrow circle I am in here, it would do no end of good to my French which I almost despair of ever improving. This is the very first time I have ever been invited out to a meal in France and I do hope it will not be the last . . .'

At the beginning of November his father and step-mother arrived for a visit. He had booked them a room at the Hôtel Voltaire on the quay near the Pont des Arts (the family hotel in which George Moore had lived in comfort while working on his Left Bank novel of love and poverty). Bertie met them at the Gare du Nord and brought them back for an informal meal at the Lemoignes' – 'their Pot au Feu, which is always nice'. Hearing his parents' 'stumbling attempts to speak the language' made him realise temporarily how much progress he himself had made. Catharine Tindall ('Mothery') seemed to have forgotten the language which she must surely, Bertie thought, have once known? Due to her aristocratic father's bigamy and therefore the family's anomalous social situation, she had spent much of her childhood in Brittany.

Albert Alfred had probably been wise to ensure a more intellectual mother for his elder children before indulging himself with Catharine, although there may have been rather more in her head than readily appeared. More than thirty-five years later, when he was dead, she at last revealed a fervent support for the Rights of Women. She had apparently been incubating this through the years in Albert Alfred's company, head bent over her darning, but had prudently kept it to herself.

Sunday was spent 'hurrying my people' round his own favourite sights of Paris, including Cluny – 'Mothery was perfectly charmed by it.' Albert Alfred escaped to 'see his agent in Montmartre'. The next day brought torrential rain, and they went to *Manon* at the Opéra Comique in the evening. 'A terrific heat, as there always seems to be in all the theatres here. Myself scarcely felt it, what with the spell of all the lovely music and splendid acting, although we had much trouble to pursuade Father not to go out in the middle, he was thinking so much of the microbes.' An odd sidelight on the preoccupations of that otherwise proverbially robust man. The result of too much haphazard contact with medical literature, perhaps. Or were the microbes a pretext because he felt hemmed in and wished to escape again? – to stroll, smoking a cigar, down the lighted boulevard, open to any chance encounter, stopping off perhaps for a drink in a café-bar glittering with cut glass, as he had done in Paris twenty-five years before when he was young and unencumbered.

On one evening the Lemoignes, true to French bourgeois style, organised a formal dinner for their guests – 'a most swell affaire . . . about 10 courses'. There was shopping for the younger children at the Bon Marché, the huge Left Bank department store depicted by Zola in *Au Bonheur des Dames*, and on the last day in the Rue de Rivoli: 'Father bought Mothery a lovely cape at the "Grand Magazin du Louvre" for 148 francs.' There were more visits, no doubt enforced by Bertie, to churches and to the Louvre, and the next day they left. 'They seem to have enjoyed themselves immensely here in spite of their bad luck in having such weather and of Mothery having such tight boots that it hurt her so much to walk that she was forced to borrow a pair of mine.' It is cheering to realise that Bertie's relationship with this undemanding stepmother was close enough for him to lend her boots.

It is consoling also to find a month later, among the sparse entries as his time in Paris drew to a close:

'Today I fixed as my last in the office, and really I am very sorry at it too, as in spite of the excessively long hours I enjoy my work thoroughly ... As a reward for my services M. Lemoigne kindly presented me with a case of Shakespeare's works in thirteen volumes, a very nice edition indeed ... This present came as a very agreeable surprise to me, as I had expected nothing ... I have learnt so much during the five months and a half I have worked for him.'

So the stay in Paris was a success after all? Well, hardly. For only three days later a real cry from the heart breaks through the carapace of dutiful gratitude, optimism and grown-up decent behaviour that Bertie had tried hard to grow round himself:

'What a cruel disappointment it is to me to know now that I must return home my object only half accomplished. Why did I not have the good fortune to fall into such good hands as I did in Erfurt to give me the power to learn French really as I wanted to, as I did German. The consciousness of a year half wasted lies heavy on my heart and I am dispirited and discouraged. Since the death of my poor mother I have never cried, until today when I sobbed like a child for half an hour, comfortless, with disappointment weighing heavy on my heart. I have learned much at business but not the French which I came for; how could I without help, without encouragement. At Erfurt, it was, I learned German so easily through the continuous intercourse with intimate friends. The Lemoignes I have never been able to make real friends much less intimate, and their greatest encouragement seems to be "I don't understand more than half you say" ...'

This diary entry goes straight on to mention having been given two tickets for the Odéon theatre by a customer, and taking Monsieur Lemoigne with him.

The reference to his mother's death, six and a half years before, surely gives the clue to much more. Whatever accumulated grief and loneliness lay beneath Bertie's sudden bout of crying, it was certainly about something other than a failure to learn fluent French. In any case, the letters that it was part of his work to compose several years later, when he was a fully fledged member of his father's staff in Covent Garden, show that his French was entirely adequate to that purpose.

The last days in Paris passed in intensive theatre-going, revisiting museums and the buying of presents, including 'a doll for the Concierge's baby'. The Lemoignes do not seem to have been on his present list, but he bought a cookery book and a chestnut pot for his stepmother, beads for the baby sister, 'music' for Maud and a compass for Howard – 'May he like it.' He packed his trunk 'which from books alone is two thirds full'. On the last evening

'We did not have dinner until after nine o'clock and then afterwards everybody sat down to read and not a word was spoken. What a difference to my last evening at Erfurt!!! The Billias [?] were so very sorry to lose [me] and all my friends but here I have no friends worth the name and the Lemoignes did not seem to mind my going at all, and I am sure their attitude to me lately makes me all the more glad to leave them.'

He left the next day in a flurry of overweight bags and the unaccustomed expenses of a cab and porters.

'Saturday, December 21st. At last I am started from that inhospitable Paris and glad I was too, to get away from it. I took the ten o'clock train from Paris to Dieppe and from there to Newhaven . . . There were very few passengers and only about 12 of the 2nd class stopped on deck, but they were very sociable and I was chatting the whole time pretty well. It was extremely cold, and a bitter wind was blowing the whole time. It was fairly smooth. The effect on the water of the constant changes in the sky were most beautiful – rainbow, snow, rain and brilliant sun.'

A family Christmas awaited him.

Chapter XIV

FAMILY MATTERS. AND A WORLD WAR

After he was fully adult, Bertie no longer kept a daily record of his doings or thoughts. Physically, the diaries continued all his life, miniature leather-bound books each about three inches by five, stacking up year after year, decade after decade. He kept them all in boxes in his attic. But in them he recorded only his daily cash expenses. Thus an ordinary weekday might read 'Lunch 11d. Papers 8d. Omnibus 1d. Tobacco 1s.2d.', while the Sunday on which his first child was born has 'Telephone 2d. Stamps and telegrams 3s.1d.' followed the next day by 'Advert. birth Morning Post 5s., Grapes for B 1s.6d.' All the days of his life, banal, joyful or tragic, were captured in his hieroglyphic, condensed form, expressing so little but redolent of much.

It seems to us now obsessional, pointless, this preoccupation with small change in a man who, once embarked on adult life, did not really need to count the pennies. But he was following a practice that, in his generation, was widespread, considered to be a good middle-class habit like a daily sponge-down in front of the washstand, or going to church on Sunday. Only right at the end of his life do the accounts waver: small sums of money are repeated, crossed out, altered, and finally the record is taken over in his last year by another hand.

By the later 1890s, after one or two educational stages in other people's offices, Bertie had joined his father full time in Henrietta Street, Covent Garden. Besides himself, Albert Alfred and Mr Cox, there were now five full-time members of staff there, including two in the basement warehouse. There was as yet no electric light, telephone or typewriter. All the letters continued to be written by hand in the 'copying ink' of the period, a preparation which, when the page was pressed into another one, produced a kind of brownish carbon-copy for record in the letter book. In other respects, paperwork seems to have been kept to a minimum. Long after, Bertie noted that there were 'no stock books, no sales were marked off, there was no stock-taking carried out and the accounts were not audited'.[1] At the end of each financial year, whatever was in the bank, after wages and other expenses had been met, was simply regarded as profit and shared out, minus any monies taken during the year, between Tindall and Cox. This primitive system must have worked adequately, as Albert Alfred and family were by then living comfortably in the new rural home near Maidstone from which he and Bertie commuted daily. Years later, however, there was some protracted wrangle about this period with the Inland Revenue: maybe Bertie's arrival in the firm was providential in saving Albert Alfred, in the end, from worse trouble.

'Fresh from an accountant's office,' Bertie wrote, 'I thought the situation to be an impossible one, and soon started stock-books etc . . . I also turned my attention to the method of keeping the authors' accounts, which was elementary in the extreme.' One may guess that some of the medical authors in the expanding publishing business, being less interested in royalties than in seeing their research and opinions in print, had not been receiving all the monies that should have been due to them.

Meanwhile, as the century that had seen unprecedented growth and change and opportunity drew to a
close, the usual copious orders for books continued to
be sent across the Channel to Lemoigne and to the
Baillières in the Rue Hautefeuille, couched in the usual
peremptory tones. By 1901, however, all the letters in
French are in Bertie's hand and the tone, though formal,
is more temperate. The first typewriter arrived in 1903,
along with a female typist. She stayed until 1919: indeed,
several staff members who joined in those years were to
stay for the rest of their working lives. Evidently Albert
Alfred's dynamic approach made subordinates feel valued;
'He did not hesitate to rebuke any author or member of
staff whom he thought to be dilatory or idle, but such
a rebuke was generally followed within a few days by an
unusually friendly letter or greeting and it was rare for
the recipient to retain a sense of grievance.'

It must have been in the early 1900s that Albert Alfred's
deafness, which had been coming on gradually for a
decade following what was probably a virus infection,
became severe. His eventual obituary in *The Medical Press*
recorded '. . . but nothing daunted he carried on his life's
work with the utmost vigour. He was by nature genial,
he enjoyed the company of his friends and was fond of
entertaining them, but his deafness compelled him to
forgo that pleasure . . . [It also] cut him off from music,
to which he was passionately devoted. He had a rich
baritone voice – there had even been talk of him taking
up music as a profession . . .'

Or the music hall, perhaps? Was that what was originally in the mind of the ambitious teenager who made
his way to London in the 1850s?

The partisan obituarist of *The Medical Press* refrained
from mentioning that he also ruthlessly made use of
his disability as a defence. When any discussion took a
line that was not to his liking, or bored him, he simply
laid down his ear trumpet – or, when one of the early

deaf-aids replaced the trumpet, he would make it whistle till conversation was impossible, and then, with an innocent expression, turn it off, declaring, 'Well, my boy, if I don't understand that at my age, how can you possibly know anything about it?'

When he was in his late eighties, and still insisted on coming into work, a member of staff who travelled the same route used to be detailed to follow him at a discreet distance. One day they chanced to meet on a traffic island in the Strand. Albert Alfred plunged into a small gap between the moving motor cars and buses regardless of danger, remarking over his shoulder to his minder, 'If you have all night to waste, my boy, I haven't.' He died in his bed at ninety-one, only a few days after his last appearance in the office.

In 1907 Bertie's younger brother Howard joined the firm too. He had been sent to Haileybury School and then, unlike Bertie, had been allowed to go on to Cambridge. His image has been fading now for ninety years: the last remaining person who recalled him in the flesh is now gone. He seems to have been, like Bertie, a rather serious, decent young man, though with a love of fun. A Cambridge photograph shows him posing in a laughing human pyramid with three other healthy-looking undergraduates in three-piece suits. He had a taste for good works – Pembroke College had what was artlessly described, in the language of the time, as 'a mission to the slums' in Lambeth – and he was good at sports, especially long-distance running. Like Bertie, he could produce fine pen and ink drawings. His main role within Baillière, Tindall & Cox was to travel around the country seeing agents, booksellers and potential authors.

By 1914 staff numbers had risen to twenty. On annual office outing snaps they stand in rows on South Coast beaches – stiff collars and fresh piqué, laced boots, eyes screwed up in jollity against forgotten suns. Later, before tea, a few boots came off for paddling. No one actually went so far as to bathe, but Albert Alfred (who, after all, had spent his unmentioned childhood by the sea, in Hastings) liked the idea that they might. Every year he brought along his own bathing suit, concealed in a folded newspaper, hoping that one of his employees would give him the excuse to plunge in too.

The firm was to have another half-century of prosperity and increase ahead of it as an independent entity, before disappearing into the maw of a huge transatlantic conglomeration in the 1960s, just a hundred years after Albert Alfred had founded his empire on hope and opportunism in one shared room off the Strand.

In 1906 Bertie got married. 'Got' is, I think, the appropriate word, as, however willingly he participated, the marriage was initially arranged by others.

Adela, one must suppose, had been dislodged from his heart or had simply been carried off elsewhere. Careful questioning of the last remaining informant produced a vague recollection of the name and the suggestion that she was some connection of Bertie's stepmother, probably a niece. This would explain why she was treated with cousinly familiarity on family holidays, but also why it might not have been considered quite decent that Bertie and she should pair off. In Victorian and Edwardian England, unlike France where the propensity was for unions that kept all the money within the family, marriages with relatives were discouraged. In any case, in the few years before the diaries proper peter out, there are many references to 'sweet, jolly girls', usually friends of Maud. Living at home, Bertie did not lack female company. But at just thirty, he was apparently heart-free. The firm was doing very well and he had recently been made a partner. Clearly the next step, from the perspective of his elders, was that he should 'settle down with some nice girl'.

*   *   *

Meanwhile, in Dublin, matters were going rather less well for the Jacob family, or at any rate for those of them that were still there. The elder children, on whose upbringing so much of Archibald Jacob's chaotically managed earnings had been spent, were now launched into life or matrimony in various far-flung places, but Archibald himself had succumbed to chronic asthma and fatigue at the beginning of 1901. His death, though predictable, was unexpected when it occurred, and his widow and the younger children were left so badly provided for that the medical world of Dublin launched a memorial fund to keep them going. This fact, never mentioned in the family, only became apparent to me through a newspaper cutting I found on file at the Royal College of Surgeons in Ireland a hundred years later.

The only Jacob son still at home was Donald, the youngest of the family, a sweet-natured, blond boy, delicately built. Aged seventeen, he was summarily despatched, in a new corduroy suit and looking woebegone, to Canada. There, it was unrealistically hoped, he might take to farming. Needless to say he did not, and it was fifteen years before anyone saw him again. He reappeared in the middle of the Great War as a private in the Canadian army. He had acquired an unfamiliar accent in the various parts of North America to which he had wandered, and a still more unfamiliar and flamboyant taste in clothes. He had also acquired, in the army, a favoured buddy ('the Kid') whose presence with him on leaves caused his rediscovered sisters some (unspoken) pondering.

By 1902 the widowed Mrs Jacob and the three daughters still with her had moved from the big house in Ely Place to a much smaller one in the Dublin suburbs. Gone now, too, was the summer home down the coast, the happy family holidays when the girls were encouraged by their doctor father to bathe every day, long hair floating out like mermaids. Gone, too, the social life centred round 'the Castle set'. Although no one voiced the fact baldly, matrimonial prospects for these girls were now not nearly as good as they had been for their elder sisters. Laura, the eldest of the remaining three and slightly deaf since childhood, was tacitly designated Mother's helpmate. Mab, the youngest, was despatched to train as a nurse, an occupation by then just about acceptable for a doctor's daughter, and to which she bravely stuck although temperamentally unsuited to it. As to Blanche, who was agreed to be the cleverest and had been their father's favourite – what to do with lively Blanche?

In the event, she seems to have spent a good deal of time with the ship-building Coote family of Liverpool, who were related to various other Cootes of Queen's County and Sligo and connected to the Jacob clan: Arthur Jacob's wife had been a Carroll-Coote. They apparently took to Blanche, and the fact that she was almost certainly a paid companion to Mrs Coote was another of those never-spoken things that only became evident to me long after all concerned were dead.

She was lucky to escape becoming a nursery governess, then the only other option readily available to middle-class girls whose own education had been sketchy and imprac-tical. Governesses only just counted as 'ladies' and were, from the Jacob point of view, perilously near slipping down that dreaded slope into the great unmentionable swamp of the lower middle classes, from which there was felt to be no ready way out into a suitable marriage or anything else.

It was a far cry from the days thirty-odd years before, when the Jacobs of Ely Place had 'tamed' Mr Tindall, graciously accepting him into their circle because he was convivial and could sing well. Did he, I wonder, feel a certain dark pleasure at the stumbling fortunes of a family who had once been in a position to patronise him? Or did he just see an excellent opportunity, a way of strength-ening his firm's connection with the Dublin medical world and acquiring for himself the entire rights to *The Medical Press*?

At any rate, in 1905 Albert Alfred suggested to Mrs Jacob, disconsolate and lost in her suburban sitting room and her crepe-trimmed toque, that Blanche might spend a holiday at the Tindall home near Maidstone. May Tindall was married now (very satisfactorily, from her father's point of view, to a Wimpole Street surgeon-gynaecologist) but Maud was still at home. Bertie, it was indicated, had seen a photo of Blanche and was 'quite smitten'.

Blanche was not really pretty but she was animated and she had abundant and lovely hair, genuinely golden, as Bertie must have seen when finally presented to her in the flesh. She was also warm, musical and, in the best Irish tradition, an amusing raconteuse with a fine Dublin vocabulary of vivid figures of speech. Like many people with more intelligence than education, she could be bossy and a troublemaker, but then Bertie was used to bossy people and had much experience of withdrawing into some inner fortress of his own till the trouble passed. In any case he too could be tactless, single-minded and – just occasionally – lost his temper spectacularly.

According to Blanche, years later, he was so shy on that first holiday in Maidstone that he spent most of the time fiddling with his bicycle and barely looked at her. No doubt his extreme self-consciousness was due to the fact that he had been told forthrightly by Albert Alfred what he was supposed to do.

Blanche too knew what she was supposed to do. She could expect no dowry beyond a little family jewellery. She was almost thirty-one, nine months older than Bertie himself. This was her big chance: no other would come.

Neither Laura nor Mab had such an opportunity. Both remained single.

*   *   *

The not so very young couple were married the following May in St Ann's Anglican church in the centre of Dublin, which had been the Jacob church in Ely Place days. Blanche wore an expensive and beautiful lace dress given to her by the Cootes. It was the Jacob family's last appearance in fashionable Dublin society.

Half a dozen years earlier, by one of those symmetric coincidences that seem to carry a message that remains opaque, the railway line that ran into Dublin from the south suffered the same grotesque accident that Bertie had seen at the Gare Montparnasse. On Valentine's Day 1900 an engine coming from Dundrum and Milltown ran too fast down the last, curving stretch from Canal Dock. At the small but elegantly Palladian terminus at the bottom of Harcourt Street, it crashed through the buffers and through a wall a yard thick to hang crazily over the street. The fireman jumped clear but the driver's right arm was crushed between engine and tender and had to be amputated to get him out.

The Jacob girls, still living then not far off in Ely Place and unaware that it was their father's last year of life, joined the crowds that passed by the scene to stare and wonder. Only years later, in assorted lifetime exile in England, did that memorable crash come to symbolise for them the destruction of the whole elegant Anglo-Irish world of which they had been a part. By then, the disappearance of that world seemed as if it had always been a fact, a death foretold. Blanche, more perceptive perhaps than some of her staunchly Unionist family, wrote long after: 'Looking back dispassionately on the people among whom my youth was spent, I can see that even in their hey-day they were doomed to extinction . . . Their end came violently, and they left Ireland with their houses burning behind them, but though it might have come more gradually and more kindly . . . it would have come inevitably.' By then, consciously distancing herself from the Ireland of the Easter Rising and the Troubles, she had largely lost her Dublin intonation, and had become what she herself ironically described as 'a fairly satisfactory example of the conventional British matron'.

Bertie and Blanche had their honeymoon in Ireland, starting in County Cork. Bertie's sundry expenses on the wedding day include 'Cycles booked 2s., porter 6d., Tickets Mallow £1.19s.2d., Tea baskets 2s.' – and, rather alarmingly, 'Smelling salts 1s.' Did he have in mind that the physical realities of the wedding night might be so alarming to Blanche that she would need reviving? Or did Blanche herself ask for salts?

Their first child was born in a London mansion flat rather less than a year later, delivered by May's husband. It was during the three-year interval that separated this birth from the subsequent one that they undertook a trip to Paris. I do not know where they stayed. Perhaps at the Hôtel Voltaire, but more likely I think, for this occasion, at somewhere grander such as the Hôtel du Louvre, a massive Right Bank establishment much favoured by English visitors. From this comfortable base, I am sure that Bertie firmly escorted Blanche round all his favourite places. This was to be her life's fate, married to a genuine lover of art and architecture, and on the whole she stood up to it nobly. She had learnt by then that Bertie was never content just to spend five or ten minutes in a church absorbing the atmosphere. Baedeker in hand, his instinct was to master the whole place. 'He always wants to see *everything*,' she was to complain in later years to their children. 'Oh Bertie dear – must we go on there now?' became in time one of her standard phrases, and, later again in life, 'Oh Bertie dear . . . my *feet*.' Small in stature and not particularly strong, she always appeared more vivacious than he, organising more social life for him than he really wanted, but she was in the end worn out by him as she had humorously predicted. She died almost twenty years before he did.[2]

It is not clear whether the couple visited the Lemoignes while they were in Paris. Bertie may well have wanted to show off his bride and his status as a grown man, but on the other hand he did not have a happy memory of his year with them and Monsieur Lemoigne had probably faded back into being a business connection. Or had he? There are suggestions, faint as foot-marks on a wet pavement, that with Matilde at any rate some sort of contact was maintained.

However much the suppressed atmosphere of the Lemoigne home had irritated and wearied Bertie, they were not an uncultured family. Monsieur Lemoigne's occupation and their Left Bank habitat exposed them to a general awareness of literature and painting at an epoch when Paris was becoming the art capital of the world. Painting, in any case, had long been a Latin Quarter occupation: the Beaux Arts institution was in the Rue Bonaparte near the family premises. The otherwise dreary Madame Lemoigne apparently knew someone who made copies of sculptures for the Louvre, for she had once taken Bertie to see his workshop. She had other artistic acquaintances, including one who had painted ceilings and frescoes in the Hôtel de Ville. (Does that explain Paul and Bertie's uncharacteristic presence there at a ball?) On one of the snowiest Sundays in the bitter winter of 1895, Bertie was taken by the Lemoignes 'to an exhibition of pictures by French ladies'. He was not impressed, and may have annoyed his hosts by making this fact apparent. 'It was . . . a very poor affair, indeed there were very few pictures worth looking at and some were simple atrocities of the noble art. Certainly I don't think much of the female talent of France if that is a fair representation of it.'

('Oh Bertie, *really*,' as Blanche would later have said,

and, in an aside to any third party who happened to be there, 'Don't take any notice, my dear. He's always so critical.')

Were the pictures really so bad? Or was it that Bertie, barely nineteen and a stickler for accurate draughtsmanship in his own work, was failing to recognise the possibilities, however tentative and amateur, that the Impressionist movement had opened up for French eyes?

Six years later he seems to have been more receptive. For in the mean time Matilde, by then in her early twenties, was taking some artistic steps. Had she been an English girl of the period, as yet unmarried, she might have absorbed her time and energies with golf, tennis, bicycling or amateur dramatics. Being a child of the Latin Quarter, she turned to brush and canvas, frequenting one of the many private studios that received young men and women for lessons and practice. Towards the end of the century the life-drawing classes in these establishments became integrated, and the Ecole des Beaux Arts, till then a bastion of riotous male studentry, started admitting women. In January 1902 Bertie appended a postscript to one of Baillière, Tindall & Cox's otherwise formal business letters to Lemoigne: *'Mes compliments à Mademoizelle Matilde sur son succès au Salon. J'ai fait écrire au secretaire de l'Exposition, mais je n'ai pas encore de réponse. J'éspère qu'elle viendra chez nous pendant l'exposition.'* ('My congratulations to Mademoiselle Matilde for her success at the Salon. I have had someone write to the secretary of the Exhibition, but haven't yet had a reply. I hope she will visit us while the exhibition is on.')

Matilde, it seems, had done well, so well that a picture or pictures by her had been selected for an exhibition in London. A whole possible future life, even if a relatively obscure one, was apparently opening up for this particular *jeune fille bien élevée*, a world beyond the cramped flat in the Rue de l'Abbaye, the closely chaperoned outings, an arranged marriage with a bored cousin – if she was lucky. I cannot tell how far her luck went, since she disappears from the patchy record. But conjecture, by a different link, suggests for her a possible continuing role in this story.

When the First World War broke on an armed but essentially unprepared Europe, it was a popular cause. Very few people, in their worst dreams, foresaw the scale of the slaughter that was to come. Like many other young men of every class, Howard Tindall soon vounteered for the Army. He was thirty, unmarried, and as the youngest partner in the family firm he could arguably be spared 'for the duration'. By the spring of 1915 he was an officer in the Royal Berkshire Regiment, and soon after that was sent to France.

Bertie, rising forty and the father of two children, came into a different category. With Mr Cox retired, Howard overseas and Albert Alfred in his mid-seventies, Bertie was now the indispensable linchpin of Baillière, Tindall & Cox. Fortunately, a number of the books the firm produced were used by the Army medical establishment, so in 1916, when conscription came in, Bertie was exempted from active service. He joined a reserve force, however, called the Old Boys Corps (read 'old boys from public schools') and spent occasional weekends, rather enjoyably, at camp, digging trenches in East Anglia or guarding government buildings in London. In Hertfordshire, where he, Blanche and the children were now living in a brand-new home with a large garden, the local great house became a convalescent home for wounded officers. Blanche bicycled off there regularly to work shifts as a VAD, a volunteer nurse organised under a government scheme. She tended (her daughter later recalled) 'young men on crutches, or with empty sleeves or jumping and twittering with shell shock'. Meanwhile her younger sister Mab and her sister-in-law Maud were both nursing in France. By that time the

very name 'France', which for a hundred years had signi-
fied a place of escape, culture, enlightenment and daring
if possibly scandalous ideas, had acquired the timbre of
doom.

As for May, she and her surgeon husband had bought
a weekend retreat near Bertie and Blanche. Why they
had chosen the same country district was not clear, since
May did not really get on with Blanche once she could
no longer patronise her as a naïve Irish bride new to
London ways. Big, handsome, clever May, her father's
daughter and a fine singer, had had no children. She thus
failed to achieve her own bizarrely limited but stated
ambition of 'one daughter, to look after me in my old
age'. Turned forty, she had become touchy and difficult,
and the family watchword was 'For goodness' sake, don't
upset May.' No offers to do anything as taxing as nursing,
or any other war work, came from her. For a life that
earlier seemed full of promise, hers was peculiarly devoid
of achievement, fulfilment or apparent happiness, though
her compact and dapper husband was everyone's favourite
uncle. He also earned a great deal of money. His fee for
removing an appendix, an oddly fashionable operation
at that time, was a hundred guineas (£105), a huge sum.
He is reputed always to have handed the extra five pounds
straight to May.

Howard came home several times on leave and stayed
with Bertie and Blanche. Blanche always remembered that
he was 'so kind to the children'. Reserved by nature, or
through his upbringing under Albert Alfred's dominion,
he did not say much about life at the Front, or about the
massacres of the Somme, which he survived. By summer
1917 he was Brigade Signalling Officer. A couple of snap-
shots, taken in July against a deceptively peaceful
background of hop fields between Poperinge and Ypres,
show a pleasant, reliable-looking soldier, moustached and
more heavily built than his elder brother. He appears more
than his age (he had just turned thirty-three) and his

expression is rather sad. At the end of that same month, on the very first day of the murderous Third Battle of Ypres, which has gone down in collective memory as Passchendaele, he was killed.

In mid-August Bertie sent a letter to their sister Maud, who was working in a French hospital. The double sheet of paper is bordered with black, and so is the small envelope. Maud evidently kept it all her life.

'My darling Maud,
    'I have not written before because I knew you would be deluged with letters.
    '. . . It is a dreadful loss for all of us and more particularly for you, dear girl, right away from everyone as you are, that it must be still harder for you to bear. I have thought of you so much during the last fortnight with the whole weight of your grief and misery on your shoulders and no one to share it with . . . May, and I believe you too, had made up your minds that the dear boy would never come through it but I was always optimistic and consequently I felt it as a real knock down blow. I have been carrying on these last 2½ years at the office as best I could, doing things in the way he liked so that he would find all in order when he came back and it has all been in vain.'

Bertie may have been right in perceiving that his younger brother had been the true inheritor of the family business, more suited to it than he, Bertie, really was.[3]

'I find it so hard to go on, knowing now that I shall never have his assistance that I had counted so much upon, but must carry on alone. A few minutes before I went off to camp on the Friday before Bankholiday I had a few lines from him practically admitting that he was going up to his death, and so simply and bravely put that you can imagine my anxiety all the time I was at camp hearing the great guns pounding away night after night and all day long . . . He was killed the day after he wrote that note . . .

'My heart goes out to you in this dreadful time, how I wish you were amongst us here instead of amidst strangers.

'Ever your loving brother, Bertie.'

Though in her heart Blanche was less conventional and probably less genuinely religious than Bertie, the letter she sent Maud conforms more than Bertie's to the received party line about dying for one's country and the Christian belief in a better life: 'I picture him now with "Bubbles" and all those other friends who have passed on. Indeed a band of Happy Warriors who have made good in the highest and noblest sense . . .' But she writes further down the page, 'It is so impossible to see good in all the frightful things that are happening that our only hope is in God.' Bertie too wrote that one could not understand 'the purpose of it all and how and when good will come out of all this evil'. This terrible suspicion, that all the destruction of precious lives might in fact be quite futile, was by that stage in the War racking middle England.

In France, too, the mood was bitter. There the heaviest losses were not among the officer class, as they were in England, but among the conscripted peasantry. In remote rural areas, whose men were perceived by the military authorities as expendable cannon fodder, whole villages were stripped of their rising generation. It is always said that the long tradition of stonemasons travelling from the Limousin, to build and rebuild Paris, was broken by that war – 'They'd killed the lot of them. None left.'

Three weeks after Howard's death, Blanche's brother Donald, he of the transatlantic accent and the fancy suits, who had already been seriously wounded the year before, was also killed, in the suicidal Canadian attempt to take Vimy Ridge. No letters survive to tell how the family coped with this double blow. Long after, Blanche said in the memoir written for her children that Donald had been ready 'to die for his country' – 'His life had been a chequered one and he did not fear losing it, and when I recall him it is always as one who had loved and suffered much.' Blanche always felt that Donald's life had been blighted at seventeen when, after their father's death, he was sent off alone to Canada. It was a source of regret and guilt to her that at the time she had not argued against this.

But Howard's life, up to the War, had been full of promise. After his death, Bertie discovered that his discreet brother had for some time been courting a 'nice, suitable girl' met through the Lambeth Mission, and that they had planned to marry. The Great War did not just destroy individual lives but whole dimensions of future family life, leaving in their place silence, a meaningless emptiness. Did the girl find another mate? I wonder. Or did she join that huge, amorphous, inter-war band of 'superfluous women' for whom there were simply not enough men to go round?

May's husband wrote – and later published himself, with other verses, in a 'slim volume' – a poem for Howard beginning:

> *Noble heroes round his grave are lying*
> *On the fatal fields of Flanders slain . . .*

More specifically, what remained of Howard ended up in Hooge Crater Cemetery, which did not yet exist at the time he met his death. Subsequent back-and-forth fighting on the Ypres Salient, which achieved next to nothing at such terrible cost, obliterated all the early, hasty battlefield burials, but shortly after the War's end

Bertie received a letter from a young Lieutenant-Colonel in Howard's regiment:

'Dear Sir, I am sorry that I do not know to whom I am writing, except that you are the next of kin of the late Lieu. H.S. Tindall . . . who was a fellow officer of mine and fell quite close to me on July 31st 1917. Shortly after the action we put up three crosses at the spot in the battlefield where Tindall, my own brother A.H. Hudson and another officer named Tarrant were killed . . .'

He went on to say that the crosses were demolished by later shelling and that he had just (early 1919) had them reinstated – he enclosed a sketch. He mentioned having got an army padre to come and read a few words, and that 'I was very glad while putting up a cross for my brother also to put one up for Tindall.'

The lack of any mention of an initial burial suggests that the three men had taken the full force of an explosion which also submerged them in the notorious quagmire that was Passchendaele. It was probably thanks to Lieutenant-Colonel Hudson's action that the remnants of these three bodies were eventually retrieved and identified. They were taken to Hooge Crater, which had become a 'concentration cemetery' for bodies collected from all over the area. Here, in a landscape of military order and gardened peace that is the antithesis to the realities of War, are commemorated almost six thousand other brothers, sons, husbands and nephews. Very many of them have as an inscription on their uniform stone simply 'A soldier of the Great War. Known unto God.' (Or 'Two soldiers of the Great War', or four or five or six or even more, so violent had been the battering of this terrain.) Among these known only to God it is possible that some vestige of Donald Jacob also lies, for the remains of many Canadian soldiers ended up in that cemetery. His name appears, among innumerable others, on the mass memorial at Loos. Howard Tindall, at least, has his own headstone. The 'other officer', Tarrant, is next to him. There is no sign of Hudson.

In lieu of the forty or fifty years of life that should have remained to Howard, a plaque was put up in St John's, Lewisham. It is below the stained-glass window that Albert Alfred gave in memory of Sophia, who had died when Howard, her youngest child, was not yet five.

The area has changed a good deal since Albert Alfred's and the Simsons' day. The jolly, down-to-earth female vicar, who unlocked the church for me one day in the 1990s, said that she had never known why the memorials were there and was glad to hear about them – it would be something to tell her Sunday school.

'Their name liveth for evermore.'

But of course it doesn't. Which is why I have tried to summon back from the very edge of oblivion one dutiful First Lieutenant among innumerable others, a great-uncle dead on the frontier of France long before I was born and who, for most of my childhood, I never even knew had existed.

Albert Alfred Tindall in old age

Rue des Carmes, early twentieth century, before it was widened, looking north toward the Place Maubert

Rue de la Parcheminerie, *c.*1900, before the demolition of the oldest houses

The Rue des Noyers, 1917, before it was absorbed into the Boulevard St Germain. Alfred de Musset's family house still standing on the left

From the diary Bertie kept during his stay in Paris, 1895

Number 12, Rue Bonaparte, where Bertie worked. When this photograph was taken in 2006, it had just ceased to be a book dealers

Maud Tindall as a young woman, *c*.1910

The Rue de l'Abbaye where Bertie lodged. Number 12 is the stone-fronted house with window arches

The Hôtel des Carmes, with the Marché des Carmes below it, 1920

The water fountain that stood in the centre of the Marché des Carmes, on the site of the original monastery well. Now removed to a small public garden at the foot of the Rue de Seine

Ursula with Tom's car, mid–1930s

'Tom' Tindall as a
young soldier in 1939

'Julia' beside the Seine, *c.*1957

A modern bus squeezes down the narrowest part of the
Rue de l'Ecole de Médecine

Part IV

MAUD: 1902–1939

Chapter XV

Maud's Secret Garden

But why was Maud Tindall working in a French hospital?

A great many British women nursed in France during the Great War. Those who, like Blanche's grumpy little sister Mab, were qualified nurses were obvious candidates for full-time paid service: Mab was sent, as a Queen Alexandra military nurse, to a British hospital behind the lines, from where she twice had to be invalided home with pneumonia. But many girls from comfortable middle- and upper-class homes, and therefore with no necessity (as it was then perceived) to work for their living, went out to France and Belgium as unpaid VADs nursing in field hospitals.

I had thought that Maud might be one of these. But the Hôpital Léon Blanc, at Aix-les-Bains, south of Geneva, which is where Bertie and Blanche's letters were addressed, was far from the British Front. In fact the town ('Aches and Pains' to soldiers) was one where battle-fatigued Allied troops were sent by train for rest and respite. In the hospital, wounded French soldiers were nursed by the French Red Cross, which at that time consisted of three voluntary organisations loosely under one umbrella, including the all-female Association des Dames Françaises.

How did Maud come to join this Association? The crumbs of information on her life that have survived are few, but significant.

Maud, like Bertie and Howard but unlike the assertive May, is said to have been bullied by their father, Albert Alfred, and therefore to have become shy and secretive. It cannot have helped that she had been the sick child who was indirectly responsible for her mother's death in Hastings. As a young woman Maud was still perceived by the family to be 'delicate'. She had abundant and pretty hair and full lips, but her face was a little heavy and pensive for the taste of the times. Her niece wrote, long after her death: 'She became a silent spinster . . . She sometimes took charge of the house when our parents were away and spent her time trying to stop us from doing anything and everything in case we damaged ourselves or the house.'

As in many families of that era, a faint story persisted that Maud had remained unmarried because she had lost a beloved Someone in the War. But there may have been an overlay here of her feelings for her dead younger brother: she had always been close to Howard, who had been a small boy when their mother died. Maud was not really one of those girls whose potential husbands disappeared into the mud of Ypres and the Somme, for she was approaching forty by the time the War was over: her state of spinster-designate must have been evident already by 1914. A good many late-Victorian and Edwardian daughters of upper middle-class families did not readily find husbands in the way their mothers and grandmothers had done, largely because standards of living had risen and bringing up a family of suitably educated children was now perceived as costly. As a result, men of the same social level were expected to delay marriage till they were financially secure. This meant in practice that many men did not marry till late in their thirties or beyond, by which time they were apt to choose women significantly younger than themselves. So a fault-line appeared in marital supply and demand, which carried on from one decade to another. Left behind each time was a cohort of women living lives essentially without a purpose. To be, like the younger Jacob daughters, unmarried and unprovided for was perhaps a worse fate; but to be dependent, however comfortably, on family money, and to have no recognised role in the world beyond being a lady, must have brought its own obscure distress.

The Great War evidently gave Maud four years of intense employment. Once it was over she spent long periods with her married sister May. The convention of the time was that a sister-in-law 'counted' as a sister to the husband too, and so could share his household with total respectability. Even if May had died an untimely death, under the Church law then prevailing Arthur Giles, May's husband, could not have married Maud. *Therefore*, the unspoken looking-glass logic went, there could be no impropriety in a domestic threesome.

Maud also shared with Arthur Giles a liking for books and a taste for poetry, and both tried their hand at writing it. He and she further shared mysterious jokes. 'They used to giggle together,' their nephew remembered, 'and May used to get cross.' ('Don't upset May!') The word in the family, one of those jocular sayings that veil an awkward truth, was that Arthur Giles had 'married the wrong one'. No doubt, from his point of view, skinny, unassuming Maud provided a welcome relief from his large, bossy wife, and it could hardly be considered his fault if Maud adored him – the other half of the semi-secret family joke. Fashionable gynaecologists are in any case accustomed to their patients falling in love with them, and in later life Maud became his patient too. He apparently operated on her 'several times' for obscure internal ailments, events which caused some further suppressed mirth to Bertie and Blanche who, like many of their generation, were less naïve than they sometimes seemed.

But this image of Maud as an archetypal comic spinster, seeking emotional and physical attentions where she could, is far from being the whole picture. Perhaps she did, actually, know more about a number of things than May did, and this was what she and Arthur Giles shared. It is even conceivable that the two of them at some point *were* lovers, a possibility that family jokes could not quite encompass. He, like most medical practitioners of that era, was a great believer in the sea air of 'Dr Brighton' as an aid to convalescence: the wealthy Gileses often rented a flat there in addition to their other abodes. Arthur Giles also had one of the early motor-cars, an elegant open tourer . . . If Maud and he did actually ever organise some private space for themselves, this would shed a different light on May's famous edginess.

But Maud had, in any case, intermittently but for many years, a quite other life across the Channel.

Her niece recorded:

'She only really came to life in France . . . There she was a different person. She had French friends, and that was why she nursed through the First World War with the French Red Cross . . . I never much liked her until, as an adult, I met her in Paris and discovered her to be both a charming woman of the world and a fluent French speaker.'[1]

If she was sufficiently integrated into French life before the War to offer her services to France rather than England, and was still at home there when her niece was grown up, in the 1930s, this suggests a long-term attachment. But to what exactly, or to whom? Apparently, once across the Channel, she changed – no, not into an obviously Kept Woman but into a French version of her

English self, without the faint connotations of joke and failure that dogged English spinsterhood. There had always been a place in French society for the woman who (it was assumed) had the independence of spirit to reject the arranged marriage, or whose family could not produce the dowry that had to accompany it. So, in France, Maud became a cultured *dame d'un certain âge* with grey cotton stockings but elegant shoes and gloves, a tendency to attend Mass and a knowledge of Parisian classical theatres and art galleries. Recitals of Brahms and Debussy at the Salle Pleyel. The occasional lecture on the Old Stones of Paris: Les Amis de la Montagne Sainte Geneviève, who published regular history bulletins, were well established by then. Apparently, like a typical Frenchwoman of that kind, she favoured the Left Bank rather than the wealthier Right. But how was her Secret Garden constituted?

Did she, at some level, make a decision after her beloved brother's death that she was not going to be defeated, here in France where she had nursed young men more fortunate than he back to health, or at least to life? The land that had been the end of all Howard's hopes and dreams, and those of so many others, was one that she would continue to cultivate, even to cherish, for his sake. Or was it something more specific that drew her back and back across the Channel over the years?

It is tempting to imagine one mysterious male presence, the classic secret love . . . Long periods apart, punctuated by almost unbearably exciting meetings in the pre-dawn cold at the Gare du Nord when the overnight boat-train drew in . . . But we are looking rather, I think, for a family, with a home in which she was made welcome. In particular we are looking – some time in the first ten years of the twentieth century when she was adult enough to cross the Channel on her own – for a young woman about her age with whom she might have formed a bond based on mutual sympathies and reticences. This unknown woman may have had sisters (but in that case would she have needed Maud to fulfil that role?). She is more likely to have had a brother or brothers, youngish men who could be called on to escort the two girls to all the places, including theatres and concerts where, by Parisian custom, they could not quite respectably go on their own. By the same token, a young man could not easily accompany on such an outing a French *jeune fille de bonne famille* even if she was essentially his sister's friend. It would have looked marked, and might have been expected to lead to a rapid proposal of marriage . . . The devastation wrought by the first War was eventually to change all this, but meanwhile a decorous family party, with Maud (with her 'free and easy English ways') making up the female side, probably suited everybody.

Was Matilde Lemoigne, I wonder, the key figure in Maud Tindall's Parisian Garden, which she kept so firmly to herself in a compartment separate from her own family in England?

I know that Bertie, after his wearying and lonely year in the Rue de l'Abbaye, never wanted to hear much of the Lemoignes again. But it is clear from the surviving letters of Baillière, Tindall & Cox that Lemoigne was still acting as chief Parisian agent in the early 1900s, and that in 1902 Bertie unbent sufficiently to send a friendly message and an invitation in a postscript to 'Mademoizelle Matilde' when there was a question of her having pictures in an exhibition in London. She had always been his preferred member of the family – 'she is the only lively figure,' he wrote in his diary, 'except for little Maurice.'

Probably Matilde did come to London on this occasion, though I can't imagine her being allowed to travel on her own. Perhaps Monsieur Lemoigne accompanied her, or her lugubrious brother Paul did: either would have reminded Bertie of the angst he had suffered seven years before. As he had had ample opportunity to observe during that year, French styles of food, clothing, manners and even moral priorities were then very different from the prevailing English ones. When Zola was staying incognito at the same period in London's suburban belt he was rendered miserable by the traditional English breakfasts, and little boys used to laugh at him in the road outside his hotel because he looked so outlandishly foreign. Perhaps, when the Lemoigne contingent actually appeared in Lewisham in their very French button boots and pince-nez, one of Bertie's fits of reserve and withdrawal came on, and so it was Maud who chiefly made them welcome. Perhaps she offered to take Matilde shopping or to a matinée. ('Bertie can't take the time off from work, you know . . .') Perhaps intelligent Maud longed to practise the French she had carefully learnt from a governess or from genteel classes. Or perhaps she simply wanted a real French friend of her own, now that she would no longer be overshadowed by May, who had got married the previous year.

Perhaps, ignoring the odd slighting remark about them from Bertie, she quietly appropriated the Lemoignes to herself, contrived to visit them in Paris and then, as relationships became consolidated, kept quieter and quieter about them, so that even her siblings were barely aware of the Lemoigne connection being maintained in this way. Monsieur Lemoigne would have been in his sixties by this time and would soon disappear from the annals of Baillière, Tindall & Cox. By 1906 Bertie was married, and Howard up at Cambridge. 'Mothery' was occupied with young Doris, her own daughter, and, being a tolerant and rather lazy woman, would have been content to let her stepdaughter, now in her late twenties, go her own sedate, secretive way. Maud had in any case long been encouraged to go away on little restorative holidays, to Folkestone or to country friends.

*   *   *

Maybe it didn't happen quite like that. Maybe Maud's secret Parisian life did not involve the Lemoignes as such. But all the scraps of evidence suggest that it involved members of a family of the same *sort* as the Lemoignes, leading a reticent but cultured and deeply French life. This life, in its very obscurity and difference from her own, combined with its parallels to her own, would have provided Maud with the chance to slip into an alternative identity. By 1912 she was sufficiently ensconced in this role to recommend a good bourgeois family in remote central France who would offer accommodation to a Jacob niece by marriage needing to acquire some French. She also preserved a programme from a multiple prize-giving ceremony at the august and prestigious Académie de France.

She was on one of her visits to Paris – or, more likely at that time of year, enjoying the country-cottage idyll at the end of the tram-ride in Châtillon – at the beginning of August 1914. When war was declared in France on the 3rd, a day earlier than it was in England, the population was caught unawares. In France, unlike England, a general mobilisation was at once announced. Fields were left unharvested as hundreds of thousands of men between eighteen and forty-eight rushed to join or rejoin regiments: since 1870, military service in youth had been a near-universal male experience. Peasant women and the wives of small shopkeepers had their hands full trying to carry on the farm or the business, but higher up the social scale wives, sisters and daughters queued to volunteer in their own way. Within a few days sixty-eight thousand women had offered their services as unpaid nurses to one of the branches of the French Red Cross. Among them, evidently, were Matilde – or a prototype Matilde – and Maud.

By November, the northernmost parts of France were invaded. The armies were literally entrenched, across the swathe of France and Belgium known as Flanders, approximately where they would remain for the next four years. The traumatic loss of husbands, brothers, sons and childhood friends had already become a reality of daily life.

By the time the War ended, the French dead numbered almost one million three hundred thousand, with another three-quarters of a million permanently disabled. Virtually every town and village in France erected a monument engraved with the names of their dead: the exceptions to this were eighteen out of the twenty Paris *arrondissements*. The excuse was that such monuments would be 'too expensive'. The only two *arrondissements* which did erect War memorials, inside their Mairies, were the eighth (which could hardly plead poverty since it contained some of the wealthiest streets in Paris) and the sixth, which covers a large slice of the Latin Quarter. The original Lemoigne flat, in the Rue de l'Abbaye, was in the sixth.

Since an anxious question must hang over the fate of all men born in the last three decades of the nineteenth century, and therefore of an age to have fought in the Great War, I sought out the Mairie's list of the dead of the sixth. In a forgotten back hall at the foot of a stair-case they stand, stone column after stone column of names, over seven and a half thousand of them from one Paris district alone. But no Paul, Emile or Maurice Lemoigne is among them, in fact no Lemoigne at all: the name is not a common one, at any rate with that spelling. Further research at Châtillon produced no dead Lemoigne either.

This, of course, proves nothing. In the twenty years since Bertie stayed with them in the Rue de l'Abbaye, the young Lemoignes would have grown up, gone out into the world, and might well have settled in other parts of Paris, France or the world. A wider internet search did produce an Emile Lemoigne who was killed in the

first months of the War. On enlistment he was registered as living in the 51st *Département*, the Marne, which
is not very far from the Paris basin. He was born in 1881,
which would accord with the impression of him in Bertie's
1995 diary as a schoolboy and would make him two years
younger than Maud. By the summer of 1914 he would
have been thirty-three. Could he, possibly, have been the
lost love to which tentative, post-War allusion was made?
But such is the extreme French reticence about personal
records, even about such commonplace public facts as
birth and death, that I was not able to access any
information about him that would enable me either to
identify him definitively as Matilde's middle brother or
to exclude him from my quest.

However, in the course of this trawl for the dead, I
came across something unexpected. I had had particular
foreboding for 'little Maurice', the other 'lively figure'
besides Matilde, since he was the youngest and therefore the most likely to have seen active service. But it
turned out that Maurice (born Paris 1883), though he
did apparently volunteer in 1914 and served throughout
the War, went on to have a distinguished career as a
microbiologist. So time has not carried him quite beyond
the reach of the living as it has borne away the rest of
his family, which is why I was able to learn the outlines
of his life. He studied agronomy, worked on trace
elements in soils and on the way bacteria break down
and eventually purify contaminated substances – in itself
an effect of time. He rose to be head of a department
at the prestigious medical Institut Pasteur in Montparnasse,
gave lectures at the Académie, that pinnacle of French
intellectual achievement, and in old age was honoured
by election as a member of its scientific section. Is this
where the relevance of Maud's otherwise unrevealing
Académie programme becomes apparent?

In the Académie archives, which are secreted in a quiet
corner of the monumental Institut de France facing the

Seine, a few minutes from the old Lemoigne business in the Rue Bonaparte, the folder marked 'Lemoigne, Maurice' contains a random collection of papers. From these I was able to glean that he had one son who, at Maurice's death in 1967, was his sole heir. So he was presumably a widower by then and, since he was eighty-five, it is likely that he was the last survivor of his generation. A *Paris-Match* photograph of him at a dinner table with others in 1961 shows a humorous, wily-looking old Parisian with a truculent bottom lip.

Why was he figuring in such a sensational, mass-circulation magazine, hardly his usual milieu? Because he had been an expert witness in a case that shook France at that time and divided scientists one from another. A widow (Marie Besnard) had been charged with murder on the evidence that when her late husband's body was exhumed, along with those of various other well-to-do relatives, all contained arsenic. However, the provincial cemetery in question sloped steeply downhill. Some biologists, including Maurice Lemoigne, took the view that the ground absorbed so much foul water drained from the built-up areas above it that bodies were apt to be contaminated with all sorts of substances which were not originally in them. Marie Besnard was eventually reprieved.

Maurice Lemoigne's obituary mentions his 'kindliness and discretion'. His air of cheery cynicism in the photo would suggest that he, like many others, thought that Marie Besnard very probably was guilty, but as a good scientist he was not going to settle for anything but the most stringent forensic proof. Arthur Jacob, treading in the same Latin Quarter streets a century and a half before, would, I think, have approved of him.

Chapter XVI

Footprints Beyond the Quarter.
And New Ones Within It

The Paris that Maud discovered in the years before the Great War, and where she began tracing paths for herself which she would tread from time to time for the next thirty years, had not undergone any great change since the 1890s. The last horse-tram ran in 1907, and then there was the replacement, year by year, of other horse-drawn traffic by the new motor-cars, but the only significant structural change had been the arrival of the Metro from 1900 on. One of the earliest lines, the Nord-Sud, from the Porte de Clignancourt to the Porte d'Orléans, crossed the Ile de la Cité and then the Latin Quarter but in a zigzag route, mainly to avoid disturbing academic institutions such as the Palais de l'Institut and also several of the ancient cemeteries known to be hidden beneath the narrow streets. All the lines were initially planned to end at the various Portes ('gates') of Paris, thus perpetuating their names for the twentieth century and beyond. Well into the 1920s, Paris proper was still corseted within the ring of the *fortifs'*. Not for another generation did the underground railway seem able to ignore this ancient but redundant barrier and prolong some lines into the suburbs.

Unlike the London Underground, which was constructed in deep tunnels, the Metro was built by cut-and-cover only just under the surface of the roadway, and therefore tends to follow a road's twists and turns as if it were a submerged tram. One of the last lines to be built before 1914 was the one that traverses the Left Bank from Auteuil in the west to the Gare d'Austerlitz in the east. It provided, and provides today, a very necessary link across a whole sweep of Paris, yet as first planned the line from Auteuil was to veer north after La Motte Picquet-Grenelle and cross to the Right Bank which was already seamed with lines. It was as if the Metro company took some time to comprehend that the inhabitants of the polite seventh *arrondissement* might ever wish to go east into the lively student quarter centred on the Odéon crossroads, let alone into the 'insalubrities' of the Place Maubert and the Montagne Sainte Geneviève.

There, old Paris slumbered largely undisturbed. Every so often a particularly dilapidated block would be pulled down: the venerable and notorious Château Rouge in the Rue Galande was one of these casualties, as were the houses with fine seventeenth-century doorways in the Rue de la Parcheminerie. The original medical amphitheatre near St Julien le Pauvre was marked for demolition, but was saved by antiquarian intervention. The inhabitants of most of the ancient buildings were left to carry on with life much as it had been lived in these streets since before the Revolution. Many never went far from their familiar labyrinth of courtyards and alleys. The modest version of *le confort moderne* that began to spread in other areas with the new century, and made more progress after the '14–'18 War (shared flush lavatories off the stairwells, individual cold water taps in the kitchens, *gaz à tous les étages*), hardly touched the lanes where Dante and Maître Albert had walked. The Rue de Bièvre still followed the course of the stream that had only been covered over within living memory. When spectacular floods occurred in Paris in 1911, in that low-lying area, river and stream between them reclaimed their ancient territory. Further along the quays the lower end of the Rue Bonaparte, too, was filled with slopping water.

An American journalist who, for many years, lived in the Rue de la Huchette, just the other side of St Julien le Pauvre and St Séverin, and who, exceptionally among his kind, spoke good French, knew his neighbours and really understood Paris wrote: 'The people . . . were fairly representative of Parisians and other Frenchmen who lived in cities. The *garçons*, chambermaids and many vegetable and fruit sellers were peasants. They treated our street as if it were a lane in the country and were bewildered by gas-light, telephones and the traffic in the Place St Michel.'[1]

But outsiders often took a rather different view of this homely district. To them, it was full of sinister nightspots and 'Apaches'. This name, borrowed incongruously from the Wild West of America, was what the popular newspapers called the local rough youths. You would think, from the language of the *Petit Journal* two or three years before the War, that these young men with striped jerseys and slouch caps, who were reputed to carry knives, really were some alien immigrant group – or degenerate indigenous tribe from an impenetrable interior: 'The Apache is the running sore of Paris. There are more than thirty thousand of these prowlers [the word employed is *rôdeur*, with its echo of *rôngeur* – rodent] as against eight thousand policemen . . . Too many young idlers – too many young criminals!' Boys were even to be seen lounging on benches during the daytime. Disgraceful.

Before the Great War, there was a chronic problem in Paris of underemployment, hence the large number of men and boys trying to sell matches, or laces, or to hold the heads of horses for coachmen who were away for a few minutes. Shabby men used to hang around the main stations and then run behind luggage-laden *fiacres* (horse-drawn cabs) all the way to distant parts of Paris in the hope – often disappointed – of earning a tip at the end for helping to carry boxes up several flights to flats. A number of them used to assemble on the Place Maubert because (as one explained to a sympathetic police officer who bought him a drink) *fiacres* came past there from both the Gare de Lyon and the Gare d'Austerlitz, heading westwards to the wealthier quarters.

One must suppose that many of these pathetic figures, along with many of the feared 'Apaches' also, disappeared definitively from Paris after 1914, first into the army and then into the shattered, muddy earth of the Marne and Verdun. After the War, the problem of 'loafers' does not seem to have preoccupied either the police or the newspapers in the same way. The perceived problem by then was the *lack* of adequate numbers of Frenchmen, either to man the industries of the suburbs or to father the next generation of cannon fodder. A draconian law was passed in the summer of 1920 making it a criminal offence to advocate or provide methods of birth control, especially to women. (Condoms still remained available, ostensibly as preventatives against VD.) The birth rate, however, remained resolutely low, which had been the tradition in France for a hundred years already. The only result of the law was that amateur abortion became an entrenched feature over a wide swathe of society, known even to those leading highly respectable lives, but rarely discussed.

As ever, peasants from remote and stony regions of France continued to make their way to Paris, where they provided a pool of cheap labour. Gérard the water-carrier was at last an extinct figure, but his kind was still in demand to carry wood and coal up flights of stairs, or to stand for twelve hours a day washing up in greasy water in restaurant back-kitchens. (George Orwell, who did this job himself, briefly, remarked on how these ill-paid 'male charwomen' took a pride in their toughness, confronting the drudgery as a masculine challenge.) The Hédevins, man and wife, came from the mountainous Lozère, France's poorest *département*. They were young and strong and earned what, for them, was good money. When a little boy was born to them in 1934 Marie Hédevin did not return with him to the old country to leave him there as her own mother would have done, but paid a neighbour a few centimes a day to look after him. Playing with other children in puddles on squalid courtyards, the healthy little boy grew and flourished.

The fact was, though there were more manufacturing jobs in and around Paris between the Wars than there had been before, people were poor. George Orwell did not deliberately seek out bug-infested hotel rooms and tiny brick-floored cafés stinking of old red wine to represent the nadir of being 'down and out'. These conditions were there as a normal part of Parisian lower-class life, and although some of the inhabitants of his street (the Rue Mouffetard, up the hill from the old Latin Quarter, behind the Panthéon) were disreputable, many of them were 'the usual respectable French shop keepers, bakers and laundresses and the like'. True, these same inter-War years saw the beginning of workers' insurance schemes. The largest of these, la Mutualité, actually established its headquarters on the Place Maubert and eventually managed to add its name to the Metro station there – 'Maubert Mutualité'. But these efforts of trades unionism and welfare were all the more necessary because France was economically at a low ebb.

Huge sums of money had been spent on the War; the Government had issued paper money to cover the deficit and so inflation had got going. By 1918 the franc had lost well over half of its pre-War value and continued to sink. Because, for the whole of the preceding hundred years, the presumed value of gold against the franc had been unaltered, the notion that it was a fixed and natural measure like the litre or the metre had become part of

French consciousness. People were ready to believe governmental promises that an eventual return to the gold standard would put everything right again. But in 1924 France abandoned the gold standard, with a substantial devaluation. It was also promised that 'German reparations' for the War would fill the national coffers again, but, with Germany's own more acute financial crisis, this did not happen, even though the French made an ill-judged expedition to try to claim the money. The value of savings, pensions and annuities – the kind of prudently hoarded income on which members of families like the Lemoignes depended – declined and declined.

Many rents had been frozen in 1914, as a protection for tenants whose breadwinners were absent, damaged or dead, and after the War this legislation was never wholly repealed. The measure helped the poor to maintain their precarious existence but did nothing to encourage them to climb out of it. At the same time it created a class of semi-bankrupt small landlords, who ceased to repair properties from which they received almost no income and whose notional value they had no way of realising. The world slump of 1929 made things worse, and France was inefficiently governed: throughout the 1930s French government after French government fell.

For all the continuing elegance of her *beaux quartiers*, the worldwide importance of her fashion industry, the buoyancy of the artistic and bohemian Paris (which had largely moved up the hill from the Latin Quarter to Montparnasse) and Paris's durable international reputation for fun and gaiety, her infrastructure became increasingly ramshackle. By 1940, when, for the third time in seventy years, German troops marched onto French soil, the capital had declined from being Haussmann's resplendent New Babylon into a battered, old-fashioned townscape, where no shutters were ever painted, nothing ever seemed to be renewed, roofs and pipes leaked, the telephone service was a bad joke, and where British and American visitors marvelled at the cheapness of food and lodging as if in some Third World state.

The once-feared 'Apache cellars' of the Montagne Sainte Geneviève became tourist attractions. A long-established dance-hall there became a cosmopolitan homosexual meeting point. By the late 1920s there were unofficially estimated to be forty thousand Americans living for the time being in Paris, although the numbers declined again after 1930 with the United States' own financial crisis. It is from this era that one can date the curious phenomenon, still observable on the Left Bank today, of an almost hermetically sealed anglophone world with its own cultural preoccupations, its own bookshop (Shakespeare & Co.), its own parties and dramas. It also has its own folk memory of former figures, from Gertrude Stein and Hemingway to the more recent Allen Ginsberg and William Styron, which hardly interacts with the French inhabitants' perceptions of the Left Bank in anything but the most superficial way. The Paris 'to which all good Americans go when they die' has always been, like the earlier 'Gay Paree', a different place from the one the local inhabitants know.

One may be fairly sure that Maud Tindall's Secret Garden did not include either the 'American bar', which was opportunistically added to the long-standing Montparnasse *guinguette* La Closerie des Lilas, or the Bal de la Montagne Sainte Geneviève, nor yet the innumerable small hotels described by George Orwell and Henry Miller.

In Paris in those years there were many other foreigners who, from necessity, integrated themselves into French society and finally merged with it, the memory of their foreignness only surviving today in family surnames. Even before 1914, when European frontiers were remarkably open, many migrants from southern and eastern Europe had made their way to France. France, unlike Great Britain, had not passed an Aliens Act in those years, and did not do so after the War, because of the perceived need for the country's economy of more labour to replace the dead. The most obvious foreign group in the 1920s were the White Russians – refugees from the Revolution of 1917 and the establishment of the Soviet Union. Laying claim, sometimes truthfully, to title and wealth in the homeland they had had to forsake, they were to be found in large numbers driving *fiacres*, or later taxis, or attempting to set up restaurants. The Ballet Russe was fashionable, so was Slav music, and these new arrivals with their heavily accented French, their ceremonial manners and their 'charm' became favourites among the more sophisticated Parisians. With the dislocations of post-War Europe they were joined by others: Hungarians, Poles, Italians, Spanish, Portuguese and, of course, eastern European Jews escaping persecution. The French capital was, for all its internal problems, seen as a mecca of freedom and civilisation.

A man who will reappear in this story, and whose parents arrived as separate hopeful youngsters before 1914, wrote to me in old age:

'My mother came from Warsaw, from a family of *petite bourgeoisie* who nevertheless appreciated art and literature. My father had also developed these tastes. With his parents, five brothers and a sister, he had left a small town in Lithuania to settle in Odessa, a prosperous centre, where, it was said, one might hope to make a good life. One has to say, however, that they were ill-informed: pogroms led by the Czar's Cossacks and their accomplices were an everyday fact of life. Again, they had to leave, taking little with them (no family jewels in my background). In the luggage they could carry were clothes, a samovar, a violin, and some books they particularly valued – a Bible, of course, and Pushkin's stories (which, much later, my father used to translate for me when I was lying in bed) and a resplendent History of Art. The family effectively split into two. Those who left for the United States (God knows how they managed it) were keen to get on materially in life, while for the others Paris, the reputed city of art and culture, was the supreme destination.'

The classic Russian-Jewish family, even to the samovar and the violin. I wonder if that was literally true or whether, over the decades, these talismanic objects had come to represent so much else intangible that had been both brought to Paris and left behind?

He went on to describe the success with which his father, having learnt good French in Odessa, managed to acquire a job in a publishing firm and married the girl from Warsaw, and how the family gradually prospered, becoming naturalised, virtually abandoning their Slav roots and also the faith of their fathers. But he added at the end: 'My parents, whose personal pasts were full of humiliations and persecutions, and who had come to France to live in peace, in the end, in this country they had chosen, had to face new horrors . . .' He, his brother and sister and their parents all survived the Second World War, thanks to a strategic change of name on their identity cards and a hasty retreat to Lyons. There were, however, uncles and aunts who, in spite of their cultural aspirations and their successes in journalism and architecture, did not survive to see the Liberation of Paris in 1944.

The Census records for Paris 1926, the earliest that are available for the capital,[2] tell their own tale about the influx of foreigners into Paris during those years, and especially in the Latin Quarter. An old house, numbered 5 Rue des Carmes, between the Marché des Carmes and the corner of the Rue des Ecoles, was now a lodging-house hotel. Many old houses, whose rooms till then had been rented unfurnished to ordinary families, had by the 1920s turned themselves into *hôtels meublés*, probably as a landlord's device for getting round the freeze on rents. Long ago, this house and its neighbour, no. 3, had reared high above the Carmelite cloister whose square shape was still expressed in the market. They seem to have belonged to the Carmelites but, facing onto the street, they would have housed stabling on the ground floor, perhaps store rooms and servants' quarters above. Cellars, ancient stone walls and beams survived, but were heavily camouflaged by nineteenth-century conversion. An iron-railed spiral staircase ran up through the centre of the building, and there were odd, blind passages, dark even at midday, like corridors in bad dreams.

On Census night in 1926 thirty-eight people were living there, singly or in pairs or in whole households. Some stated French as their nationality, but there were also Russians, Poles, Armenians, Hungarians, an Egyptian, a Rumanian, some apparent refugees from the collapsed Hapsburg Empire who called themselves by the new term 'Jugoslavian', and another from the same quarter of Europe styling himself Austrian. Among the stated professions were 'employed in a restaurant' (Russians), a cook, a lawyer's clerk, a *'professeur'*, a *'docteur'*, a hairdresser, a cabinet-maker, a draughtsman and an alarmingly named *'coupeur de dames'* who was presumably in the hairdressing business too. The family groups had a number of young children between them, and there were also several students. A full house, vibrating with the footsteps, low-toned conversations behind closed doors and sudden cries: carefully maintained separate lives going in every corner of its ancient structure. Arthur Jacob would have recognised his old haunts.

A few years earlier an Italian poet, Guiseppe Ungaretti, had lodged here for six months. A contemporary description of another hotel nearby, which had a similarly cosmopolitan population but at a lower social level, stresses an Italian presence. It mentions 'five floors, divided and sub-divided into such small cubicles as could only have been conceived by gross avarice [on the part of the hotel owner] . . . Rickety tables and chests of drawers whose open drawers disgorge a jumble of colourful clothes and vegetables, especially tomatoes. In the centre of the room family and friends are crowded around a stove with no top and no chimney which is fed with charcoal for heating and cooking.' The author is censorious, predicting that the bad smells and the lack of 'air' will surely be the death of some of the occupants. The book in which this description appears was published by Baillière et Fils, still a fixture in the Rue Hautefeuille.

In the Rue Basse des Carmes – a narrow alley wrapped around the market building – a more stable and conventionally French working-class population was to be found in the 1920s, the families of bakers, metal workers, postmen, a musician, an accordion-player, hat-makers, builders, an elderly dressmaker and an ice-cream seller. In the Paris of those days, as in every era before, ordinary people could find, in the interstices of the humming city, a modest room or two in which to roost, within their means. It was a precious, taken-for-granted freedom that the prosperity of the later twentieth century, in Paris as in London and in other cities around the world, has destroyed.

So where, in the mid-1920s, were the surviving Lemoignes living? Thirty years had elapsed since Bertie's stay with them: it would be reasonable to assume that, by then, both of the elder Lemoignes were dead. The Census for 1926 shows no trace of the family in the Rue de l'Abbaye, though the kind of tenant does not seem to have changed. The stone-faced house sheltered, probably in the Lemoignes' old apartment, a staff member of a magazine publishing company, his wife and two servants, and on another floor an accountant of some sort lived with two big sons. An elderly painter and his wife lived on the top floor. St Germain des Prés was still a *petit quartier* of modest commerce with a slight bookish, artistic and antiquarian flavour. The large café on the Place, the Deux Magots, had as yet no particular fame attached to it. Many ordinary little grocers, bakers, *blanchisseries* and cobblers plied their trades down the Rue Bonaparte. At no. 12 Lemoigne's antiquarian book business was being carried on by someone from eastern France styled, in the Census, simply as 'expert'. There was a draughtsman's studio at the same address where his son and brother-in-law worked, and the concierge's husband was the 'packer for a publishing firm'.

But St Germain des Prés, which adjoined the still exclusive Faubourg St Germain, was the polite end of the Latin Quarter. As you moved east, although the boulevards with their Haussmann apartment blocks remained respectable, grubby little drinking shops, second-hand clothes dealers and fusty working-class licensed brothels multiplied in the old side streets. The once-illustrious Café Procope was now a *bouillon*, literally a soup kitchen, in practice a cheap restaurant serving fixed-price meals of soup, main course, dessert and unlimited bread to a clientele of students and underpaid clerks. There was another *bouillon*, belonging to a chain, further along towards Maubert, and on the old Place itself the growing presence of the Mutualité made that crossroads a natural rallying point for the noisy left wing demonstrations and marches that characterised the early 1930s.

I do not think that any of the younger generation of Lemoignes moved in that direction. I see them, rather, after about 1910, when Monsieur Lemoigne was retired, migrating away from the shabby, 'airless' old streets of the Latin Quarter, up the hill a little towards Montparnasse (conveniently near the Institut Pasteur). This was where the artistic life of Paris now had its epicentre, in the Dôme and the Rotonde cafés at the junction of the Boulevards Montparnasse and Raspail. I don't imagine that the Lemoignes had any direct contact with such figures of Montparnasse's heyday as Modigliani or Picasso, or that they joined the 'shrieking hordes of poseurs' on the café terraces that Orwell noted there in the late 1920s. But the pleasant, respectable streets between the Luxembourg Gardens and the big Montparnasse Cemetery had, in a more general sense, become Paris's Hampstead or Greenwich Village, and people like Matilde Lemoigne (and Maud) felt at home there. Simone de Beauvoir was growing up there in those years. Not till the German invaders of 1940 made the central crossroads of Montparnasse their playground for the next four years did the currents of literary and artistic Paris flow down the hill again and recolonise St Germain des Prés.

Or should I locate the surviving, unmarried Lemoignes, rather, in the little house at Châtillon? No Metro ran out in that direction till the end of the 1930s, but the electrification of the trams had made the journey in and out of town quick and easy. Châtillon had become a suburb, but still a pretty one because of its hilltop situation. On the Avenue de Paris gabled houses faced in heavy, mock-rustic stone alternated with provincial-style stores and the remains of much older cottages and stables. There were market gardens, and in side lanes with names like 'Impasse des Champs Fleuris' two-storeyed modern villas, set in shady gardens with the remnants of old orchards, still made possible the rural dream.

The young couple mentioned earlier, both from eastern Europe, who had met in Paris during the First World War, married soon after the Armistice. Leaving their ageing parents to their respectable but essentially Slav and immigrant world near the Gare de l'Est (the point of arrival in the city), the couple migrated to the fresh air and *petit bourgeois* French innocence of Châtillon. From there, the husband could readily travel in and out to the editorial work he had now secured in a series of magazines: fashion, art, the new cinema . . . Three children were born to them within six years. When they grew older, they might travel in to Parisian *lycées* if, as seemed likely, their own tastes too proved literary and artistic. The couple had achieved what they had left their homelands to seek: they were happy. The youngest son – let us call him Serge – recalled till the end of his own life jolly family evenings with the violin and Russian songs, but wrote:

'As regards social life, my parents' friends were by now almost all French. I only heard Yiddish or Russian spoken when we visited my grandparents. My parents, I think, had taken a deliberate decision to live *à la française* and to turn away from what they had earlier suffered. Yes, a page was turned, as if history had been forgotten. But that was in the end revealed to have been a fundamental mistake . . .'

Long after that, too, was over, and the War and its consequences had scattered the three children to different parts of the world and made them almost strangers to one another, Serge described unearthing a photo of these pretty, dark-eyed children grouped together with their parents in a flowery garden. He, a man who had never much liked his brother once they were past infancy, had neither wanted nor had any children of his own, and to whom his far-off nephews and nieces were little more than names, found, to his embarrassment, that the photo made him want to cry.

* * *

One odd, persistent memory of my own inclines me to the notion that the 'ramshackle old place' in Châtillon, where Bertie gardened furiously, did remain in the possession of some of the Lemoignes between the Wars. Though they may well have sold off most of the garden to a developer as the value of their savings declined.

One weekend in the mid-1950s a teenage girl – whom I can see clearly but as if she were someone else from a distant era – was wandering round the flea market just inside the Porte de Vanves. Unknown Châtillon was on its hill above. A slum of corrugated-iron shanties occupied part of the site of the fortifications, where the Périphérique motorway would later be built. But the girl who was me focused only on the foreground, where a feast of stalls and ground-sheets displayed china, glass, old clothes, shoes, horned wind-up gramophones, antique cooking stoves, abused dolls, washstand sets, dressmaker's and shop-window dummies, crude oil paintings, bolsters, flaccid and stained red eiderdowns, books, used prams, sepia photographs of places now unrecognisable and embossed albums containing forgotten people.

The girl must have picked up one of the albums, for the next memory is its board-thick pages. The cloud of youthful self-absorption that enveloped her was momentarily pierced by a faint shaft of imaginative interest, the feeble first stirrings of an empathy with the past: low waists, drooping stockinette, strapped granny shoes, cloche hats, hair screwed up in buns or cutely shingled *à la garçonne*, young faces mismatched above what now seemed aged styles as in a children's joke book . . . She felt sorry for them, disinherited as they were. Someone, once, had known them well enough to keep their pictures, to write names under them, and it had (she thought, not understanding that time carries everything away) all been in vain.

A page or two of faces in old-fashioned nurses' uniforms, caps well down on brows . . .

A youngish man in a high-collared military tunic and medals. A tiny spray of very ancient, yellowed box leaves pressed onto this page, leaving its ghostly imprint . . .

'A Châtillon . . . Chez Madame Vaurin . . . Avec nos amis Leclair au Petit Robinson . . . Avec nos amis russes . . .
'Avec Maud, notre amie anglaise.'

But, knowing nothing of Maud, the girl idly went on turning over the pages. Then the stallholder was approaching her. Blackened teeth in a cavernous mouth and an ingratiating smile. Reek of old sweat, Gauloises and garlic. She put the book down. In her small, scuffed shoes and cotton skirt with rattling nylon petticoats underneath it, she retreated to pore over a stall selling cheap North African jewellery.

Of course Maud was a common name then. Might have been anyone.

But still, recalling this remote fragment of retrieved time, trying in vain to bring it into clearer focus, I have a small ache of frustration, a regret.

I do not think that Maud was still visiting Paris in the 1950s. At the start of the Second World War in 1939 she would have been too old, at sixty, to resume her nursing activities with any Red Cross, either French or English. I have the impression that her long involvement with France died out during that War and in the years following it, when no foreign travel was possible for ordinary British subjects.

In any case, after that ten-year gap, it may have been that her particular friends were dead, and the house in Châtillon – or the flat off the Boulevard Raspail or the Rue de Rennes – given up.

Perhaps the cross-Channel relationship subtly changed with time, wearing thin like an old garment. In the War, when France was occupied, no boat services ran and no letters could pass to and fro. The long British relationship with Paris itself hung in suspension, just as it had during the Napoleonic Wars of a hundred and thirty years earlier, though, for many, Paris still remained a lodestar. 'Lost love, lost youth, lost Paris – remorse and folly. Aie!' wrote Cyril Connolly in wartime London. 'Tout mon mal vient de Paris. There befell the original sin and the original ecstasy; there were the holy places . . .'[3] In 1942, when the outcome of the War still hung in the balance, far away in New York the American journalist Elliot Paul, who had lived for many years in the Rue de la Huchette, getting to know it intimately – 'the beds, stoves, meals and draperies; the soaps and olive oil; the wine, the bread, the piety and wit; the crimes and sacrifices; the knowledge, ignorance, love and hate' – wrote in anguished nostalgia: 'If only that tiny thoroughfare, a few hundred yards in length, could be resurrected, there would be enough of France alive today to stir a spark of hope in the hearts of men.'

As we know, in the end Paris was given back undestroyed to the Parisians and to the world at large. But for some Parisians and for some visitors things had changed. Betrayals had occurred. Ageing people, who remembered the useless sacrifices and losses of the previous War, were more likely to have pinned their hopes, during the Occupation, on Pétain's Vichy government than on the clandestine and faction-ridden Resistance movement. And there was the Mers el Kebir business, when the British navy scuttled the French fleet . . . Some French citizens never felt the same about the British after that. In mutual reticence, disapproval, embarrassment and eventual silence, a number of long-term friendships ended in the years after 1945. And some British felt quietly but profoundly shocked when it eventually became apparent that Parisian Jews at every social level had been deported wholesale to their deaths with very few hands or voices raised to save them. The endemic anti-Semitism of Catholic France, which had manifested itself so strikingly in the Dreyfus case at the end of the previous century, combined by 1940 with the vague resentments fostered by decades of unrestrained immigration. The effect was lethal. Many of the Jews who had believed, half a lifetime ago, that the Gare de l'Est was their gateway to freedom and security found they had another journey to make – to the Gare d'Austerlitz.

On that station today a plaque reads:[4]

> *De la Gare de Paris-Austerlitz*
> *Furent dirigés sur les camps*
> *de Pithviers et de Beaune-la-Rolande,*
> *avant d'être déportés et assassinés à Auschwitz:*
> *3700 juifs, tous les hommes, le 14 mai 1941,*
> *et du 19 au 22 juillet 1942*
> *7800 juifs, dont les 4000 enfants de*
> *La rafle du Vélodrome d'Hiver,*
> *arrêtés dans l'agglomération parisienne*
> *à la demande de l'occupant allemand*
> *par la police de l'autorité de fait*
> *dite 'Gouvernement de l'Etat Français'*
> *N'oublions jamais!*

*

Arthur Giles had died before the Second World War. He was ten years older than his wife. Through the War and afterwards, till May's own death in the 1950s, the two sisters lived together in a small house in Sussex on the borders of Ashdown Forest.

May, though balked of a daughter, as usual got her own way. She had the younger Maud to look after her till the end.

Maud, who had been supposed to be 'delicate', lived on a great many more years. My one image of her – I do not think I had ever met her before – dates from about 1970. She was having tea with her brother Bertie, two very old, tall, thin, beaky-faced survivors in a world that seemed to them changed out of all recognition. Bertie had had a stroke and had given up talking much, since he tended to forget what he wanted to say, but they seemed nevertheless to be complicitly enjoying themselves over fruit cake and Earl Grey. A year or so later, Bertie had gone, but still in 1973 Maud, who must then have been rising ninety-four, could write a good, cogent letter to her nephew in a clear hand. She regretted, she said, that she knew so little about her father's side. She mentioned a family crest, and the possibility of the Tindalls having been descended, eight centuries back, 'from the widow of King Stephen – this I gleaned from my old friend of the Lake District before she died. She too was a Tindall.' As to Albert Alfred's father's occupation, she agreed that there had been a persistent family tradition that he had at one time driven the Dover coach, but after that – '*I* always understood that he had his own livery stables.'[5]

This incidental letter, and a few plangent poems by Maud, mainly about nature, have through time and chance survived. Streams ripple, dew drops glisten and meadows have a tendency to be flower-bedecked, but her own sense of beauty and wonder comes through; so it does in a fairy story she wrote for children appealingly called 'When Everything was White'. There is also a manuscript ghost story (with a phantom coach) whose narrator is a busy London surgeon with a motor-car; and a third story, set in Canada, which she actually wrote in fluent, if not totally correct, French. This has been corrected for her in pencil in a different, classically French hand. There is also a notebook into which she evidently transcribed for her own use a wide vocabulary of idiomatic French words and phrases, such as one might acquire from daily contact with native speakers.

Along with these few survivals is a copy, in Maud's handwriting, of Swinburne's passionate poem 'At Parting'. Also a finely executed pen and ink drawing of an Italianate building, signed by Howard and dated 1903 when he must have been about eighteen. Apart from photographs of the brothers and sisters in childhood, nothing else remains.

Maud died, apparently without fuss, the year after the letter to her nephew was written.

Her long but obscure life, that led nowhere and left so little lasting trace, was full of integrity, decency, private emotion and secret effort. Like innumerable others of her kind, she passed over personal disappointments and frustrations in silence, and made a life for herself with what was available to her. Childless, in old age she gave financial help to the daughter of her half-sister Doris, when the young woman's husband left her on her own with three children. An emblematic British spinster aunt, she nevertheless found another country of the mind across the Channel. The alchemy of Paris turned her from a stock joke into 'a charming woman of the world' and of her own secret world also.

Part V

JULIA: 1955–2008

Chapter XVII

THE CHILD OF THE METRO

So we are back, through all the different imprints of time and place, with the expanses of Ashdown Forest, where a Wartime child walked beside her mother and was given a lift in a cart.

That child and her mother lived then, and for a good many years afterwards, on the side of the Forest that extends towards the Kentish Weald; the aunts May and Maud lived on the far side, to the south-west. Everyone took buses in those needy, car-less years, and green-and-cream double-deckers trundled regularly up and down hills, past chalk and heather and bracken, dropping passengers off at isolated stops with names like Hindleap Warren, Wych Cross and Nutley. Why did the aunts never visit? More to the point, since they were old, why were they never visited?

Children accept things as they are. The mother was long dead, and the child a grown-up herself for years, before the oddity of this circumstance occurred to her. The mother's parents lived nearby: every Sunday without fail lunch or tea was eaten at their house, even after the young man in the photograph called 'Daddy' came back from the War. But his own parents, Bertie and Blanche, who had also moved to Sussex in old age, were visited only two or three times a year. And everyone else in that once-extensive and clannish family was, to the child, unknown.

It became clear to her much later that some sort of family fracture had occurred. Such visits as were made to Bertie and Blanche (who were addressed, with supreme tactlessness, as 'Other Granny' and 'Other Grandpa') were animated but filled with tension. Hardly ever did their daughter-in-law say anything about them afterwards that was not critical. Blanche, no doubt, was not the easiest of mothers-in-law. She tended to dominate any conversation, without meaning to. She probably thought (rightly) that her cherished only son had married, too young, someone who, though apparently suitable, was not the right sort of person for him. But there was nothing Blanche could have done, in her teasing, voluble, Anglo-Irish way, or yet Bertie with his didactic organising tendencies, that could have permanently alienated a daughter-in-law who wanted to like them and be liked by them.

Ursula was their daughter-in-law and she did not want to like them. That commonplace responsibility was seemingly beyond her. If questioned about them, she would probably have used words like 'conventional', 'Victorian' and 'stuffy', the all-purpose terms casually applied by those who grew up after the First World War to stigmatise those of an age to have been supposedly responsible for that War. Of all the long shadows cast by the slaughter between 1914 and 1918, a casual, wholesale contempt for the values of previous generations was one of the most insidious and longest-lasting.

The Bright Young Modern pose, which had no doubt irritated Bertie and Blanche in the twenty-year-old Ursula, was indeed no more than a pose. But it was not abandoned as she grew older. The central truth was probably that she did not really want to be an adult woman at all. She resisted, with a kind of panic-stricken myopia that was self-defeating, the idea that she was, like everyone else, in thrall to time and chance. How could she, Ursula, become *middle-aged*? It was like a personal attack on her.

She had been happy as a child: a tiny home-made magazine, which her own mother kept all her life as a memento, suggests a bright, clever little girl. She had been especially happy as a teenage schoolgirl. She was very happy too when her family, who were cultured and indulgent, sent her to Paris to be 'finished'. Such was the image of harmless, rather old-fashioned elegance that Paris had among well-to-do English families between the Wars. Her father was a Treasury knight: with his influence, she was readily admitted to a women's college in Oxford, which was not then the intellectual powerhouse for undergraduates it would later become. These prolongations of boarding school life, with their carefully sheltered modicums of fun and freedom, were, to her, the ideal existence. All subsequent periods of her life were measured against this standard and found wanting. And for coping with life's blows she developed no strategies at all.

Though in love with the young man she had met at Oxford and carried away by his eagerness to marry her, she did not adapt well to the married state. Expecting protection as of right, she yet strained mockingly away from most of the concepts embodied in the marriage vows, defending her own 'unconventionality' and 'independence' while doing nothing to validate these claims. The significant events of the 1930s made little impact on her. Fatally, the Second World War then inserted five years of distance and different experience between her and her young husband, and consolidated her self-image as someone unjustly held back from the life she preferred. Genuinely loving to read, and believing herself therefore intellectual and already enlightened, she let the War pass her largely by, perceiving only its privations and none of its opportunities for growth and change.

'Of course I couldn't volunteer for anything with you around,' she said later to her daughter. But she had always had resident domestic help, and her own mother lived nearby. She wrote (and published, in those days of voracious lending library readers) a handful of 'amusing modern novels', slackly constructed, showing a distinct minor talent for dialogue and for the apposite word or phrase, and little insight into the human mind or heart. One reviewer, more perceptive than most at that time, remarked that the characters' personalities seemed stuck in 1930.

She had not been keen to have a child, but when her little daughter was born she adopted her passionately as an alter ego. Very young, the child (whom I have called Julia) was talked to almost as an adult, had complicated stories and good poetry read to her. For years, Julia thrived on this loving partnership, though distanced from other children by the grown-up vocabulary she acquired and by her ineptitude at childish games. Only later in childhood, when she began to realise she was expected to replicate her mother's life and tastes entirely – 'Oh you'll love tennis, darling! I always have . . . Don't worry about boring arithmetic, darling, people like us are never any good at that sort of thing' – did a degree of unease set in. Forebodings which increased as she began to notice how shaky Ursula's grasp of current events actually was. But Mummy always knew so much about some other things, so how could one ever explain . . .

Ursula took refuge in daydreams. Julia, till she was old enough to evolve coherent and separate daydreams of her own, shared these too, as the offered way out of the present that was supposed, in some never-quite-stated way, to have something wrong with it that was not fair. The daydream called 'One day you and I will go to Paris together, darling' continued to be a favourite. Now that Julia was a little older, the white-and-gold-towered fairy-tale Paris by a bright sea was replaced by one even more exotic. To introduce her daughter to French (something not taught at the cranky and 'enlightened' progressive school to which she had sent Julia) Ursula bought her children's books in that language. This was a good idea: indeed her daughter was sadly to reflect, long after, that if only Ursula had had to go to work as a teacher then her talents and qualities might have found a proper outlet. Julia was briefly charmed by favourite characters from infancy reappearing as *La Famille Flopsaut* and *Noisy-Noisette*, but the book that particularly caught her imagination was called *L'Enfant du Métro*.

Lavishly illustrated in colour, at a time when in England most children's books were still appearing in restricted, monochrome 1940s editions, this told the story of a small boy roaming, lost, in the white-glazed corridors of the Paris underground. He discovered to his delight that he had somehow slipped through an automatic barrier (*Attention au portillon!*) into an alternative Metro in which each station resembled its name. Porte des Lilas, of course, was an ancient gateway hung about with succulent mauve flowers, and Place des Fêtes on the same line was a jolly fairground, but others had a more eccentric charm. At Gare d'Austerlitz, Napoleon and a posse of toy soldiers in white képis flourished sabres on a railway platform full of unconcerned passengers, while in Chambre des Députés elderly, bearded gentlemen with pince-nez lay neatly tucked up in rows of camp-beds under a gilded ceiling. With the sonorous and incongruous pairings that have long entertained Metro-lovers, the book's creator really got into his stride. At Denfert-Rochereau a sinister devil in *vie de bohème* dress prowled in a rocky landscape, while at Sèvres-Babylone eastern-looking people with long, curling beards disported themselves amid tiers of expensive china. A memory survives of a jolly gentleman waving a welcome from a landscape of classic gods and goddesses (Montparnasse-Bienvenue), and sheep grazing with labels round their necks on a brilliantly green pasture (Mouton-Duvernet). But was there really pictured – or has adult imagination supplied? – a station at Réaumur-Sébastopol in which a huge thermometer-building dominated a fortified town, rising above walls at which a force of tiny men in mid-nineteenth-century clothes were aiming cannons? It is well over half a century since the book disappeared, and it seems to be known to no one and unfindable on any website.[1]

'You do know, don't you, darling,' said Ursula fondly to Julia, 'that Paris isn't really like this?' But the Paris she now described to her daughter, a shining, tidy city in which people, when they were not playing tennis or going for boat trips on the lake in the Bois de Boulogne, sat having fun and coloured drinks on café terraces, was almost as far from the reality. In her Paris, time had surely stood still, and she would once again be reunited there with her real identity as a clever young English Miss.

No one in England could get to Paris in the years immediately after the War, except the wily and privileged: no foreign exchange was generally available till 1949. Ursula's dream was therefore, for the time being, well protected. Tales that did filter back, from lucky travellers to the Continent, suggested a Paris unchanged by four years of Occupation, a city without the bombed ruins that pockmarked London, and where meat, eggs, cream, wine and pretty clothes were there for the asking. To a stringently rationed England, held for several years more in the prudent grip of what was known as Austerity, with stodgy food and bread itself in short supply, it was not surprising that Paris appeared as a lost Eden. The fact that, in unregulated France, the franc was now falling in value month by month, reducing many Parisians to penury, was not widely realised across the Channel.

Ursula's Parisian experience, at eighteen, had been of life in the large Montparnasse apartment of one of

France's innumerable black-clad ladies whose husbands had been killed at Verdun or on the Marne. Madame Bazin (as I will call her) took in, two or three at a time, English girls *de bonnes familles*, and had nephews and nieces whom she also entertained when they were not studying for their *bac*. From these friendly playmates (who were later to turn into ambitious and slightly eccentric adults) Ursula quickly picked up French, and this accomplishment possibly went to her head. To talk fluently in a foreign language requires a heightened level of concentration that is apt to make the speaker feel he or she is living with a special intelligence and intensity. Years later, Julia discovered this for herself. But as a child, listening to her mother's accounts of 'the *fun* we had, darling!', and slightly baffled because the animated recitals of trivial excursions did not seem to amount to anything she had come to think of as grown-up and exciting, she formed the impression that she was being told about children of much her own age.

Having at last been sent to an ordinary school where French was taught, she now had a French lesson book that seemed to cover the same territory. In it, Pierre and Solange lived in an over-furnished apartment with their Maman and Papa, a fluffy white dog called Plonplon and a black-clad servant called Liliane. When not involved in perpetual preparation of *études* and *devoirs*, Pierre and Solange promenaded in the park (neat box hedges surrounding gravel and a képi-ed policeman in charge) or – more daringly – *jouaient au tennis*. Meanwhile Papa went to his unspecified *bureau* while Maman *allait aux grands magasins*, or, as an occasional respite from the burden of shopping for sewing silks and hat-trimmings, *prenait du thé* with female friends. On Sunday, the family *prenait un tramway* for *une sortie à la campagne*, where Papa pointed out various birds to them by name.

The only charm of this boring non-story, as far as Julia was concerned, was that it existed in two different versions, both of them antiquated. Of the twenty-odd battered copies that had been handed round the class by the French Mam'zelle at the beginning of term, about half showed Papa in a bowler and spats (like Babar the Elephant) and Maman in a waistless dress and cloche hat. Solange, similarly waistless, had white socks and a drooping hair ribbon, and Pierre very short shorts, white socks too and a Breton cap. But in the rest of the copies, still more tattered wrecks of a yet earlier edition, with pages chaotically adrift from what had once been the spine, Papa, bearded, was in a frock coat and top hat, and Maman was in a floor-length and much-frilled dress with a hint of bustle. Solange, similarly befrilled but in a shorter version, had stockings, button boots and long ringlets, and Pierre wore a sailor suit. The cumbersome décor of the flat, however, seemed much the same, as indeed did the appearance of Liliane and the eternal Plonplon. In the older edition, the tennis chapter was missing ('You will have to share books for this lesson, girls') but otherwise nothing at all beyond the clothes had apparently changed in bourgeois Parisian life between 1880 and 1930. And of course the participants had not grown any older.

In the tedium of lessons usefully devoted to irregular verbs, Julia formed the dreamy impression that in the Paris to which she and her mother would one day be transported, time did indeed run differently. Everyone her mother knew there would still be young. Mummy had no doubt lived in that very flat, or one entirely similar, with people dressed in those same clothes. One day soon they would make the epic journey to see it.

Julia knew nothing of the Lemoignes, but it occurs to me today that the atmosphere of oppressive respectability and lack of physical space, which was breathed out from the dog-eared, scribbled-on pages of that ancient French primer, accurately portrayed what Bertie had encountered in his own youthful stay in Paris.

But Ursula's Pierre and Solange were evidently more entertaining than Bertie's version, and through the 1930s contact with them had been maintained. Like huge numbers of Parisians in every era, the family came from elsewhere in France. Their roots were in the Basque country near the Pyrenees, where they still had parents, uncles and aunts. Since Biarritz, the main town of the area, had become a fashionable resort much favoured by British visitors, it was there that jolly holiday reunions took place. *Ils jouaient au tennis*, no doubt, and there were more boat trips, and swims, and of course sessions on café terraces over drinks that were now *gin-fizz* and *side-cars*. Being *très modernes* (unlike, they thought, all the generations behind them), the Pierre-Solanges and their entourage were not going to agree to arranged marriages. Elaborate clandestine and not entirely clandestine relationships were carried on. These were generally described as *flirts*, an English term imported from more innocent times and somehow fossilised in colloquial French: this no doubt enabled the older generation in Biarritz comfortably to close their eyes to what *modernité* might actually entail.

Little of this impinged on Ursula, however, once she had turned up in a sports car with her handsome, if rather shy, young English husband. The Pierre-Solanges were pleased for her: that was just the sort of partner, and car, that chatty English girls were supposed to have. They were even more generously pleased when a mysterious *crise de foie*, that blighted one holiday and required the attentions of a doctor-uncle, turned out to be the first signs of a pregnancy. Julia had been conceived.

But the holidays in Biarritz or Paris were then almost at an end. Not because of the baby – middle-class mothers at the end of the 1930s still had uniformed nannies 'in sole charge' – but for larger reasons. On the far side of those Pyrenees that were shadows in the sky above the café terraces of Biarritz, the Spanish Civil War had already sent another wave of political refugees into the supposed safety of France. In early September 1939 came the declaration of the Second World War. This time round, at least, French farmers had been able to get the harvest in before being summoned to their regiments. Those English who were still nonchalantly holidaying in French resorts ('War? Well, we're poo-pooers. I mean – Chamberlain won't let it happen, will he?') hastily regained the British Isles by whatever boats were available.

Later that autumn, Ursula's husband was in uniform. Like his Uncle Howard in the previous War, he thought it best to volunteer before the decision was taken out of his hands, much to the grief and anxiety of his parents who feared a terrible repetition of the previous slaughter. In addition, Tom (as I will call him, in an approximation to his mother's baby name for him, which stuck throughout his life) had been fragile as a child. Bertie and Blanche had been afraid, early on, that he might not live. Though he had grown into a happy, intelligent young man, and a good tennis player, there was still the family feeling that Tom was more delicate and sensitive than other young men. How would he cope with Army life? Blanche, in particular, was inclined to see in her son the wistful, blue-eyed ghost of her youngest brother, Donald, whom she had failed to save from exile in Canada almost forty years before.

Ursula always loudly maintained that Tom had been 'horribly spoilt' by his mother. While this assertion was part and parcel of her general enmity towards her in-laws, she may have been right about it. For Tom, though universally acknowledged to be a sweet-natured fellow, was also admitted to be rather young and silly still for a married man now rising thirty. Like Bertie before him, and with similar lack of real enthusiasm, he had dutifully gone into the family firm, but he was not, at that stage, cutting a particularly convincing figure there, and he knew it.

Bertie, always fair-minded, had tried to equip his son for the job as well or better than he himself had been. So, before Tom spent his three years in Oxford falling in love and obtaining a not very good degree, he too had been sent to spend six months in France and six in Germany – though with rather different results from those Bertie had experienced. In the suburbs of Paris, not yet eighteen and without his father's artistic passions, Tom seems to have been too much of a shy schoolboy to derive any benefit from his stay, but Germany was a different matter. Like Bertie, Tom flourished there, but for a quite different reason and one certainly unknown to Bertie: he was rapidly seduced by the lady of the household who received him. His months there, near Dresden, were therefore some of the happiest and most instructive of his young life. It was only, perhaps, rather a pity that this boyish idyll, self-enhancing but free of any responsibility, set a pattern for him. It was one he would try to recapture throughout life.

So, late in 1939, Tom said goodbye to Ursula and to his eighteen-month-old daughter. He and Ursula were to meet for one or two hurried leaves spent in provincial hotels in that first, freezing winter of the War, but he was not to see Julia again till she was rising six. Perhaps this was the main reason that (as he himself once ruefully remarked) he never seemed to develop quite the kind of paternal feeling he noted in other men. Later in her childhood he treated her as one might a favourite niece, rather than as someone for whom he was centrally responsible.

In the chilly, provisional Army quarters requisitioned somewhere in the Midlands by the Ordnance Corps, Tom proved no more convincing as a soldier than he had been as a medical publisher. It was some time before he was recommended for the commission which might have been expected to follow on his background and education. Meanwhile, his feet bled in Army boots on field marches, Sergeant-majors cursed him for inefficiency and the officers in charge did not know what to do with him. Someone eventually enquired what his job had been in civvy street – 'Oh, medical stuff? Good . . . Because the CO says we need someone to give this mob lectures on VD. You can do that, can't you?'

An appeal by Tom to his father and cousin at Baillière, Tindall & Cox produced some books with suitably graphic illustrations of ulcerated genitals. 'After I showed them these,' Tom used to recount happily afterwards, 'those tough chaps fainted in rows.' He also managed to teach the rudiments of reading to some who seemed hardly to have encountered the skill before.

His stock with his superiors went up; the long winter ended and he was sent, attached to a cavalry regiment, to Palestine. So he embarked on what, in the end, turned out to be, in the phrase of the time, 'a good War', which was to say one full of movement, experience, new skills learnt, new friendships and a degree of personal success. Fate, in the form of the Eighth Army, took him from Palestine to the desert War in North Africa, with periods in Cairo and Alexandria, and eventually to the maelstrom of the Salerno landings in 1943. The following year a broken leg providentially kept him out of the first and most lethal wave of the landings in Normandy. He followed up the Allied invasion in the second wave, reaching Belgium and finally Germany, where he became part of the army of occupation. Five years of military life, a narrow escape in Italy and the rank of Captain (Acting Major) had by then endowed him with an assurance and know-how that he would never have gained in other circumstances.

Engaged in a 'mopping up' operation near Bayeux in the autumn of 1944, in pursuit of the retreating and fragmented German forces, the Company to which he was attached was ordered next to Brussels. 'I knew our tanks would take at least four days to get to Belgium,' he recounted afterwards, 'and it seemed an absolute waste of time to traipse along behind them. So I and my driver went to Paris for a couple of nights. I had a wonderful time there. We caught up again with our convoy before they reached Lille.'

Paris, which had been liberated at the end of August, was for a horde of British and Allied forces living up to its traditional reputation for gaiety. More than ever before in its long history it figured as the place of freedom and rejoicing, almost as a Celestial City where one might hope to meet again those one had thought lost for ever. On a more realistic level, it was bursting with people, many of whom were free of daily fear for the first time in four years, and many of whom were searching for others whom they were not, as it turned out, destined to find.

Tom had no such anxieties as he went looking for his old friends. But great was his delight when, in a gathering full of different uniforms, he suddenly came face to face with his favourite of the Solanges. She had the insignia of the Forces Françaises de l'Intérieur on her shoulders – the erstwhile Resistance, now triumphantly in charge – and she was just as pleased to see him.

'Just imagine,' she said to Julia long after, 'there, suddenly, before my eyes, was your dear father. What joy! And he was not timid any longer. He had developed so much. In fact, so much the victorious one – the *sexful soldier*, you know – that it took me a minute to recognise him.' The English phrase 'sexful soldier', inserted into an otherwise French sentence, left Julia uncertain as to whether Solange, whose English was always more exploratory than accurate, actually meant 'full of sex' or 'successful' or a mixture of the two, but the general message was clear.

*   *   *

The War was over, and presently a little brother was born. There were, after all, some times of family life, of shared interests: of mild, decent happiness.

By the end of the decade it was even possible to go on foreign holidays again. The new, bloodless invasion of the coasts of Europe, which would be in full swing by the mid-1950s, was already, insignificantly, beginning. Well-organised middle-class English families ventured to Normandy and Brittany. But, for whatever reason, Ursula and Tom did not take their children abroad on holiday. They did not even take a brief few days together in Paris. Paris, apparently, was still mysteriously inaccessible to Ursula, a land of lost content that could not be regained.

When Julia, now just in her teens, bored and frustrated, mentioned hopefully to her mother their old dream of visiting Paris together, she was offered excuses that even to her seemed inadequate: 'Oh well, no, darling, I wouldn't want to – not with the stingy foreign exchange restrictions. Only £25. On that we wouldn't be able to drink in cafés, you see.'

The truth was that, after 1939, in the sixteen years of life that remained to her, Ursula never crossed the Channel again.

The dream was not going to be tested. By and by the fantasy of Paris as a place where her lovely, real life awaited her was dropped from Ursula's repertoire. Julia, missing it, continued it secretly in her own way. In the lonely prison of boarding school ('Oh, Julia loves school,' Ursula insisted to her friends) she wrote part of a secret novel, during Prep or in ill-lit lavatories after Lights Out. It was set in Paris, at some vaguely determined period that was probably late seventeenth or eighteenth century (carriages, silk breeches, low-necked bosoms, mud, beggars, monks, swords, crucifixes . . .) Local verisimilitude was added with the names of streets and of important buildings such as had occurred in the Pierre-Solange readers. Only, as Julia had never seen a map of Paris, the carefully mentioned 'Rue St Honoré' or 'Place du Panthéon' bore no relation to the real city. The 'Château de Vincennes', with a vague recollection of the now-lost *Enfant du Métro*, was where the King lived, and the 'Tour Eiffel' (having escaped from its late-nineteenth-century moorings and become a stone tower) housed a beautiful female prisoner.

The schoolmistress who caught Julia writing the novel said it was indecent and silly, and anyway it was deeply deceitful to write a novel in school exercise books when you were supposed to be doing Prep for the next day – 'I hope you're thoroughly ashamed of yourself.' She tore it up.

At home, Ursula was now officially diagnosed with depression. She reinterpreted this in her own terms. 'Depression', she explained to her daughter, was an external blight like flu. It 'could happen to absolutely anybody' and had little connection with anything one had done or failed to do. It certainly wasn't one's fault. Although it might be partly other people's fault for somehow conspiring to make one live in a place where one's real self – intellectual, enlightened, etc. – could not flourish. Or, alternatively, it might be due to something called 'the change of life', which was another blight ('like adolescence, you know, darling – that, of course, is why *you're* fed up') which apparently descended from nowhere on one's fortieth birthday.

As if to allow room for this depression which, like an unpleasant lodger, seemed to have moved into the house, Ursula withdrew further. She went to bed earlier and earlier, had 'rests' after lunch, and so encountered insomnia in the small hours. Trying to write plays now instead of novels, she nevertheless tended to resist suggestions about theatre trips to London – 'Too tiring.' Too tiring and difficult now also, apparently, were walks on the Forest, riding, swimming and almost everything else she had enjoyed in earlier days, including tennis. Paradoxically, this woman in the prime of life who was afraid of middle age, was now acquiring the mental and physical outlook of an old woman.

By and by there were visits to psychiatric hospitals for abrupt doses of 'treatment'. (This was before the era of psychotropic drugs.) In a panic-stricken way, she did very much want to 'do something' about herself. But the same life-view that had created her problem also prevented her from confronting it honestly.

As the nemesis that had been in the making for the last twenty years began to close in on Ursula, Tom too became enmeshed in her bogus world of mechanistic excuses and hasty rationalisations. Kind by nature and accustomed to regard his wife as a strong character, he was quite ill equipped to cope with the emotional burden now being laid on him. He was also now the key partner in the family firm. It was all too much for him; he had neither time nor energy to think about the children too. Their small son was despatched for a long stay with cousins and then to boarding school.

At much the same time Julia managed to leave her own boarding school, mainly by refusing, in a storm of tears, to return there. (No one had apparently noticed before that she did not like it there.) She was almost sixteen, and it was decided that perhaps she could continue her education at a crammer's. In any case, truth to tell, she was needed at home, now that her mother was so frequently unable to get out of bed. This chimed with a half-formed, egocentric perception of Julia's own that perhaps, in some less specific way, her mother did need her presence. They had been close during Julia's earlier childhood – all those books and stories, all those shared times with no one else there – and it was when Julia had been sent away to school that Ursula had begun to fall to bits.

It is just possible that Julia was right about this. But,

too old now to be her mother's soul mate, she was too young to offer objective advice or comment. Meanwhile, the responsibilities thrust on her were almost more than she could manage. At her father's increasingly desperate but oddly unexplained request – 'Try not to leave Mummy alone more than you can help' – she found herself minding a woman who did things that were, to her, inexplicable. Once, Ursula was brought home by an anxious stationmaster, who knew the family because Tom travelled daily by train to his office in London. She had been wandering back and forth across the railway lines. Another time she returned in a police car. She had been found at the top of a high building in a nearby town. Julia continued not to understand, but felt cross because she had wanted to go into the town herself to mooch round the shops and perhaps run into that boy again who was often in the Kardomah . . . Why hadn't Mummy, always so fussy and critical about Julia's own movements, told her she was going in? Two days later, Julia went there by bus, and returned to find her mother trailing about the house with soaking hair. 'I tried to drown myself in the bath,' she confided miserably.

It should have been revelatory, yet it still was not, not quite. An otherwise able-bodied woman cannot drown herself in a bath, as Julia correctly perceived, and therefore she was inclined to regard her mother's desperate act as a piece of melodramatic showing off.

If that sounds as if Julia was hard-hearted and did not love her mother, that is unfortunate. But it is no more unfortunate than the fact that the self-absorption of depressives tends to drive those who care for them into stoniness in sheer self-protection. Not only was it impressed on Julia that she was not allowed to say to her mother, 'For Heaven's sake, pull yourself together,' she believed she was not allowed to think it, either.

Teenagers are, by force of nature, self-centred themselves, necessarily looking outwards to the world in store for them. It is not good for them to be asked to sympathise interminably with the plight of someone who has failed at the enterprise of living. During those weeks and months and years Julia held her peace and did her best, but her capacity for compassion was strained beyond its limits and took many years to recover.

She retreated into work for A-levels, and from that official activity into reading the dated novels with which the house was well supplied. Encountering Margaret Kennedy's *The Constant Nymph*, she daydreamed of dying, like its heroine, in the arms of a secret lover in a Brussels boarding house. By and by she began turning the story into a play in French, an activity which she thought of as a private escape from Milton and Carlyle. Only long afterwards did she realise, between amusement and puzzlement at her younger self, that this endeavour had been rather remarkable in a teenager who had never yet been abroad. Perhaps a specific gene-for-French, inherited from Aunt Maud, had been making its presence felt in her . . . But of Aunt Maud herself, the teenage Julia knew nothing.

As for Ursula, instead of the old dream of Paris as the lost Eden, London now began to figure on her mental map as the place where she might find again her true self. London was only an hour and a quarter away by rail; she could have spent every day there, had she wished, as her husband did – but the idea of the great life-changing move was put into action. The task of finding a new London home and organising it distracted her satisfactorily for some months, but as Moving Day approached she must have begun to realise (with what misery and panic one can only surmise) that London held out no magic remedy. A further dramatic collapse took place. Julia and her father had to organise the move on their own.

Ursula reappeared from hospital, to be welcomed into the new home. She complained, very much, because in the move her fountain pen had disappeared. How could she be a writer without her fountain pen? It must be somebody else's fault. Six days later, having by the move severed further the ties that had held her to life – and having, incidentally, taken her family away from all its supports and accustomed surroundings – she made another suicide attempt which, this time, was fatal. She was not found for two days.

To Purgatory fire thou com'st at last,
And Christ receive thy soul . . .

No one, I think, can measure the real distress that must lead someone 'with everything to live for' to such an end. It seems self-evident that the suicidal impulse can be overwhelming. But even now, more than fifty years later, when the dead woman that I recall is young enough to be my daughter, I find myself appalled by the manner in which she chose to carry it out, and in particular by the lack of any scribbled word of apology or grief or love for either of her children.

I also find it odd. In her own distorted way Ursula was conscientious, sometimes obsessively so. Julia was within a month of taking her Oxford entrance exams ('Oh you'll love Oxford, darling – I did'). In choosing such a moment for her traumatic exit, did she, as Julia darkly wondered afterwards, have some destructive intent towards her daughter? Because she was so unhappy herself and felt a failure, did she, at some level, need Julia to be so too?

But the simpler answer, I have come to suspect over the years, is that she thought she was going to be rescued. Only the day before, she had bestirred herself to go shopping, buying two new nightdresses which were found after her death still in their cellophane wrapping. She probably imagined that the garage with the sports car where she hid herself would be opened in time, that there would be an ambulance, and once more the blessed cocoon of hospital and concerned voices. Once again she would be looked after and told it wasn't her fault. Once again she would be an indulged schoolgirl, safely organised by other people, a *jeune fille de bonne famille*, clever favourite daughter of a clever father. It would all be all right, and she would never – quite – have to face the realities of ongoing time and change and inevitable loss, the wavelength on which real life is lived generation after generation.

Chapter XVIII

ESCAPES

Three years later Simone de Beauvoir's *Mémoires d'une Jeune Fille Rangée* was published. Julia read it. The last sentence, following on the quasi-suicide of de Beauvoir's greatest childhood friend, Zaza, runs '. . . *et j'ai pensé longtemps que j'avais payé ma liberté avec de sa mort*' ('. . . and I thought for a long time that my freedom had been bought at the cost of her death').

The words struck at a section of Julia's heart which, almost all the time, she managed to keep shut off from her current life. She seldom, at that period, thought of her mother at all, and it seemed to her, reading de Beauvoir's words, that such a bargain with fate had been struck in her own life too. Ursula's death had surely been the necessary price of her own freedom?

'*J'ai pensé longtemps . . .*' Not till she was older and a mother herself did she understand what a terrible act it is for a mother deliberately to abandon a young child. And not for a number of years more did she know that to abandon a child who is just growing up is almost as great a betrayal of responsibility and trust, of love itself.

A suicide is not just a tragic event fixed in time, as a fatal accident or illness that has come from without. By its willed destruction, it changes the entire perception of that life, casting a retrospective shadow over the whole, implicitly calling in question all the aspirations of the life, all the values by which it was lived. This much was clear to Julia within days of Ursula's funeral. Yet there seemed to be a general, if uncoordinated adult effort to treat the suicide as if it had just been a relatively brief, unfortunate and rather embarrassing corollary to a life otherwise unaffected by it. A tragic event, of course, but you must try to put it out of your mind, Julia dear, and remember your mother as she was not long ago, before All This started . . . Tom, punch-drunk with his own mixture of grief, guilt and new-found freedom, awkwardly joined in the unconvincing chorus.

This was before the days of counselling. Phrases such as 'grief therapy' and 'post-traumatic stress' did not yet trip off anyone's tongue. In that era, the working-class reaction to a suicide in the family tended to be one of shamed secrecy. The middle classes did not exactly write the suicide out of the script in that way, but took refuge in the stiff upper lip, the getting on with normal life, the not-brooding and the keeping-busy that had been the coping strategy through two world wars. Dwelling on death was morbid – Victorian, indeed – and Ursula's children must be prevented from doing so. Her little boy, who had lost not only his mother but his childhood home in Sussex, must stay at his boarding school. As Bertie, another child deprived suddenly of his mother, had done seventy years before. Julia, of whom so much adult understanding and responsibility had recently been expected, must somehow be thrust back into a more suitably juvenile role. Tom seemed in a hurry to remake his life, and she was now in the way. She had, of course, managed splendidly with cooking and so forth while poor Ursula, yes, tch, tch . . . But she would be off to Oxford soon, wouldn't she? And before that, of course, she was going to be sent to spend a few months in Paris, what a lucky girl! That was always to have been the plan, no reason to change it. Poor Ursula had wanted Julia to spend some time in Paris with some nice suitable family just as she had.

So it was that, five months and one week after her mother's death, Julia found herself despatched to Paris. She had not asked to go there.

The old daydream of Paris, which had been nurtured in her from childhood, was now, like the rest of that childhood, consigned wholesale to a fear-haunted, decomposing rubbish dump, shoved away out of sight along with her mother's photo. In the last few months, she had managed to cobble together some sort of different life in London, a territory without a past or envisaged future. She read nothing, wrote nothing. Infinitely remote, now, seemed the great calm expanses of Ashdown Forest, its folded hills and dips, its white-sand streams. Instead, there was the crushed, much-populated grass of Hyde Park where she rolled around with an unsuitable boyfriend.

Just once or twice, when alone, she found herself overtaken by an inexplicable burst of tears. She took this to be a physical symptom, like crying over onions, so divorced did it seem to her to be from anything she consciously felt or thought.

She was not consulted about the arrangements for Paris. In an inappropriate attempt at the social patterns of the past, which were going rapidly out of date by the mid-1950s, the traditional-widow-taking-in-nice-girls-of-good-family was found for her. Apparently it did not occur to anyone that her experiences of the last twelve months, indeed of the last several years, might have unfitted her for docile acquiescence to such a scheme.

The apartment was off a dull avenue near the Eiffel Tower. The drawing room seemed full of the furniture and cabinets of china already familiar to Julia from the pages of Pierre-Solange. The dining room, opening out of it through mirror-glassed doors, occupied a central position at the corner of the building: its pot-bellied balcony hung over the street and avenue as if to invite a heady plunge four floors down. There, in an atmosphere of darned table napkins the size of babies' sheets, tarnished silver fork-rests and weary constraint, meals were served by a black-clad and overworked cook-maid called – what else? – Liliane. The rest of the apartment was dark and cramped. Off a corridor with no daylight but haunted by more mirror glass, the bedrooms, insufficient in number, overlooked a narrow courtyard and the twin apartment on the other side. The widow had a Second Empire, falsely aristocratic *de* to her name and the peremptory, over-emphatic manner of her kind. She owned a turreted château in need of repair somewhere in Normandy, and had several daughters to marry. These shared small rooms, or bedded down at night in the dining room, while the largest and best-equipped bedroom was left to the foreign girls on whose payments, it seemed, the whole household subsisted. Julia found herself sharing this room with a wordless Canadian girl and an older Belgian who smelt faintly, and who told nightly stories, in a nasal whisper, about men who followed her in the street. This quickly improved Julia's spoken French, but did nothing to resign her to the circumstances in which she found herself. A weekly bath was permitted, and there was one lavatory, the door of which Madame de B complained foreign girls tended to leave ajar.

Madame de B no doubt had many troubles and cares. Her only son, never seen, was said to be handicapped and was, like the crumbling Château, 'in the country'. Her eldest daughter was engaged and was tacitly allowed to have her fiancé in her room far into the night because there was no acknowledgement that he was in the flat at all, but the young man was said by the Belgian, with heavy innuendo, to be 'getting bored'. Even had Madame de B had the inclination to organise a pleasant and inclusive life for her paying guests, she had neither the energy nor the mental resources. She was, in fact, taking them on under false pretences.

Once this had dawned on Julia it became, as far as she was concerned, the only advantage of her present situation. She had been, up to that point, invaded by sudden moments of misery and disorientation whose intensity stunned her. She had felt herself thrust into a false position, neither welcome guest nor autonomous lodger. She was darkly relieved when she realised that Madame de B's initial assurances to her father, that she kept an eye on where her guests went and whom they saw, were empty. Madame de B showed no sign at all of being interested in what Julia was doing, provided she was there at mealtimes. In that case, Julia thought, she, Julia, need feel under no obligation to stay. It was barely a month after her arrival that she told Madame de B she had found somewhere else to live. Fending off Madame's indignant protests and then her more craven pleas about her need for money, she waited till her hostess was visiting the Normandy ruin, then packed her case and left.

In later life, on the rare occasions when she recalled this event, Julia was rather amazed that she had managed to carry it off. Evidently, the degree of ruthlessness, the stony refusal to be sucked into the prison of another person's needs which she had evolved in self-protection over the last three or four years had come in useful.

From distant London, no significant protest was raised. Tom too had made an escape and was now busy with his own emotional needs.

So it happened that Julia, not yet eighteen, was living on her own in Paris. First she stayed in a bed-and-breakfast place in the polite Invalides district recommended to her by a Dutch girl she had met at the notional Sorbonne 'course' they were both following. She ate in subsidised student restaurants off metal food-trays – '*Ne gaspillez pas le pain!*' notices said. 'There are some who don't have any.' At this rate, the money in the bank which would not now go to Madame de B would last for ages, Julia thought happily.

She had found herself drawn into the Latin Quarter through circumstances, without awareness. But soon it began to exercise on her the pull it had had for innumerable others before her, turning gradually from a collection of battered streets into a country of the mind with its own inherent contours. The shortest way to the Sorbonne from the bus stop where she got off at the Odéon crossroads lay up the Rue de l'Ecole de Médecine: her feet trod daily where her great-great grandfather's had a hundred and forty years before. She had barely heard of Arthur Jacob, but something in her began to respond to the gravitas of the medical schools, whose fortress walls were decorated with a huge, antique injunction not to stick up posters (*Loi du 29 juillet 1881 . . .*) She liked, too, the way the august street narrowed abruptly into an alley with the murky windows of the Dupuytren museum on one side. Many things, she sensed, had happened here, but she did not yet know quite what.

In her first weeks in Paris she had dawdled along the Boulevard St Germain and the Boulevard St Michel, looking into shop windows at flat sandals and green eye-shadow and the whitish lipstick that was fashionable in that far-off, Juliette Gréco, pre-Beatnik spring, but now she paced the side streets with their insistent suggestion of other and hidden lives. She discovered the tiny, zinc-countered cafés of the Rue Hautefeuille, and the one in the Cour de Commerce which sold cabbage soup and *petit salé aux lentilles* and leathery steaks from the butcher's with two gilded horse heads in the Buci market. One day she left her lodging in the bland vistas of the seventh *arrondissement* and moved into a room in a modest hotel not far from the Ecoles de Médecine and the Odéon theatre. It stood in the slanting Rue Monsieur le Prince, which ran – though she did not know this then – right down the line of Paris's thirteenth-century wall.

From this new base, she explored more easily. Wandering a few hundred metres further east one day, beyond the point where the Sorbonne-bound crowds thinned away and the buildings in the back streets became scabrous and a little sinister, she passed through Maubert and came upon the steep, winding route up the Montagne Sainte Geneviève. She climbed up, slightly heady in the spring sunshine, beguiled by the ancient and ramshackle buildings she passed. Though far more ignorant of architecture than her grandfather had been some sixty years before, like him she discovered with delight the eccentric beauty of St Etienne and its stained-glass windows. She knew nothing then of Bertie's time in Paris. It was not till several years later, when she had returned to Paris as a genuine grown-up, that he asked her for news of the tram terminus in the Place St Germain. Now, she simply wondered why no one had told her that this was what Paris was really like – the Paris into which you felt you could go deeper and deeper, far from the Champs Elysées, the Eiffel Tower and dull apartments near the Champ de Mars. The fantasy Parises of her childhood, too, fell away from her, forgotten as if they had never been.

By and by, like a young animal staking out its territory, she ventured further. She sought out the old Portes St Martin and St Denis, marooned in the crowded boulevards of the Right Bank. She came upon the quiet Marais, and wondered in ignorance why the garment trade signs in the dilapidated Place des Vosges were so weather-faded, and why there were shut-up kosher butchers and a derelict synagogue in the Rue des Rosiers. She travelled to the ends of Metro lines that were not yet extended beyond the line of Paris's now-demolished fortifications, and wandered around the wide spaces littered with bric-à-brac at the Porte de Clignancourt and the Porte de Vanves. Objects there called mutely to her, but she turned away. To travel lightly through life, physically as well as emotionally, that was surely the best plan? Someone advised her enthusiastically to go to Montmartre, but there were American tourists there in the Place du Tertre having their portraits sketched by much-bearded and jerseyed artists. She left, and went back to the Latin Quarter.

When high summer came, and the hotel near the Odéon terminated the lets of lodgers such as her so as to rent the rooms in July and August to foreign visitors who would pay more, it seemed natural to look eastwards again. After some searching, she found herself a room high up in the Hôtel des Carmes. It cost three hundred old francs a night, two hundred less than the other hotel. Since the franc had by then inflated to the weightlessness of a pre-War centime, this worked out at two pounds seven shillings a week. Julia knew by hearsay, from her few months in London, that this was rather less than a bedsitter there would cost in any comparable position. Not that there *was* anything comparable in London, she thought. By leaning perilously out of her attic window she could see the towers of Notre Dame one way and the other way, uphill, the dome of the Panthéon. This, now, was her life, the only reality she had. To both the fear-haunted past and the yawning, unknowable future she closed her mind.

Chapter XIX

ANOTHER LIFE IN PARIS

L ong afterwards, when she looked back on this brief
period with a detached nostalgia, as if at a time
abandoned to history, Julia saw that the middle
years of the 1950s had been the ending of an era. It was
still, just, the Paris of the Liberation on which her eyes
and her spirit opened fully for the first time. It was physically and mentally the Paris that had seen street-fighting
on barricades in August 1944. There had been one
between St Julien le Pauvre and the river quay, and there
were small plaques on walls here and there throughout
the Quarter commemorating dead fighters barely older
than herself. But the city was, indeed, the same Paris
that had hardly changed since before the First World
War, merely growing a little shabbier and more cynical
in the years between, stagnating economically behind
peeling shutters, waiting for its fortunes to be revived
by the next turn of history.

In a year or two General de Gaulle would be summoned
back into office and changes would begin. In a year or
two the streets and boulevards would begin to fill with
traffic, its fumes invisibly tainting the air, wheels a
continual noise on the old cobbles. But for the time being
many of the Haussmann arteries of Paris were great open
spaces, traversed mainly by antique vegetable-laden

lorries, by bouncing canvas-roofed Deux Chevaux, by the wide-based black Citroëns that had been the emblematic vehicle of the Liberation, by bicycles – and by handcarts. The handcart, piled with goods to be delivered or sold, or sometimes with household chairs, basins and mattresses being removed from one minimal lodging to another by a tired-looking man in an old alpaca jacket, was still the insignificant workhorse of the older quarters.

Few people owned cars, any more than they owned telephones. The standard means of rapid communication was the *pneumatique*, a late-nineteenth-century invention that used vacuum pressure to suck small, folded missives along a network of special tunnels to all districts of Paris, as if the city were one huge department store. You bought a small, blueish letter-card (a *petit bleu*) at any post office, inscribed it with a message of instructions, protestation, love, regret or reproach, sealed it and dropped it in the slot provided. From there it would make its way to the appropriate district and be delivered by a messenger on a bicycle, all within an hour or two. Like the Metro, it managed to be admirably efficient and very old-fashioned at the same time.

The Metro was crowded at most hours and in the early evening was packed tight. Its centre carriage was always the First Class one, which cost more and was therefore less full. *Des jeunes filles*, Madame de B had said, were well advised to travel First Class at busy times, advice which Julia naturally did not take. The trains were also full again after midnight, as the time neared for the last one – *le dernier métro*, a term still impregnated with the drama and fear of the Occupation curfew, when to miss it was to risk arrest. The trains travelled slowly, grumbling along on wheels that did not yet have rubber tyres. Passengers, coming down the stairs, would hear the last train approaching and begin frantically to run. You had to get to the platform before it was actually in, or a heavy automatic *portillon* would grind shut in your face.

The Metro authority seemed to have a fixed fear – eventually abandoned – of people trying to jump into the train at the last moment.

The *portillons* were in addition to the human guardians of the Metro, usually female, who sat by barriers at each end of every platform and punched holes in passengers' tickets. Each ticket could be used twice, and the punched-out tiny circles of yellow littered the platform ends like confetti. The hint of gaiety was illusory, for this was recognised to be a job undertaken only by those who could aspire to nothing better, and the *poinçonneuses* were proverbially ill-tempered. They knitted, to pass the otherwise dreary, draughty hours, and occasionally two on opposite platforms would hold loud, complaining conversations across the rails. With almost three hundred stations, many of them with multiple platform entries, needing to be manned from five in the morning till past midnight seven days a week, the number of *poinçonneuses* must have been counted in thousands. Yet with the modernisation of the Metro and some reconfiguring of its maze-like passages, they began to disappear. There were no more left after 1970, and in the folklore of Paris they figure with an affection they never attracted in life. In the same way, the instantly recognisable smell of the Metro, which wafted up even through gratings in the street and seemed to be composed of garlic, dust and tobacco (although the Metro trains all forbade you to smoke), is remembered with nostalgia now that it, too, has gone.

Gone as well are the meticulous notices on both Metro trains and buses stating who had priority over seats and in what order: First, War cripples (*mutilés de guerre*), second, civilian cripples and the blind . . . Those with heavy parcels or young children ranked only fifth. Since the Second World War produced few French cripples and in fact few military dead, owing to France's rapid collapse and capitulation in 1940, it was the spirit of

1918 that was incarnated in these orders. The buses themselves, with their slatted wooden seats, open platforms
at the back and pull-chain bells, were still in the 1950s
the same early motor design that Maud Tindall had found
in Paris when she returned from nursing in 1918.

In the 1950s, too, the *pissoirs* (more genteelly known
as *vespasiennes*), that had been first introduced by Préfet
Rambuteau in the 1830s[1] and redesigned circa 1900,
continued to stand jauntily at street junctions. In wrought
iron, usually round over a round grating and divided
internally into three triangular stalls, they screened the
user from shoulders to calves. No doubt their coming
had originally seemed a hygienic advance, finally modi-
fying the age-old Parisian habit of relieving oneself just
anywhere, but their very obvious purpose, lack of overall concealment and characteristic reek meant that
effectively the habit of urinating in public was given indef-
inite sanction. A perfectly respectable man, when walking
in female company, would not hesitate to dive into a
pissoir with a murmured *Excusez-moi*, make use of it while
hardly breaking off conversation, and emerge buttoning
himself. (The *pissoirs*, of course, were not designed for
women. Women, presumably, had never been much given
to relieving themselves in the street, so the need to
accommodate females had not been perceived.) Alas for
male comfort and ease, General de Gaulle – or possibly
Madame de Gaulle – disapproved of the *pissoirs*. They
were said to encourage male homosexuality, and after
1960 began to disappear quite rapidly. The one that had
been installed on the remnant of Place Maubert in the
early 1900s, along with the statue of Etienne Dolet, in
an effort to make that ancient expanse of Parisian earth
more respectable, was replaced with a small, purely decorative fountain.

Visible in the streets of the Latin Quarter, as Julia first
knew it, was the Paris that had existed for hundreds of

years but would do so for very little longer. In that Paris, most of the ordinary working people still lived within an embracing culture of poverty. One-woman laundries full of steam occupied basement rooms; cobblers, tapping nails into soles, sat in triangular shelters inserted into any odd corner where one old building protruded further than its neighbour. In other corners, hot-chestnut sellers, as in Bertie's time, did a steady trade among the chilled and hungry. Meanwhile, those who had slipped from the world of work into destitution, through ill luck, folly or too heavy an attachment to the eternal *coup de rouge*, slept undisturbed on Metro gratings through which came the dragon's breath of the tunnels. Others bivouacked under bridges on the quays where, as yet, no politician had had the bad idea of constructing motorways.

It was still the world in which the Hédevins worked long hours in menial jobs in the restaurant trade, and nursed the dream of one day retiring back to the Lozère. Their small son Paul had been taken there for safety, to grandparents, in 1940, abruptly exchanging the freedom of the streets for that of the hills, rocks and trees that had cradled his ancestors. He had been returned to Paris after the War as a cheerful but almost illiterate eleven-year-old. In the Lozère people had had priorities other than school attendance, and on the farm a boy was always useful. Although he was to settle and marry in Paris, and make his way in turn in the restaurant and hotel business, his identity and values continued all his life to draw upon the peasant roots from which he had come. In the maze of the city he had his own pathways, his own routines.

But then many born Parisians too continued, throughout the twentieth century, to treat their particular quarter as a known village set in wilder country which they seldom penetrated. Typical in this way was the journalist and novelist Henri Calet. He was born in 1904 in the Montparnasse hospital that received unmarried mothers, grew up to travel the world but always returned to his natal landscape. His most enduring book, *Le Tout sur le Tout* ('All About Everything'), takes Montparnasse, just up the hill from the Latin Quarter, as his sacred ground of memory, at once the microcosm of the globe and the sum total of his inheritance.

The Rue de la Huchette, Elliot Paul's adopted sacred ground, was in the 1950s still lined with small businesses sellings things in small quantities: grocers, ironmongers, drapers, seedsmen, all characteristic of provincial France, as it had been when the American had lived there twenty-five years before. Milk was ladled from churns into customers' own cans, yoghurt was sold in earthenware pots which were to be returned. A tiny theatre, newly started in an old warehouse, was the only sign of changes to come. Night after night, two plays by Ionesco were applauded by an audience that had filtered over from a kilometre to the west. Since the end of the War, St Germain des Prés had become the epicentre of fashionably Bohemian Paris.

Fifty years later the very same plays, *La Leçon* and *La Cantatrice Chauve*, are still part of the repertoire at the Théâtre de la Huchette: they are a cherished tradition there. But all around in the street, and in the adjoining alleys of St Séverin, towards St Julien le Pauvre, the scene is transformed. The modest shops have become North African restaurants, take-away counters and Italian pizza bars. You could say that Huchette has, in the very long perspective, regained its old identity, for in the twelfth century it was the street where the mutton-roasters plied their trade. But the present-day loud music, the necklaces of lights, and the grazing hordes of American, German and Dutch tourists that now fill the narrow street are redolent of nothing but the blurring of national cultures and the loss of habitat for ordinary Parisians.

*　　*　　*

In the 1950s a few remaining old-fashioned restaurants still advertised *plats à emporter*, usually stewed meat and vegetables, handed out in covered metal bowls on which a deposit was taken. Otherwise, frankfurter sausages with fried potatoes, wrapped in paper, were the only take-away food on sale. These were not eaten in the street, but were carried off to be consumed in shabby rooms. In the Rue Maître Albert, and in the Rues des Anglais, des Rats and de Bièvre, tenants still settled for years in homes whose only water supply was an ornate, verdigris-encrusted tap several flights below. There, in their own kingdom of interconnected courtyards, grubby children in traditional blue or black pinafores played happily in permanent puddles. In such pockets, the bugs that George Orwell had recorded in cheap lodgings twenty-five years before were still a fact of life.

Elsewhere, bugs and non-existent plumbing had been more or less remedied after the War without pulling down the buildings. But on the grounds of *insalubrité*, that sonorous word of official French condemnation, there was still extant the long-term plan, carried over from the nineteenth century, to demolish the entire Maubert district. Traditionally, the designation 'insalubrious' was based on the local death rate from tuberculosis, and hence on the by then obsolete notion that tuberculosis was caught from buildings rather than from people. In addition, for many years after the War the tuberculosis figures themselves were out of date: the most recent ones available derived from the early 1930s.

However, this did not prevent them from being used for the Grand Plan that was drawn up in 1950 and ratified a full eight years later. Marked for extinction, along with Maubert, were great swathes of traditional working-class habitat in the north of Paris, in the 15th *arrondissement* behind Montparnasse and in the 13th behind the Gare d'Austerlitz. Fortunately for the Latin Quarter, the engines of destruction first turned their attention to these larger schemes. Many of the unfortunate working-class citizens in the designated areas were removed to tower blocks a long way out of town, which in a few years more became the breeding ground for newer social evils than insalubriousness.

In the 1950s Julia knew nothing of the guerrilla warfare then continuing between preservers of old Paris and would-be developers. The high houses of Maubert and the Montagne Sainte Geneviève, palpably so much older than anything surviving in London, seemed to her eternal, as if the irregular buildings were natural rock formations in a mountainous landscape. In those days, entry codes were unknown. Concierges might keep intermittent watch from behind net curtains, but the great courtyard doors for bygone coaches and carts opened readily. You could walk in, as if into a public space, in any daylight hour, and explore further doorways, climb flights of worn stone stairs, admire half-obliterated carvings and the lettering of defunct trades, peer from old windows onto still more hidden inner yards and rooftop views. If you proceeded quietly but purposefully, Julia discovered, looking as if you knew where you were going, no one was likely to question you.

The Rue des Carmes itself, always a cut above neighbouring Maubert, had not entirely escaped twentieth-century attentions. At its foot, the last of the Rue des Noyers including Alfred de Musset's birthplace had finally been pulled down, in spite of protestations, in 1930. 'This is progress,' wrote a local antiquarian at the time, 'ignoble progress, and the so-called exigencies of public health, the mania for straight lines, and the urban planners who, on the pretext of renovating a city, smother its soul and its memories.'[2] In place of the house and others adjoining was erected the headquarters of a Technical School of Building, in uncompromising Bauhaus brick. Just one stone-fronted house of the same style as the de Mussets' remained, and remains to this day, along with the surviving trace of the Rue des Noyers in the form of a lowered piece of pavement at the foot of the Rue Jean de Beauvais. A similar drop outside two ancient shops on the opposite side of the Boulevard St Germain indicates the original level of the Place Maubert.

The upper reaches of the Rue des Carmes lost its old houses on one side to road-widening in the 1920s, but the section below the Rue des Ecoles, which had already undergone some late-nineteenth-century straightening, remained untouched in the 1950s. The Hôtel des Carmes, and another lodging house alongside, hung over the Rue Basse des Carmes and the remains of Napoleon's covered market, where chickens, old clothes and bicycles were still bought and sold. Not till after the Left Bank riots of 1968 would the market site be rebuilt again with another four-square, cloister-shaped building. This is the concrete blockhouse of a new district police station, a classic example of the architecture of paranoia.

Opposite the Hôtel des Carmes, when Julia took up her abode there, was the house of a Dominican order, almost the last relic of the religious foundations that had once crowded the immediate district. Rebuilt in the 1860s in heavy Gothic-revival style, set back from the street around the remnant of a much older cloister, it was a sunless place of dwindling, ageing occupants, but added an old-world respectability to that section of the Carmes.[3]

Like most small hotels then that provided long-term accommodation, the Hôtel des Carmes had no proper lobby or desk. You walked straight in from the street, along a corridor, past an alcove where unwatched keys hung on pegs and there was a bell just in case you should want to summon someone, and then to the spiral staircase that went up six floors to the top of the house. The rest of the ground floor, one-time stabling or storehouse for the monks of the Carmes cloister, was occupied by the family that managed the hotel. Underneath, in the deep cellars, was a jazz club. It had been established there shortly after the War, and in 1948 the film maker Jacques Becker used it as a setting for his *Rendez-vous de Juillet*. This confirmed and spread the fashion for jazz-cellars, and by the 1950s St Germain des Prés (now conflated in many people's minds with the Latin Quarter) was celebrated for these seductive, smoky holes.

The hotel was still very much as it had been when it had sheltered thirty-eight people from many different countries in 1926. But the numbers had increased, and in thirty years the ethnic base had shifted. Now Arab music wailed in some corners, and among the layered smells of damp washing, bought fried potatoes and methylated spirit stoves were those of couscous and spice. Once away from the staircase, down which a faint light penetrated through grimy panes of glass high above, the labyrinthine corridors were completely dark. They burrowed round corners, through big old rooms that had been partitioned into smaller ones, and no two floors were the same. Coming and going between the street and her own eyrie, Julia never learnt the layout of most of the floors in between. Turning the heavy old key to push open the door of her room was like emerging from a forest climb onto a sunlit upland at the top.

She had a window high above the street, looking over the Dominicans. She had a round table, discarded from some more elegant setting, and two chairs. She had a sagging bed with a bolster, twill sheets and an old feather quilt, a wardrobe with a mirror and some curtained shelves. Behind a screen was a basin with taps that produced cold water and, sometimes in the mornings, warm water too, tinted brown. Underneath the basin was a doll-sized enamel bidet on a stand, with a jug to fill it. The hotel had no bathrooms, and if any of the rooms on the lower floors had shower cabins Julia neither knew nor cared. The lavatories, one to each floor, were by the stairwell, the site to which all Parisian plumbing had naturally gravitated with the invention of the soil pipe, since that had to go down somewhere. Each convenience consisted of a hole in the floor with two ridged surfaces for the squatter's feet. This, as one of Julia's new acquaintances said, was 'more hygienic' than the pedestal sort, since '*ainsi tu ne mets pas ton derrière sur n'importe quoi.*'

Of course she got to know new people all the time, superficially. In the hotel itself were a band of rather noisy French male students who greeted her cheerfully – '*Bonjour la petite anglaise!*' – often followed by some unintelligible joke or query she felt it best to ignore. She was wary of their slang and their deliberately coarse shouts as they bounded up and down the stairs, but half wanted to know them better: they seemed so vital and sure of themselves. In the room opposite hers there were two Brazilian girls who exchanged the odd friendly word with her: one of them was pregnant, and one night came up the stairs sobbing steadily. Later, there were cries, and running feet, but by that time Julia was almost asleep.

There were other students, Arab these, who led their own life in a sort of kasbah at the back of the first floor, and an older Moroccan who always greeted Julia politely on the stairs, once carried a heavy bag up for her, and once invited her into his room for a glass of mint tea. She sat nervously on the edge of the bed, alert for the moment when he would make a lunge at her. Her rapidly accumulating experience of life led her to expect this would happen, but he just spoke nostalgically of his wife and children in Rabat, and of the sadness of separation. She avoided him, rather, after that. Her own neediness had little to offer to his.

Her days were, in any case, increasingly populated by young and not so young men. She was pretty, and though her air of concealed desperation must have put some off, it undoubtedly drew others to her. In those days (or so it seemed to Julia) it was the general rule that a man would, of course, try to go to bed with a girl, and it was equally accepted that she would do her best to resist him. The two conventions struck her as rather irrational and extreme, and led to exhausting wrangles, but she went along with them. She struggled, giggling, kissing, demurring, on quiet evening quays by the river – and, once, on the green banks of the Marne where, in an expedition redolent of working-class Paris life before the War, a not so young man had taken her on his motorbike for a Sunday picnic. One evening, a distinguished-looking man rather older than her own father took her to a brothel behind St Séverin. It would, he said, be interesting for her to visit such a place. She was sufficiently aware to guess that he had something more in mind, but she said, poker-faced, How kind it was of him – Yes, it had been very interesting, and now she must go home.

She had met this gentleman, most respectably, in the home of one of the Pierre-Solange contingent. From some sense of honour, or simple embarrassment, she never told the Pierre-Solanges of this further experience with him.

She felt herself to be buoyant, managing well. She had escaped from many things.

Then one night she had a terrible dream.

She was in the hotel, but could not for some reason reach her own room. She was in one of the lower corridors, in the dark, and could not go back: possibly the stairs were not there any longer, or perhaps some hostile presence was behind her. She could only grope her way forward. But, as she did so, she became aware that in the room at the end of the corridor lay something dreadful, something on which she did not want to open the door. It was a body. It lay on the floor and must, she began to realise, have been there for a long time. Decomposing. No one had found it till now. She knew whose the body was. Horror seized her.

She woke with a cry. The quilt was twisted round her. She lay there unmoving in the dark. She wanted to go to the hole by the top of the stairs, but was too frightened to get out of bed. Who knew what was lurking behind any of these doors? Or what she might find when she came back . . .

At last the short summer night began to bleach into day at the edges of the shutters. She crept out of bed and opened them, breathed the morning air. Far below in the street someone was brushing water about with a twig broom. On the edge of the wall by the dormer window, scored into the old plaster, was an elaborate pierced heart with initials: she had never looked hard at it before. How long had it been there – months? Many years? The walls were lumpy, their paint faded, marked here and there with old nails and stains.

All at once she knew that beneath the present layer of paint and plaster lay other hearts, other messages, crude drawings and sentimental ciphers, the grimy prints of other hands. Innumerable people, she realised, had been happy and unhappy here before, making love or submitting to another's needs, wrangling about money, celebrating survival, clinging to one another or plotting escape, being homesick for distant places. They too had looked from this window, whose frame from an unimaginably distant tree was now petrified silver with time. Perhaps people had even died in this room, long before it was a hotel, of consumption or cholera or –? Or abortion. Or despair. Babies may have been born here too, children grown here year by year. Underneath the present layer on the walls might lie their pencilled heights and names, messages of hope for a future now all past.

Exhausted by the night, overwhelmed with intimations of a life ahead she could hardly compass, let alone plan, she huddled on her clothes and went out to look for a cup of coffee. But the richness of the vertiginously populated past had reached out and touched her. Although she did not yet know it, it was to shape her own future.

*   *   *

The Pierre-Solanges, as they admitted to her long after, were rather worried about Julia. What was their old friend Tommee thinking of, to leave his little girl kicking around Paris on her own? But they were busy people and did not want to stir up trouble – and perhaps in England, famed for modernity, these things were viewed differently. They contented themselves with inviting her sometimes to lunch, when she ate ravenously and they complimented her on her increasing fluency in French, or to the occasional early evening party at which their sophisticated middle-aged friends found her crude but fetching.

It was, in fact, through some ostensibly respectable contact met through the Pierre-Solanges that her life changed once again, though later she could never recall just what the tenuous social links had been.

She remembered an agreed meeting in a dark bar off St Germain des Prés. She remembered a rapid drive westwards out of Paris in a car crowded with three men and two other women. She remembered a strange house, with music and laughter and a great deal to drink, and then finding herself alone in a bedroom with one of the men. Rescued just in time by the most resourceful of the women, she was eventually driven back to Paris by another of the men, who seemed to have constituted himself her protector. He was young, though a good deal older than her, since everyone then was older than she was. He was short and muscular, big-nosed, with curling dark hair. He seemed to her over-voluble; he made jokes she could not follow. His name was Serge. She liked him simply because he had been kind to her.

The next morning he sent her an affectionate *pneumatique*, asking her to meet him that evening for dinner and go with him to the Théâtre de la Huchette. She accepted readily. More nice food. Oh, good.

Three days later it was the fourteenth of July, Bastille Day, when traditionally Parisians take to the squares and crossroads for evening dancing. The blast of amplified rock music that would fill the night skies of Paris on that fête by the end of the century lay in the unguessed future. The music then was provided, as it had been for the previous hundred years, by firemen's brass bands or by accordions. Waltzing far into the summer night in Serge's arms, to the perpetual shuffle of shoes around them on the cobbled ground, Julia was conscious of participating in a very long-standing Parisian ritual, probably far older than the Revolution it ostensibly commemorated. Serge assured her, with joky solemnity, that it would continue long after they were both dead and gone. She liked being included in this way, by him.

That same night, just up the hill in Montparnasse, something occurred that was unknown to Serge at the time and hence to Julia. This was the death of Henri Calet, the writer who had taken his particular personal square mile of Paris to represent the entire world. He was only fifty-two but his heart gave out, quietly and all at once, as the beat of the band went gaily on in the street below.

It was three in the morning when, after a long walk to the Halles district and back for night-time onion soup, Julia finally convinced Serge to take her back to the Hôtel des Carmes. At that late hour the street door was shut, something Julia had not expected. At midnight, at one o'clock, even, when the last Metro was running, she had always found it open, but now . . . .

She did not have the experience to know that, had she pressed the bell, a somnolent member of the manager's family would have aroused himself enough to buzz the door open for her. Serge did not tell her. So she went helplessly back with him to his flat in Montparnasse and yet another new life began for her.

Some time after, Serge was to say to her, in a tone of faint but honest apology:

'I thought, *tu vois*, that if it wasn't me it would very soon be someone else, so it might as well be me.'

Each had got the other wrong, as they were to agree years afterwards, meeting again for lunch. Serge had initially taken her to be yet another sweet but rather silly girl, fine for a brief liaison but nothing more. Julia, on her side, had grabbed unthinkingly at the chance – as she had grabbed at any chance in her makeshift life – to experience in Serge's company a socially grander, more lavish and more interesting Paris life than she had been able to find so far on her own. Each was surprised, and a little disorientated, as they were forced to know one another better. Beneath the surface, their separate insecurities reached out to each other.

More than ten years after the Liberation of Paris, Serge, under a man-about-town air, was still fragile from the fear and humiliations that had haunted his Wartime teens. The family's flight to Lyons, the assumed name and the false identity cards, the veiled taunts and glances, the elder brother deported for forced labour in Germany, the aunts and uncles who disappeared never to be seen again . . . All these things had marked him, indeed were to mark him, faintly and indelibly, for the rest of his long life.

One day, having learnt the little of Julia's recent past that she could bring herself to tell him, he said in genuine puzzlement:

'But, *ma chérie*, didn't your father want you to stay at home with him, after what he has lived through?' (*après tout qu'il a vécu*).

Julia's throat constricted. How to explain that the answer was No? She had no ready explanation, either for herself or for anyone else, for the way in which her mother's ending had managed to complete its destruction by blowing her father and herself apart. She had fetched up in this strange, alternative life. And of the little brother, abandoned to boarding school, she hardly dared think.

* * *

Not very long after, however, she received a summons home. She had been half agreeing to go with Serge to Brittany, where his parents, to whom he seemed much attached, had rented a house. But apparently exile was now suddenly over and she must return to London. Apparently a simulacrum of family life there was about to be arbitrarily resumed. In a new form and with a new member of the cast.

A rather hastily chosen newcomer, one might think, and it seemed that some people did think. 'You see, dear,' one relative wrote nervously to Julia, 'your father has had such a rotten time for years, poor boy . . . And after all, he's still quite a young man . . .'

Young man-in-love. It was a role in which Tom had always readily seen himself, ever since his idyll in Germany at eighteen. Clearly, it would be useless for Julia to stake any claim in that department herself. The map of Paris that she had been constructing for months as her new country of the mind and heart was to be rolled up again.

More literally, an eighteenth-century map was to be rolled up, one by Boisseau, which she had bought (with Serge's encouragement) from one of the dealers' stalls on the quays. It was her very first purchase of a kind of which, later in life, she was to make many more.

AFTERWARDS

J ulia was to come back often to Paris, and to live there
again for most of a year in her early twenties, but
although Paris gave her much it was never, quite, the
same. She had grown up, and seen other places and known
other people.

Paris was changing too. The shanty towns at
Clignancourt and Vanvës were removed. The years passed,
and in place of the huts made of tarpaulin and old petrol
drums there was eventually built a roaring, raised, circular
motorway, as much of a visual barrier round Paris as the
old *fortifs* had been. Meanwhile the North African families who had made some sort of life for themselves in
the huts had been deported further out, to the same serried
ranks of slab buildings that were housing the dispossessed
Parisian poor – an architecture that, in the worst tradition of French grandeur, despises the human scale. Metro
lines were extended, and by and by once-pretty suburbs
like Châtillon were invaded by shopping complexes and
high-rise office blocks.

Serge's elderly parents had long since migrated from
Châtillon back to central Paris; his brother and sister
had abandoned France for good in favour of America,
for reasons not hard to understand. The promise of the
three young children in the flowery garden at Châtillon

had not, after all, been fulfilled in France where their parents had settled with so much hope. Was it really for lost Châtillon that Serge felt a momentary pang when he discovered an old photograph? Or for the loss of the future that had once been planned.

Within Paris the Halles, the one-time central markets with their wrought-iron pavilions, were summarily demolished in 1971 under the Grand Plan, in spite of many protests. The Halle aux Vins, the wholesale wine market that had been built on the Left Bank by the first Napoleon between the Maubert Quarter and the Jardin des Plantes, was replaced by a complex of wind-trapping skyscrapers housing the university's science faculty. Another new tower, enormously high and black, rose on the site of the old Gare Montparnasse, where the famous locomotive had crashed through the buffers in 1895. Soon other huge blocks and towers began to rise further west, filling the open view beyond the Arc de Triomphe at the top of Paris's grandest boulevard. Motorways usurped the ancient river quays.

There were many larger schemes at this time to transform Paris into a version of New York, but President Pompidou, the chief enthusiast for this implausible project, died prematurely in 1974. Indignation by this time was loud, and was expressed not just by architectural historians but by large numbers of ordinary Parisians. Haussmann Paris, that had once appeared so alarming and modern in itself, had over the past century and more acquired a patina and become loved for its own sake. One of the first acts of Pompidou's successor, Valéry Giscard d'Estaing, was to decree that no more skyscrapers should be built within Paris proper. At the same time, public opinion was so overwhelmingly opposed to the loss of any more of the beloved back-street fabric that at last a number of long-maintained schemes were finally abandoned. These included a particularly noxious one for the entire Latin Quarter that would have gouged out an extension of the Rue de Rennes as far as the Seine, obliterating the Rue Bonaparte. It would have eviscerated with a huge criss-cross road system the remaining old streets between there and the Boulevard St Michel, and (of course) destroyed the Maubert area. So, fully reprieved for the first time in almost two hundred years, the Rue St André des Arts, the Rues Hautefeuille, Huchette, St Séverin, Maître Albert and all the others began to be rehabilitated.

It was probably inevitable that this rehabilitation should involve the stones and timbers of the buildings rather than the lives of those who had been living there. Paris was at last, for better or worse, largely liberated from rent control. Market forces took over, and the whole nature of the Maubert area began to change. Gone were the playing children, the old women in broken-down shoes who fed stray cats, the cafés that sold wood and coal as well as wine and working-class cigarettes in yellow *papier maïs*. Accreted layers of old plaster, cement and pebble-dash were removed from façades, exposing to the light of a new day great seamed oak beams, hardened through their load-bearing centuries to the consistency of rock. Actual rocks, hand cut to size by thirteenth- and four-teenth-century workmen, were discovered round doors and windows, cleaned up and set off by fresh rendering in buttery hues. Carved street names and niches for tiny saints were disinterred. Meanwhile, inside the buildings, total transformations were taking place, as partitions, false ceilings, shaky glass-paned doors, flights of iron steps, obsolete sinks in dark corners, enamel pails, floor tiles, washing lines, dangerous loops of amateur electric wiring, corroded bird cages, flower pots with the dry ghosts of geraniums, collections of dusty bottles, the paraphernalia of a hundred different minor trades and all the rest of the humble clutter of past habitation was flung down into skips. By the 1980s, President François Mitterrand himself had a pied-à-terre in the Rue de Bièvre.

*   *   *

Julia lived for half a year in the Rue Bonaparte, and it was to this address that her grandfather wrote and told her of his own stay in the Quarter. She did not then realise, however, that the antiquarian book-dealers at no. 12, with a particular line in medical volumes, was the very business where he had worked. She used to look in its windows as she pattered homeward from the noisy cafés of St Germain des Prés. Sometimes, in addition to the books, there were objects for sale. For several weeks, on top of a pile of gold-embossed medical encyclopaedias, was an ivory woman about twenty centimetres long, in a loose gown, lying on a plinth. She had a pretty, rather chinless eighteenth-century face surrounded by beautifully sculpted tendrils of curling hair. She lay supine, her stomach protruding upwards, for she was nine months pregnant. The arch of her stomach, shaped like a tea-pot lid, had been lifted off, to display within a complete set of exquisitely carved reproductive organs and a baby ready in position to be born: tiny hands and feet, rope-like cord, spongy placenta. The expression of infantile confidence and docility on its miniature face matched the smug contentment on its mother's. No apprehension of the biblical Great Pain and Peril of Childbirth was to be suggested here.

Julia was very tempted to buy this artefact but did not, for it was expensive and what (she said to herself) would she do with it? She realised that it was intended to serve as a medical illustration and teaching aid, from an era when such things were works of art constructed with loving skill, but she herself had embarked on a career as a writer, not a doctor.

Most of a lifetime was to pass before she was to see that unbought, lost ivory lady as something that had stretched out from the past and touched her. It had been a message from the Paris world of her great-great grandfather, Arthur Jacob, there in the window of her grandfather's place of work, silently calling to her as she followed unknowingly in his tracks.

The years accumulated. Julia settled back in England, married, and created the family home she had missed in childhood; but France, as the archetypal Other Place, the point of reference and the parallel other existence she might have had, intermittently haunted her work. For many years she was visited by the fantasy that an alternative self was continuing its own existence somewhere on the Left Bank.

This was not like her mother's fantasy of a lovely 'real life' continuing elsewhere. Julia did not envy her own doppelgänger. She was wary of her, and inclined to think that she had chosen a false path, but the increasingly alien ghost proved as resistant to oblivion as she apparently was to change. Passing through Paris, Julia would get sudden whiffs of her, almost-sightings. She apparently lived in one of those tiny apartments now being carved out of the old houses somewhere near St Germain des Prés – or, later, as the tide of gentrification moved eastwards, behind Place Maubert. She was not a writer, but perhaps worked in a publishing house, Julia thought. Or, this being Paris, more likely an art gallery. 'Moving in creative circles' rather than creating at first hand, as if her talent had been siphoned off into recreating herself. The actual nature of her work would not be as important to her as the sheer fact of being in Paris and having constructed a life there. She 'knew interesting people' and made a point of keeping up with cultural events. ('*This is the penalty of leaving your native land. It means transferring your roots into a shallower soil . . .*') She gave carefully planned little dinner parties, beautifully cooked. She dressed well, this ghost, more expensively than her English equivalent, hair nicely cut, make-up attended to, always the right scarf. No children, of course. And no husbands, or none that lasted . . .

Julia would sometimes think with guilty amusement that she was being unfair to the ghost, whose life might in practice have led her into paths of which she, Julia, was ignorant. But no more unfair than the ghost was to her. For ghost-Julia (Julia was sure) had based her life in Paris very substantially on the idea of having had a lucky escape from England, which to her remained a land of fog and custard and hypocrisy and drearily garish clothes and people who moaned on about depression . . . Huh, said Julia unkindly to the helpless ghost, you'd better watch it! What will you do with your cherished, interesting, cultured Left Bank life when all the people you've been despising in England have been dead and gone for years, and your assorted lovers are dead too, or rendered inoperative by age, or retired to places like Meung-sur-Loing with their wives? If depression should one day catch up with you after all, *ma semblable, ma sœur* . . . But this line of unforgiving fantasy seemed so dark that Julia retreated from it in shame. On one occasion, the pathos of this fossilised creature that she had invented almost overwhelmed her.

In any case, in the real world the real Julia had shifted her personal French territory away from Paris, to the still older rural France that many Parisians continue to carry within them. She adopted as her country of the mind a small segment of this deeply traditional France, whose only constant change was that of the seasons with their constant renewal. Putting down roots into this compost, she began to work on the history of the area and its people, and so, in a back-to-front way, constructed a French setting for herself. The child, who had trudged in the rain across Ashdown Forest and had been given a lift in a cart, witnessing an ancient way of life then on the verge of extinction, surfaced in her in another guise. She found that she had the capacity to offer back to the people of France their own vulnerable, receding pasts, and that they were grateful for this. The moment in the

Hôtel des Carmes, when the populated past had first touched her with some intimation of her own future and what her task might be, had been a true one.

And in the day-to-day world, too, the Latin Quarter was changing. Spared now the external devastation that was visited on some less famous quarters, internally it was subject to a huge dismantling. By the 1990s streets that had, for centuries, sheltered workshops and small laundries, grocers and bakers, and still did when Julia lived in the Rue Bonaparte, gradually filled with businesses selling pictures, *objets d'art* and expensive clothes. The premises on the corner of the Rue Bonaparte and the Rue de l'Abbaye, which in Bertie's day had housed an employment agency for servants and a florist ('Wreaths a speciality'), was by the end of the twentieth century a retail outlet for Dior. Lemoigne's old book-dealing premises long remained in the same trade, but today its forlorn windows offer minimalist designer furniture. In the Rue Maître Albert, at the other end of the Latin Quarter, a grocer's survives, run by Vietnamese, but in place of the wine shop and the old clothes dealer there is an art gallery and a house-agent advertising flats for sums approaching a million euros.

For the first time in the thousand-year history of the Quarter, the students at its institutions of learning can no longer afford its rents, and nor even can the teachers. A pity, when general awareness of its long history of scholarship has never been higher. In the hot summer of 2005 some wit went round the Maubert area in the steps of Abelard, Agrippa and Dante, neatly pasting blue-and-white alternative street signs over existing ones. *Via Anglicorum* (Rue des Anglais), they read, *Vicus Beveris* (Place of the Beavers – the supposed origin of Rue de Bièvre). And *Vicus Romanus* – Latin Quarter. Because the sites chosen were high up, and because the labels were designed to look, at a glance, like standard street names, it took the municipality a while to notice them all and remove them.

Many of the time-honoured small hotels of the area are still where they always were, under the same names. But their essential nature has changed. No longer are they the long-term lodgings of foreign workers, students, retired language teachers or jazz musicians: they are tourist hotels, and charge tourist rates. They are not approached up ill-lit staircases, but have front desks in tastefully furnished lobbies with brochures advertising Parisian Sights. There, callers are expected to sit and wait for residents to descend, for keys are not left in doors nor are visitors free to come and go unchallenged.

Staying at the Hôtel des Carmes occasionally over the years, Julia could chart the gradual progress of this change. The old lavatories, where *tu ne mets pas ton derrière sur n'importe quoi*, were replaced by the pedestal sort. At the same time, some of the labyrinthine passages and partitions were reorganised and a few bathrooms (*Bain 3 francs. sur réservation*) appeared. Better timed light-switches were fixed on the stairs. Nightmares were to be banished, along with cries and murmurs. Then, in the early 1970s, came a change of owner and a larger shake-up, at about the time that the remains of the Marché des Carmes were being pulled down to build the fortified police station. The hotel reclaimed its ground floor from small shops and was done up throughout. A tiny lift arrived. So did carpets in some of the rooms, and telephones.

A little later again the bigger rooms, including Julia's old eyrie at the top, were divided into two or even three. Space was now too much of a luxury for a modest Left Bank hotel to offer, but more and more individual shower cubicles were installed. Then, in the 1990s, the whole house was done over again. The traces of its long human history were suppressed, along with old beams and stones and messages scratched in plaster, under layers of insulation, sealing, polystyrene, paint – and carpet every-where, even on the walls of the new, larger lift. Each room had its own self-contained bathroom now, its own television, its own standard furnishings and colour scheme.

Yet something of the innumerable past lives it had sheltered still beat, a buried memory deep inside the building. And when Julia stood leaning out of one of the top windows, she could still see, looking down to the river, the illuminated towers of Notre Dame. Looking up the hill the other way she could see the Panthéon, as tenants of the house did when it was the new church of Sainte Geneviève and the market gardens and orchards began just beyond it.

At some point in the late 1980s the Hédevin family became involved in running the Hôtel des Carmes.

The hard-working, robust couple who had travelled from the Lozère to Paris to seek their fortunes in the 1920s were now dead and gone, part of the rich Parisian earth, fading from human memory. Their son Paul was a man in his fifties, content with a piecemeal life through restaurant kitchens and hotel baggage rooms, ambitious only for his daughter Véronique for whom he had ensured a 'proper' Parisian education. So it was that Véronique, competent, firm but welcoming, became the Carmes's young manageress. Two or three other cheerful, reliable people joined her and, feeling comfortable, remained for many years. Even the night porter, traditionally on the Left Bank a job for transient students, was a known and trusted fixture. By and by Paul too came to frequent the now well-lit passages, tool bag in hand, whiling his retire-ment away attending to showers the guests had blocked or electric plugs they had mysteriously damaged. The Carmes was a true success, much appreciated by regular customers. Early in the twenty-first century it developed an enthusiastic internet following. If Julia half regretted the long-ago Carmes, with its floors of wide, splintery old wood or worn red tiles, its cooking smells and all its freedoms, she kept the fact to herself.

She has stayed briefly at the Carmes a number of times in the last few years. One visit followed an invitation from the Société Française d'Histoire de la Médecine to represent, at a conference in the Ecoles de Médecine, the English connection of *'cette grande maison d'édition médicale française Jean-Baptiste Baillière et Fils'*. Tom, very old by now, had been pleased to hear of her appearance in that role. Guiltily, he always seemed a little puzzled, if gratified, that she had turned out as she had. Once, quite spontaneously, he apologised for having neglected her so. She said that it did not matter now, for by that time it hardly did.

By a poignant coincidence that he would probably not have appreciated, she happened to be in the Hôtel des Carmes again two years later, when she received a phone call with news of his sudden death. Once again, she thought with worn affection, Tom had managed to escape her.

Another visit too was connected with a death. Julia was summoned by the remnants of the Pierre-Solanges. Her favourite Solange was dead at last at over ninety, and again she was required to 'represent the English interest'. Solange, her great-nephews and -nieces knew, had always been fond of England. *Le fair play. La marmelade. Le pudding de Noël. Agatha Christie* . . . And there had been the haven of the Free French domain in Carlton Gardens, London, during the War. *N'oublions jamais* . . .

So it is that Julia finds herself standing up one morning in a big, old Left Bank church addressing in French a respectful congregation. A small green ribbon, bestowed on her by the French government in a fit of generosity towards those interested in obscure French history, adorns the jacket of her most sober suit. As she speaks, she feels pangs for Solange, almost her oldest friend, who will not be replaceable. But she also feels a sudden pang for the Julia who had first been welcomed by Solange, so long ago. She wishes she could tell that far-off, desperate Julia that, in spite of everything she might have seen or been told so far, life was going to be all right.

That night, in the now insulated and double-glazed security of the Hôtel des Carmes, she has another dream.

She knows she is in Paris, and in the deeply familiar territory of the Latin Quarter. Yet not far from Place Maubert, just where the land rises up the Montagne Sainte Geneviève, the terrain is not as she remembers it. The streets here give way to a great, undulating heathland with tracts of heather and bracken and broom, dotted with clumps of trees. Yet this wild landscape seems once to have been used as a graveyard, for here and there stand weathered tombstones, modest but permanent.

And somewhere over on the far side, glimmering on the horizon, is a shoreline, the edge of the land.

Her dreaming mind tries to rationalise this heath, this shore ... Has a section of rural France perhaps been there all the time in the familiar street plan of the fifth *arrondissement*, and she has simply failed to notice it before?

Only while consuming coffee and rolls the following morning in the Carmes' breakfast room does she suddenly understand that the heath was Ashdown Forest. It had been quite recognisable, actually.

Dreams know no chronology, perpetually attempting to conflate different periods into one. She knows that, in the dream, the tombs of different sizes and ages standing among the birch trees raised no fear. Arthur Jacob ... Albert Alfred Tindall ... Bertie ... Maud ... the Lemoignes ... Yes. Those are the people whose harmless memorial stones she herself has discovered in Paris, in the landscape of time.

As for the distant seacoast, that must be the last vestige of the dream Paris, the unreachable after-the-War Paris that Julia was told about on those forest walks as a very small child. The Paris of white towers and a bright blue sea with ships and swans. Only a faint memory now, almost below the horizon. The long walk across Ashdown Forest is over.

She finishes breakfast, and goes out once again into the well-trodden morning streets of Paris to have another look.

Notes

Part I

Chapter II
1 Once, when he was visiting the home of a Dublin associate, a little daughter of the house ran in and flung her arms round her father. Surprisingly, John Jacob said 'I would give all I have for one of my children to greet me like that.' The little girl grew up to marry one of his nephew's – Arthur's son.
2 The distant cousin who covered himself with military honour, and after whom Jacobabad is named, was of a subsequent generation.

Chapter III
1 Sir Charles Hastings, 1794–1866. Founder of the British Medical Association.
2 *Statutes and Rules for the Government and Conduct of the General Infirmary for the Relief of Sick and Lame Poor at Northampton.* 1813.

Chapter V
1 John Scott, the editor of *The London Magazine*.
2 *Un Grand Homme de Province à Paris*, 1839.
3 Rue des Noyers would eventually be almost annihilated by the Boulevard St Germain.
4 It disappeared when the wide streets of Monge and Jussieu were cut through the district in the 1860s,

though the steeply slanting Rue des Boulangers still traces its outline.

5 Today it has been removed about a kilometre away to the small garden at the foot of the Rue Mazarine.

Chapter VI

1 Since obliterated, like so much else, by the Boulevard St Germain.
2 Various historians and commentators have claimed addresses for Marat in the part of the ancient street that is still standing, near the junction with the Rue Hautefeuille, but in reality it seems that his address, then no. 30 Rue des Cordeliers, was one of the many houses that disappeared with the construction of the Boulevard St Germain.
3 Although the Terror tends to be seen by history as a largely Parisian phenomenon, another 1400 overall were guillotined in provincial France.
4 Much of it is there today, though embedded within the more extensive buildings of the late nineteenth century.
5 Quoted in *The Royal College of Surgeons in Ireland and Its Medical School 1784–1984*, by J.D.H. Widdess.
6 *Mémoires d'un Bourgeois de Paris*, by L. Véron, 1856. Louis-Désiré Véron studied medicine under Guillaume Dupuytren, but later made a fortune out of a patent remedy and took to journalism and politics.

Chapter VII

1 Today the two ancient foundations form one hospital in large, modern buildings near the Gare d'Austerlitz, not far from the original sites of both.
2 The manuscript pages are today in the Wellcome Library.
3 Not to be confused with the later Hôtel Voltaire by the Seine.

Notes

Chapter VIII

1 Quoted by J.D.H. Widdess. Op. cit.
2 Manuscript memoir of Arthur's granddaughter, Blanche Jacob.
3 Unfortunately no letters between them survive from the famine period two or three years later, though there must have been some.
4 Information from Patrick F. Meehan, writing in *The Laois Yearbook* in 1983.

Part II

Chapter IX

1 *Etudes sur la Transformation du XII Arrondissement*, 1855.
2 Henri Meding, *Paris Médical*, 1852.
3 *Coins de Paris*, 1905.
4 Lawyer, newly elected member of the Corps Législatif, and later and most famously Minister of Education under the Third Republic.

Chapter X

1 Pierre Mazerolles, *La Misère de Paris, les Mauvais Gîtes*.
2 A character in the popular songs of Pierre-Jean Béranger.
3 Daphne du Maurier, *The du Mauriers*, 1937.
4 Also known as *Fiesta*.

Part III

Chapter XI

1 All the Tindalls in the area, however they spelt themselves, appear to have been descended from a John Tindall/Tendall who owned a small amount of land in Ticehurst in the mid-eighteenth century. 'Tindalls Cottage', which stood there till the 1970s when it was demolished for the contruction of a reservoir, survives as a heap of numbered bricks and timbers in the storehouse of the Weald and Downland Open

Air Museum at Singleton, West Sussex. At the time of writing, its re-erection is planned 'soon'.

2   In the UK, the full Census records may not be consulted till one hundred years have passed.

3   I am indebted for this insight to Kathryn Hughes, in *The Short Life and Long Times of Mrs Beeton*, 2005.

4   The University of Reading.

5   Manuscript memoir of his granddaughter, Monica Campbell née Tindall.

Chapter XII

1   Manuscript memoir of Monica Campbell.

2   Since the 1970s, the Boulevard Périphérique has occupied the ring round Paris traced by the old fortifications. This urban motorway preserves, in its signs, the memory of the old gateways in and out of Paris that used to punctuate the customs wall.

3   This contemporary view of the statue is now hard to evaluate, since it disappeared, along with many others, in the early 1940s, melted down by the occupying Germans.

Chapter XIII

1   H. Dabot, *Calendrier d'un Bourgeois du Quartier Latin*, vol. 2, 1905.

2   Quoted by Marguerite Perrot, *Le Mode de Vie des Familles Bourgeoises 1873–1953*, thesis 1961.

Chapter XIV

1   Quoted in *A Short History of Baillière Tindall* by D.H. Tindall.

2   He did, however, love her very much. Letters abandoned in a barn, which only came to light as this book was being printed, show that for their entire married life, whenever they were apart, he wrote her a loving and chatty letter every single evening.

3   In 1920 a nephew from the Jacob side, who had also

been in the trenches in Flanders but survived, was taken into the family firm to fill Howard's empty place. He fortunately proved very able.

Chapter XV
1 Manuscript memoir of Monica Campbell.

Part IV

Chapter XVI
1 Elliot Paul, *The Narrow Street*, 1942.
2 In virtually every provincial *département* of France, as in Great Britain, Census records from about 1840 onwards are available for consultation, and in France these may be consulted for up to thirty years before the present date. The records of the twenty *arrondissements* that make up Paris seem, however, to have been largely lost. Various excuses are offered by local archivists – that the reorganisation of Paris proper circa 1860 led to a loss or misplacement of documents, that records disappeared wholesale in the burning of the Hôtel de Ville in 1871 – but none of these theories explains the absence of material for the later 1870s to the 1920s. One is forced to conclude that the doctrinaire left-wing nature of most Parisian Councils over many decades has led to the unthinking destruction, in the name of progress, of paper testimony to past lives that should have been kept.
3 *The Unquiet Grave*, 1944.
4 'From the Paris railway station of Austerlitz there were sent to the camps of Pithviers and Beaune-la-Rolande, and from there deported and murdered in Auschwitz, 3700 Jews, all male, on 14th May 1941. From 19th to 22nd July 1942 a further 7800 Jews were transported, four thousand of them children seized in the Vélodrome d'Hiver raid, arrested within Paris on the order of the occupying German forces by the police accredited by

the authority then in charge. This was done in the name of the "Government of the French State".

    'Let us never forget!'

5   Research in the Hastings street directories does not support this belief.

Part V

Chapter XVII

1   For a while I tried asking literate acquaintances, both French and English, if they had any faint memory of such a book, but abandoned this quest when I found the invariable response was to assume that I must mean Raymond Queneau's *Zazie dans le Métro*, which dates from a generation later and is anyway excessively well known.

Chapter XIX

1   The public began mockingly to refer to these objects as *rambuteaux*, so the Préfet responded by baptising them after the Roman emperor who had also installed such conveniences.

2   Paul Farry, Secretary to L'Association des Amis de la Montagne Sainte Geneviève.

3   Today the building, vacated by the Order, is divided into expensive flats, still sunless, and the premises of a 'dermatological institute of beauty'.

Books Consulted and Other Sources

While it would not be possible for me to cite all the books in my life that have contributed, in some measure, to the present one, here follow two fairly comprehensive, if heterogeneous, lists of books and other material that I know I have consulted over the last three years. One list relates to France and the other to the British Isles.

Except where otherwise stated, the books written in French were published in Paris, and those in English in London.

For France

Anon. *Le 5ième Arrondissement, itinéraires d'histoire et d'architecture*, Mairie de Paris, 2000

Anon. *Le Bulletin de l'Association des Amis de la Montagne Sainte Geneviève*, 1895–1902, 1909–1912, 1920–1938 – essays and notes contributed by members of the Association des Amis de la Montagne Sainte Geneviève

Baldick, Robert, *The First Bohemian: The Life of Henry Murger*, 1961

Balzac, Honoré de, *Un Grand Homme de province à Paris*, 1839

Bancquart, Marie-Claire, *Images littéraires du Paris 'fin de siècle'*, 1979

Barsky, Hannah K., *Guillaume Dupuytren: A Surgeon in His Place and Time*, New York, 1984

Beaurepaire, Edmond, *La Chronique des rues*, 1900

Birkbeck, Morris, *Notes on a Journey through France, 1814*, 1815

Borgé, Jacques, and Viasnoff, Nicolas (editors), *Archives de Paris*, 1993

Burge, James, *Heloise and Abelard, a Twelfth Century Love Story*, 2003

Cain, Georges, *Coins de Paris*, 1905

Calet, Henri, *Le Tout sur le tout*, 1948

Caron, Jean-Claude, *Générations romantiques: les étudiants de Paris et le quartier latin (1814–1914)*, 1991

Chadych, Danielle, and Le Borgne, Dominique, *Atlas de Paris, evolution d'un paysage urbain*, 1999

Chevalier, Louis, *Le Choléra à Paris*, 1858

Christiansen, Rupert, *Tales of the New Babylon, Paris in the Mid-Nineteenth Century*, 1994

Clébert, Jean-Paul, *Promenades dans les rues de Paris, Rive gauche 1, 2* (après Félix, Marquis de Rochegude, 1910), 1958

Books Consulted and Other Sources

Cramouzaud, Eugène, *Etudes sur la transformation du XII arrondissement*, 1855

Dabot, H., *Calendrier d'un bourgeois du quartier latin*, vol. 2, 1905

De Moncan, Patrice, and Heurteux, Claude, *Le Paris de Haussmann*, 2002

De Musset, Alfred, *Une porte doit être ouverte ou fermée* (play), 1834

Des Cars, Jean, and Pinon, Pierre, *Paris Haussmann*, 1991

Dickens, Charles, *The Uncommercial Traveller*, 1860

Du Camp, Maxime, *Paris, ses organes, ses fonctions et sa vie*, 1894

Du Maurier, Daphne, *The Du Mauriers*, 1937

Du Maurier, Gerald, *Trilby*, 1894

Du Mesnil, Dr Octave, *L'Habitation du pauvre à Paris*, 1890

Duveau, Georges, *La Vie ouvrière en France sous le second Empire*, 1946

Dyer, Colin, *Population and Society in Twentieth Century France*, 1978

Elliot, Paul, *A Narrow Street*, 1942

Evenson, Norma, *Paris: A Century of Change 1878–1978*, 1979

Gady, André, *La Montagne Sainte Geneviève et le quartier latin*, 1998

Gaussen, Frédéric, *Le 5ième Arrondissement vu par les peintres*, 1998

Gibson, Robert, *Best of Enemies: Anglo-French Relations Since the Norman Conquest*, 1995

Gourdon de Genouillac, H., *Paris à trayers les siècles*, 1881

Griscom, John, *A Year in Europe 1818–19*, New York, 1923

Guerrand, Roger-Henri, *Mœurs citadines – les lieux, histoire des commodités*, 1992

Hansen, Arlen J., *Expatriate Paris: A Cultural and Literary Guide to Paris of the 1920s*, 1990

Hillairet, Jacques, *Dictionnaire historique des rues de Paris*, 2 vols., 10th ed., 1997

Horne, Alistair, *The Fall of Paris*, 1965; *Seven Ages of Paris*, 2002

Hussey, Andrew, *Paris: The Secret History*, 2006

Huysmans, Joris-Karl, *Croquis parisiens*, 1886; *La Bièvre et St Séverin*, 1890

Jaillot, Hubert, Géographe du Roi, *Recherches critiques, historiques et topographiques sur la ville de Paris*, 1775

Krief, Philippe, *Paris Rive gauche, petites histoires et grands secrets*, 2004

Lemaire, G.G., *Les Cafés littéraires*, 1997

Le Notre, G. (editor), *Le Vieux Paris, souvenirs et vieilles demeures*, 1911

Loyer, François, *Paris XIX siècle: l'immeuble et la rue*, 1986

Maneglier, Hervé, *Paris-Imperial: la vie quotidienne sous le second Empire*, 1990

Mansel, Philip, *Paris Between Empires*, 2001

Mazerolles, Pierre, *La Misère de Paris, les mauvais gîtes*, 1875

Meding, Dr Henri, *Paris médical*, 1852

Mellet, Philippe, *Paris disparu 1845–1930*, 2000

Mercier, Louis-Sébastien (in English translation), *Paris Delineated, short account of the principal edifices and curiosities*, 4th edition, 1802

Moore, George, *A Modern Lover*, 1889

Morizet, André, *Du Vieux Paris à Paris moderne, Haussmann et ses prédécesseurs*, 1932

Books Consulted and Other Sources

Nadaud, Martin, *Les Mémoires de Léonard, un garçon maçon*, 1895, re-edited 1976

Olsen, Donald J., *The City as a Work of Art: London, Paris, Vienna*, 1986

Orwell, George, *Down and Out in Paris and London*, 1933; *Inside the Whale*, 1940

Perrot, Marguerite, *Le Mode de vie des familles bourgeoises 1873–1953*, unpublished thesis 1961, lodged with the Bibliothèque de la Ville de Paris

Pillemont, Georges, *Paris disparu*, 1966

Pitt, Leonard (translated by Yves Emsette), *Promenades dans le Paris disparu, un voyage dans le temps au cœur de Paris historique*, 2002

Planta, Edward, *A New Picture of Paris, or the Stranger's Guide to the French Metropolis*, 6th edition, 1817

Radwan, Anna, *Mémoire des rues, Paris 5e arrondissement 1900–1940*, 2005

Rambuteau, Claude-Philibert Berthelot, *Mémoires du comte de Rambuteau publiés par son petit fils*, 1905

Réau, Louis, *Histoire du vandalisme: les monuments détruits de l'art français*, 1994

Régnier, Dr Christian, 'Jean-Baptiste Baillière', article in *Medicographia*; vol. 27, no. 1, 2005

Renault, Georges, and Le Rouge, Gustave, *Le Quartier latin*, 1899

Richardson, Joanna, *The Bohemians, La Vie de Bohème in Paris, 1830–1914*, 1969

Robert, Jean, *Les Tramways parisiens*, 1992

Sand, George, *Histoire de ma vie*, 1855

Scott, John, *A Visit to Paris in 1814*, 1815

Simonds, Charles (editor), *Paris de 1800–1900*, 1900

Texier, Edmond, *Tableau de Paris*, c. 1855

Tombs, Robert, *France 1814–1914*, 1996

Tomel, Guy, *Le Bas du pavé parisien*, 1894

Uzanne, Octave, *Parisiennes de ce temps*, 1910

Valdour, Jacques, *La Vie ouvrière*, 1921

Véron, Dr Louis-Désiré, *Mémoires d'un bourgeois de Paris*, 1856

Vinen, Richard, *The Unfree French*, 2006

Ware, John N., *How to Find Old Paris*, 1927

Weber, Eugen, *France fin de siècle*, 1986

Zola, Emile, *La Curée*, 1872

For Great Britain

Earnest, Dr Robert, *Synopsis of Medical and Surgical Care at the Sheffield General Infirmary during 22 years*, Sheffield, 1820*

Forbes, John (editor), *Cyclopaedia of Practical Medicine*, 1830s

Gibbs, *Dr Denis D.*, 'The Physician's Pulse Watch', article in, *Medical History*, vol. 5, 1971; 'The Almshouses of Lichfield, Cradles of Pulse Timing', article in the *Journal of Medical Biology*, vol. 2, 1994

Guthrie, G.J., *Lectures on the Operative Surgery of the Eye*, 1830

Hughes, Kathryn, *The Short Life and Long Times of Mrs Beeton*, 2005

Books Consulted and Other Sources

Jacob, Archibald, and Glascott, John H., *An Historical & Genealogical Narrative of the Families of Jacob from AD 1275 to 1875*, published privately in Dublin, 1875

Lyons, J.B., *Brief Lives of Irish Doctors 1600–1965*, Dublin, 1978

O'Brien, Eoin, *Conscience and Conflict: A Biography of Sir Dominic Corrigan 1802–1880*, Dublin, 1983

Manwaring Baines, J., *Outline of Hastings History*, Hastings, 1989

Robinson, Victor, *Victory over Pain, A History of Anesthesia*, New York, 1946

Rowlette, Robert, *The Medical Press and Circular 1839–1939: A Hundred Years in the Life of a Medical Journal*, 1939

Smith, Henry Lilley, *Observations on the Prevailing Practice of Supplying Medical Assistance to the Poor*, Warwick, 1819*

Smith, G.M., *A History of the Bristol Royal Infirmary*, Bristol, 1917

Tindall, D.H., *A Short History of Baillière Tindall*, 1983

Widdess, J.D.H., *The Royal College of Surgeons in Ireland and Its Medical School 1784–1984*, 3rd edition, Dublin, 1984

Winchester, Simon, *The Map that Changed the World*, 2001

*These items form part of a collection of 'Tracts on Hospitals' made in the 1840s and now in the Rare Book Room of the British Library.

Other sources

Arthur Jacob's papers (letters, articles, obituary notices, etc.) in the archives of the Royal College of Surgeons in Ireland; also his library which is housed there.

Baillière, Tindall & Cox archive in the University of Reading, consisting of twenty-one volumes of copy-out letters, 1875–1910.

MS diary and letters, listed in the Wellcome Foundation Library as 'Journal compiled by unknown English traveller in 1818', subsequently identified as being by John Sims.

MS pocket diaries of 'Bertie', A.A. Tindall, numerous, various dates between 1895 and 1969, in the author's possession.

MS note by Jean-Baptiste Baillière, concerning his origins and early life, copy in the possession of Michel and Annie Roux Dessarps.

MS memoir of Blanche Tindall, née Jacob, written c.1930, in the author's possession.

MS memoir of Monica Campbell, née Tindall, written c.1985, in the author's possession.

MS stories and poems by Maud Tindall, in the possession of David Waddell and Claire Metson.

Archival Sources and Acknowledgements

My main source for much of the material used in this book has been the **Bibliothèque Historique de la Ville de Paris**, delightfully housed in the Marais in what was, in the sixteenth century, a private mansion. Its pleasantly antiquated card-index catalogue, its relaxed attitude towards those who wish to browse its capacious open shelves and its large collection of maps more than make up for certain inefficiencies and for its long-time-inoperative photocopier. I shall be sorry when a threatened modernisation occurs. I owe a particular debt of gratitude to its archivist Madame Claude Billaud, who, having interested herself in what I was doing, actually made me a present of a complete set of modern-reproduction eighteenth-century Jaillot maps of Paris, of which the library had a surplus. These have been invaluable to me, and have formed the basis for the street plans in this book, along with documents in the same library relating to the transformations of Baron Haussmann.

Other Haussmann schemes for compulsory purchase I consulted in the **Archives Nationales**, once also in an old house in the Marais but now exiled to a large concrete block on the Boulevard Sérurier. This has also been my source for such Census returns as the Paris region has managed to preserve. My grateful thanks to Mesdames Filloles and Monardie for guiding me through the system.

It is generally agreed among researchers that any architectural deficiencies of Boulevard Sérurier (such as a roof that tends to leak) pale into insignificance in comparison with the defects of the new and monumental **Bibliothèque Nationale** east of the Gare d'Austerlitz, with its four exposed towers of books, its wind- and rain-swept podium, its subterranean reading rooms, its multiple useless armoured doors, its lack of adequate on-site cafés and its overcomplex and frequently defective computer system. My thanks, nevertheless, to the librarians, who battle bravely and politely with these fundamental faults in design: I only wish I could have faced using the place more often. And I am more than ever grateful for our own **British Library** at St Pancras, whose modest red-brick interior conceals such a well-thought-out interior and whose staff were, as ever, helpful during my sessions in the Rare Book Room. My thanks also to the staff of the **London Library**, the institution that enables its members to carry off expensive and scarce volumes to study at home and keep them there for months if they are not needed elsewhere. And especial thanks to Chantal Morel of the library of the **Institut Français** in London, who, knowing that a great many no-longer-catalogued books had ended up in its basement, conducted me down there and allowed me to browse at will.

Gratitude, too, to the archivists of the redoubtable **Institut de France**, who welcomed me into their modest office and quickly found for me a file relating to the Académicien Maurice Lemoigne. Also, and especially, to two archivists of the library in the **Royal College of Surgeons in Ireland**, Eileen Phillips and Mary O'Doherty, both of whom went to great trouble to show me what they hold relating to Arthur Jacob and his brother John. Thanks, also, to Mary Fitzpatrick of the archive department of **Laois County Library**, and to those in charge of the publishing archive at the **University of Reading** library, especially Brian Ryder. Also, and especially, to Richard Aspin of the **Wellcome Foundation Library**, who, when he heard about my project, produced for me exactly the manuscript document I needed, and also directed me to a companion publication to be found in another library.

Thanks, as well, to the staffs of **Hastings Public Library**, the Hastings **Old Town Hall Museum** and also the **East Sussex Record Office** in Lewes, resources that enabled me to reconstruct the obscure history of the Tindalls. Also to the **Weald and Downland Open Air Museum** in West Sussex, especially to Richard Harris who confirmed to me that 'Tindalls Cottage' was indeed connected with my research, and to Danae Tankard who very kindly made available to me a copy of an informative paper she had written on the cottage in question. I do hope, one day soon, to see it re-erected.

Like most researchers today, I have made intermittent use of the internet to check basic facts on well-known figures or events. I am particularly grateful to the website of the **Commonwealth War Graves Commission**: it has enabled me to trace and visit the grave of Howard Tindall, which no living family member knew existed.

As with previous books, a number of individuals beyond those mentioned above have, at different moments, been kind enough to offer me support, interest, specialised information, advice, introductions or – in certain cases – their own memories. They are Dr Philippe Albou, Madame Claire Berche of the (resurrected) l'Association de la Montagne Sainte Geneviève, Dr Edward Brett, Roger Cazalet, Peter Conradi, Sara Davies, Juliet Gardiner, Dr Dennis Gibbs, Lavinia Greacen, my editor Penelope Hoare, Victor Laks, Paul and Virginie Lutyens, Douglas Matthews, Richard Mayne, Robin Price, Michel, Annie and Marie-Agnès Roux Dessarps, Colin Thubron, Professor Maurice Vaisse, David Waddell and his stepdaughter Claire Metson. My thanks to all of them, and my hopes that they will get something back from this book.

Also, and especially, to my husband Richard Lansdown, who accompanied me with his camera on several excursions in the footsteps of Arthur, Bertie or Maud; and to Robin and Inge Hyman who were so generous as to allow me to borrow their flat in the Quarter on several occasions. A final mention, too, is due to the family now in charge of the Hôtel des Carmes, who do not wish their real name to be used but who have taken an informed interest in the promise of this book.

Timeline

1789	Start of French Revolution.	Arthur Jacob born.
1792	The Terror.	
1799	Napoleon Bonaparte appoints himself First Consul.	
1804	Napoleon becomes Emperor. Important town projects set in train.	Jean-Baptiste Baillière arrives in Paris as an apprentice bookseller.
1814	Napoleon defeated and sent to Elba. Bourbon monarchy restored.	Arthur Jacob takes his MD in Edinburgh and walks to Paris.
1815	Spring, Napoleon escapes back to France. His 'Hundred Days'. Bourbons retreat again till Napoleon defeated at Waterloo in June. Second restoration – Louis XVIII.	
1824	Louis dies, succeeded by Charles X.	Arthur Jacob marries, starts a family.
1830	The July Revolution. Charles deposed. Louis-Philippe becomes last French king.	
1830s	Social unrest in Paris. Cholera appears.	Arthur's fourth son, Archibald, born in Dublin.
1840s	Paris enlarged with new customs wall. First railways built. Significant road schemes begun.	Albert Alfred Tindall born in Hastings.
1848	Revolution. Louis-Philippe deposed. Napoleon's nephew, Louis-Napoleon comes to power. Second Republic.	
1851	December, Louis-Napoleon becomes Emperor Napoleon III. Second Empire begins.	

Timeline

1850s–60s	
Paris substantially rebuilt and reorganised under Préfet Haussmann.	Archibald Jacob marries, starts a large family. A.A. Tindall making his way in London in the print trade. Visits Drs Jacob in Dublin. Hippolyte Baillière, of London, dies.
1869 Haussmann dismissed.	
1870 Napoleon III makes war on Prussia. September, French army substantially defeated at battle of Sedan. Emperor escapes to England. Third Republic established.	A.A. Tindall associated with Baillière firm.
1870–71	
Winter, Siege of Paris by Prussians.	
1871 Siege lifted. May, popular insurrection, known as the Commune, bloodily repressed.	A.A. Tindall marries Sophia Simson. May Tindall born. Arthur Jacob dies.
1870s French society being modernised.	Blanche Jacob born. Bertie Tindall born. Maud Tindall born. Family publishing house now well established.
1879 Third Republic consolidated.	
1880s	Howard Tindall born. Sophia dies.
1895 Railway engine crashes at Gare Montparnasse.	Bertie spends the year in Paris.
1898 Paris Metro begins to be built.	Bertie joins the family firm. Archibald Jacob dies.
1900s	Bertie marries Blanche Jacob. Their daughter is born. 'Tom' is born.

Timeline

1914	Start of First World War. Northern France invaded by Germany.	Maud nursing with French Red Cross. Howard Tindall and Donald Jacob both killed in third Ypres offensive.
1918	War ends in Armistice.	
1920s	Fortifications round Paris demolished.	'Serge' born in Paris.
1930s	Wide political divisions in French society.	Albert Alfred Tindall dies. 'Tom' marries Ursula.
1939	Start of Second World War.	'Julia' born.
1940	France invaded by Germany. Paris occupied. Puppet government installed in Vichy in so-called Free Zone.	'Tom' away on active service.
1942	November, all France under German rule.	
1944	June, France liberated in stages after Allies land in Normandy. Paris liberated 26th Aug.	
1946	Fourth Republic formed.	
Late 1940s–50s	Series of unsustainable governments.	Ursula dies. 'Julia' first in Paris.
1958	General de Gaulle voted in as President of Fifth Republic.	
1968	May, extensive riots in Paris.	
1969	De Gaulle resigns, succeeded by Pompidou.	
Early 1970s	Pompidou's programme of high-rise blocks and urban motorways for Paris.	Bertie dies. Maud dies.
1973	Boulevard Périphérique opened on line of old fortifications.	
1974	Pompidou dies. His successor rescinds all plans for further skyscrapers within Paris proper.	

Index

Index

Index

Ireland: Jacob family in, 17–21, 109–10; conditions, 109; and Great War (1914–19), 110–11; Jacob family leaves, 214–15; *see also* Dublin

Jacob family: activities in Ireland, 17–21, 109–10; Diaries, 110–11; leaves Ireland, 214–15

Jacob, Archibald (Arthur's son): marriage, 105–6; character and manner, 107; meets Albert Alfred Tindall, 158; in Ireland, 160; asthma and death, 211; *The History of the Jacob Families*, 17–18

Jacob, Arthur: walks from Edinburgh to Paris, 12, 15–16, 25–7, 29–34, 36; medical training and career, 15, 22–4, 80, 100; origins and background, 17–18, 20; medical work in Maryborough, 19; birth, 20; appearance and dress, 21, 31–2, 103–4; visits hospitals., 29–31; religious scepticism, 33–4; life and studies in Paris, 47–8, 50–4, 61–2, 76–7, 84–5, 87, 92, 95, 98, 186, 237, 312; book collection, 48, 95–6; in Dublin, 48; and use of bodies for dissection, 80–1; specialises in eye and skin diseases, 88, 90–1; acquires pulse-glass, 97–8; character and personality, 100–3; working routine, 101; marriage and family, 102–3, 105–6; lecturing, 103–4; revisits Paris and France, 103, 124; interest in zoology and pet animals, 104–5; retires to Barrow-in-Furness, 107, 160; intervenes in Irish murder case, 108–9; meets Albert Alfred Tindall, 158; *Dr Jacob's Essays – Anatomical, Zoological, Surgical and Miscellaneous*, 97

Jacob, David (Arthur's nephew), 110

Jacob, Donald (Archibald's son), 211, 221–3

Jacob, Florence (*née* McClean; Archibald's wife): marriage and children, 106–7; moves house in widowhood, 211; and daughter Blanche, 213

and construction work, 13, 62, 130; published guide to, 35–6, 39, 41, 51; pre-Haussmann developments, 46–7, 51–2, 116–18, 122–3; Arthur's life in, 47–8, 50–4, 61–2, 76–7, 84–5, 87, 92, 95, 98; foreign visitors and migrants, 48, 65–6, 174, 244–8, 250–1; medical studies, 53–5, 76–8, 81–2, 85–6; houses, 61; Jews in, 61–2, 245–6; water supply and sanitation, 63–4, 116, 126–7; wood-burning, 63; river activities, 64–5; effect of Revolution in, 75; explosion and fire (1794), 75; hospitals, 83–4, 87–8; Napoleon returns to (1815), 92; restaurants introduced, 93–4; cheap living, 94–5; street entertainment, 98–9; Arthur revisits, 103, 124; Haussmann develops, 116, 118–19, 125–6, 130, 167–8, 289; *pissoirs* (*vespasiennes*; public urinals), 116, 292; the poor in, 119–21, 132–5, 242–3, 293; rubbish collection and disposal, 121;

Commune (1871), 126, 170, 190; Metro (underground railway system), 127, 181, 238–9, 290–2; drinking places, 133–4; student and artistic life in, 135–7; bohemianism, 138–43; prostitution in, 139, 175–6; besieged in Franco-Prussian War, 167–8, 170; Albert Alfred in, 172–3, 176, 201–2; Folies Bergères, 173–4; as 'Gay Paree', 173–5; Bertie in, 178–80, 182–94, 198–9, 201–2, 268; suburbs, 181, 196–7; transport, 181, 190, 195–7, 290; statues, 182; cold winters, 188; privacy in, 191–2; Gare Montparnasse train accident, 199–200; Bertie leaves, 203–5; Bertie revisits with Blanche, 215–16; Maud Tindall's life in, 231–2, 234, 238; First World War memorials, 235; later changes and development, 239, 308–10, 315; floods (1911), 240; under-employment and underclass in, 240–1;

Paris – cont.
cheap labour, 241;
under occupation in
Second World War,
243, 250, 254;
Americans in, 244;
Census records (1926),
246–9; Julia's first vision
of, 264–8; depicted in
L'Enfant du Métro, 265;
Allied troops visit in
Second World War,
273; Julia stays in after
mother's death, 283–9,
292–3, 296–303, 312;
pneumatique, 290;
Grand Plan (1950–58),
295, 310; Left Bank
riots (1968), 297; Julia
revisits, 308, 313,
316–18, 320; Les Halles
demolished, 309;
development modified
by Giscard d'Estaing,
310–11; Julia's imagi-
nary life in, 313–14
Buildings, Streets and
Locations: Abbaye de St
Germain (St Germain
des Prés), 68–70, 149,
294, 298; Boulevard St
Germain, 127–8, 132;
Boulevard St Michel,
127; Cordeliers District,
71–2, 122; Ecole des
Beaux Arts, 217;
Hôpital de la Pitié, 83,

138; Hôtel de Ville,
189–90; Hôtel des
Carmes, 297–8, 316–19;
Hôtel Dieu, 85; Ile St
Louis, 187, 193; Jardin
des Plantes, 83–4, 99,
104; Latin Quarter, 14,
45–7, 53, 65, 67–8, 78,
124, 127–9, 133–5, 143,
182, 286, 295, 310,
315–16; Left Bank,
116–19, 127, 143;
Montagne Sainte
Geneviève, 8–19, 244;
Montparnasse, 250,
294; Moulin de la
Galette, 173; Moulin
Rouge, 173; Notre
Dame (cathedral), 43;
Opera House, 167;
Panthéon, 78, 118;
Place Maubert (and
district), 56–7, 59, 66,
70, 118–21, 123, 132,
182, 241, 249, 295–7,
311; Rue de l'Ecole de
Médecine, 122–3; Rue
des Carmes, 121–2,
296–7; Rue des Ecoles,
121–2; Sacré Coeur,
187; St Julien le Pauvre
(church), 132; Sainte
Chapelle, 187;
Salpêtrière, 84;
Sorbonne, 79, 136;
Théâtre de la
Huchette, 294

Index

Pasteur, Louis, 199
Paul, Elliot, 254, 294
Perrymond (left-wing
  idealist), 119
Philippe Auguste, King of
  France, 43
Pierre-Solange family,
  283, 300, 302, 318
Pompidou, Georges, 310
Poubelle, Préfet (1880s),
  121
Procope, Café, 68, 93,
  249
prostitution: in Paris, 139,
  175–6
Puccini, Giacomo: *La
  Bohème*, 137, 189

Radcliffe, John, 30
rag-pickers (*chiffoniers*),
  120–1
railways: development,
  152, 155
Rambuteau, Claude-
  Philibert Barthelot,
  comte de, 116–17, 292
resurrectionists, 80–1
Richelieu, Cardinal
  Armand Jean Duplessis,
  duc de: head, 79
Robespierre, Maximilien,
  68, 76
Romantic Movement,
  135–6
Rousseau, Jean-Jacques,
  68
Royal College of

Surgeons in Ireland:
  Arthur's involvement
  with, 48, 103

St Helena (island), 115
St Vincent de Paul,
  Sisters of (Order), 42
Saint-Just, Louis Antoine
  Léon Florelle de, 74
Sand, George (*nee*
  Aurore Dupin), 60, 99,
  122
Sarrazin, Pierre, 122
Scott, John, 65, 83, 98
Second Empire (French),
  122, 124, 130, 132,
  167–8
Second World War
  (1939–45): French occu-
  pation and isolation,
  253–4; outbreak, 270
Serge (Parisian), 302–5,
  308–9
Shakespeare & Co. (Paris
  bookshop), 244
Sims, Dr John, 84, 86–7,
  91–3
Smellie, Mrs (Edinburgh
  landlady), 23
Smith, William, 27–8
Société Française
  d'Histoire de la
  Médecine, 318
Spanish Civil War, 270
Stein, Gertrude, 244
Stendhal (Marie-Henri
  Beyle), 135

mother's death, 283–9,
292–3, 296–303, 312;
dreams, 300, 319;
romance with Serge,
302–4; returns to
England, 305; revisits
Paris, 308, 313, 316–18,
320; subsequent life
and career, 312–13;
imaginary Paris life,
313–14; life in rural
France, 314; attends
conference of Société
Française d'Histoire de
la Médecine, 318
Tindall, Maud (Albert
Alfred's daughter): birth
and childhood, 163–6;
sends tie to Bertie, 168;
Bertie takes present
from Paris, 204; at
home, 213; nursing in
France in First World
War, 218, 227–8, 230–1,
234–5; and death of
brother Howard in war,
220, 228; background
and career, 228–9;
remains unmarried, 228;
lives with May and
Arthur Giles, 229–30;
life in France, 230–4,
250, 253; shares home
in sister May's
widowhood, 255, 261;
in old age, 256; writings,
256; death, 257

Tindall, May (Albert
Alfred's daughter) *see*
Giles, May
Tindall, Nicholas (Julia's
brother), 304
Tindall, Sarah (*née*
Pearce; Stephen's wife),
153
Tindall, Sophia (*née*
Simson; Albert Alfred's
wife), 151, 161–5,
203–4
Tindall, Stephen (Albert
Alfred's father), 37,
151–3
Tindall, 'Tom' (Julia's
father): marriage to
Ursula, 262–3, 269;
military service in
Second World War,
270–3; upbringing and
career, 270–1, 276; and
Ursula's depression,
276–7; and Ursula's
death, 282; makes new
life, 285; and Julia's
absence in Paris, 304;
remarries, 305; death,
318; and Julia's later
career, 318
Tindall, Ursula (*née*
Orange; Tom's first
wife): background and
character, 262–4; and
daughter's birth and
upbringing, 264–6,
269; idealises Paris,

Index

264–8, 274; accuses Blanche of spoiling son Tom, 270; never visits France after 1939, 274; clinical depression, 276–7; moves to London, 278–9; suicide, 279–82
tuberculosis, 295

Ungaretti, Giuseppe, 248

Victoria, Queen, 169
Victoria, Princess Royal (*later* Empress of Germany), 161
Vie Parisienne, La (magazine), 174
Villon, François, 56, 139
Voltaire, François Marie Arouet, 57, 68, 120

Waterloo, Battle of (1815), 37, 65, 92
Wellington, Arthur Wellesley, Duke of, 92
White Russians: in Paris, 245
Wilde, Jane Frances, Lady ('Speranza'), 88–9
Wilde, Sir William, 88–9, 102
women: in bourgeois Paris, 193–4; nursing in First World War, 227, 234; and marriage, 228–9
Worcester Infirmary, 31
Wordsworth, William, 31

Zola, Emile, 168, 233; *L'Assommoir*, 190; *Au Bonheur des Dames*, 202